OOPS!
I NEVER THOUGHT OF THAT!

Surprises in Creativity

Key to Effectiveness
In the Arts, Sciences and Everyday Life

Edgar E. Hardy

Illustrations by Kay Hardy

a **TECHNOMIC**® publication
TECHNOMIC Publishing Co., Inc.
265 W. State St., Westport, Conn. 06880

OOPS!
I NEVER THOUGHT OF THAT!

Surprises In Creativity

©TECHNOMIC Publishing Co., Inc., 1975
265 W. State St., Westport, CT 06880

a TECHNOMIC® publication

Printed in U.S.A.

Library of Congress Card No. 75-16995

Standard Book No. 0-87762-162-4

This book would not be complete without my sincere thanks to Dr. Samuel Steingiser for instigating it, Tom Linxweiler for his many valuable suggestions and Les Krambeal for his many hours of typing.

Edgar E. Hardy

TABLE OF CONTENTS

Just a word, before . . . .
Participation is a must. "Reading" this book is not enough.

Chapter	Title	Page
1	Creativity: Your potential!	1
2	Originality: Effective surprise!	25
3	Perception: Doors to awareness.	44
4	Problems have many answers.	63
5	Building blocks for creativity.	80
6	Ideas, many, many.	99
7	Incubation: Time out for creative digestion.	114
8	Solution, surprises, action!	127
9	The creative group. Multiplication or division?	139
10	Communication: Do you hear what he is saying?	151
11	Creative media: Writing, speaking, listening.	170
12	Octopus world: Organizing for progress.	187
13	Discovery, invention and innovation.	202
14	A creative lifestyle: The place in the sun!	217

Just a word, after . . . .
Feedback is a must. "Reading" this book is not enough.

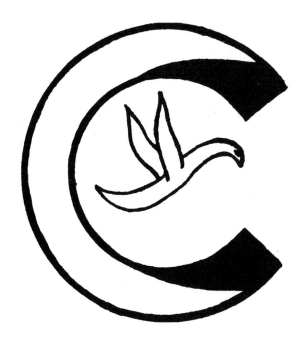

Creativity: Like a bird projected from the human cage to contribute to the world...

Just a word before . . .

"Oops . . . "I never thought of that!"

"I really did not expect that. I am surprised, delighted, shocked! I am laughing. . .I see a solution, I see a way to do it!" Just like great works of art, inventions, discoveries, innovations. . .the everyday solutions to our problems are not accidents. They are the results of the creative process!

By honing of our natural creative skills; by stimulating and training our ability to perform with imagination, we can assure our fulfillment and a constructive life.

Human beings are unique in their power to effect change. Each individual can move mountains. Together we can move the world to new heights. To do so, however, we must perform at high levels of capabilities. We must maximize our effectiveness. Let us get away from limited use of our being, to full living, full contribution, full awareness, full performance, and thus fullest utilization of our potential.

Imagination, creativity, surprises, effectiveness in the arts, sciences, and everyday life, that is our goal.

Life can be a successful and a pleasant adventure. Creativity is a door to such human satisfaction and enhanced productivity. Encourage your imagination.

Cultivating your senses can bring you unexpected results. At work and at play, creative behavior is the bridge that leads to results. Just as important, creativity knows no barrier... it serves all! Engineers, scientists, businessmen, housewives... creative imagination helps them all.

Cultivate creativity and problems disappear as if by magic, understanding flourishes and progress comes easy. Never forget, this God-given talent can be encouraged. It can be stimulated, it can be trained. This is what we are going to do together. Even in today's world with its grim realities and many pressures towards uniformity, routine performance and machine influences, imagination can and will be the wedge to new solutions.

A book is a very limited medium for communication between human beings. Communication is a cyclic process. At its best, it is a back and forth process between people. Communication is a give-and-take from both sides which reinforces itself, growing to establish a significant bond, to generate understanding between individuals. Good communication, like a snowball rolled across the snow, keeps growing to reinforce itself, to increase in size and gain significant dimensions.

This book tries to build a true communication with its user. It wants, it requires, it demands of them participation, feedback, action. True feedback to the author can only be limited, but reader feedback to the content of the various chapters has been made easy.

Whether used as a text in a group effort of stimulating and training the creativity of the participants or whether intended and used for reawakening of your own individual capabilities, whether used as a class guide or an individual instrument to assist you personally in making fuller use of your potential, this book wants your action. It wants to motivate you, not only to read on, but to exercise, to practice your senses, your creative abilities.

This book wants to introduce you to other interesting, stimulating, and more detailed accounts on how to carry out specific tasks in a novel way. It wants to open to you the doors to the substantial and significant literature aimed at creativity training, development and reawakening of your fullest potential.

Even more important, there are exercises. Here is where substantial feedback between you and the author's attempts at assisting you is possible. Try the suggested exercises. Expand on them. Play with them. Enjoy them. Practice them. Invent and add your own supplementary training devices. Find out what would help you the most in developing your own style, and then do it. Practice it again and again until it becomes part of you, part of your way of doing it, part of your way of giving your creative potential the fullest rein. Remember, creativity is the road to successful and constructive change.

CHAPTER 1
CREATIVITY: YOUR POTENTIAL

The world we live in   Reality and imagination
Complexity and change   Conflict or synergism
Nature of creativity   Discovery, invention & innovation
A human talent   Nature of human progress
Multiplying your potential   Motivation and "can do"
Action, originality and value   Creativity training
Applied creativity, a universal need   A creative life style

CREATIVITY: THE NEED

Creativity is a tool to be used in facing the world competently and productively. Understanding, exercising, practicing creativity allows us humans to contribute in life more effectively, more successfully, and with greater pleasure.

Spaceship Earth is populated with the most interesting beings. Two-legged, large, small, fat, and thin. They are capable of the most astounding feats.They visit the moon in tiny capsules. They travel around their planet in that thin shell of air protecting it. They create pyramids, atomic submarines and skyscrapers. They create symphonies, operas and murals. They leave their mark on this fascinating, ever changing spaceship Earth. They are unique. They are human beings.

The human individual has an urge not only to survive but to progress, to contribute, to create, to bring about something of value to himself, to others and to the total system that he is born into. The combination of these urges is the energy that fuels progress and survival.

Whether street cleaner, professional, entrepreneur, plodder or genius, we all have an important contribution to make. If spaceship Earth is not kept clean, the genius may drown in garbage rather than initiate a breakthrough for mankind. The success of the professional lays the foundation for the entrepreneur to build a new enterprise. The progress of our system, the forward movement of spaceship Earth, in every respect is a function of the individual contribution of each human, each unique active creative individual.

We live in a world of miracles. Man has come a long way. Our knowledge of the life's mystery is expanding. Today a surgeon can repair a living heart and save a younster who ten years ago would have had little chance to live a normal life.

We live in a world of change. Our store of knowledge increases and becomes more complex every day. It is a crowded world, people working closely side by side. People live on top of each other in apartment buildings, tenements and the small lots of the suburbs. They impinge upon each other to a much greater degree than ever before in the history of human civilization.

Chronic high speed communication and especially the ever present television add a mental crowding to the physical crowding that we experience. The world crowds into our living room. Snatches of far away events intrude on our conscious activity every day of our lives.

This world of miracles we live in is characterized by complexity and change, by ever increasing new and different problems and demands. Knowledge learned today is out of date tomorrow. With such rapid change, yesterday's problems, yesterday's demands, and yesterday's knowledge seem like messages from a far distant past.

If it were only a question of complexity and change, technology, as in the past, might be able to keep pace with both of these facets of modern life. However, due to high speed communication, a third and equally important factor has appeared — that is, human expectations and the impatience to see these expectations fulfilled forthwith.

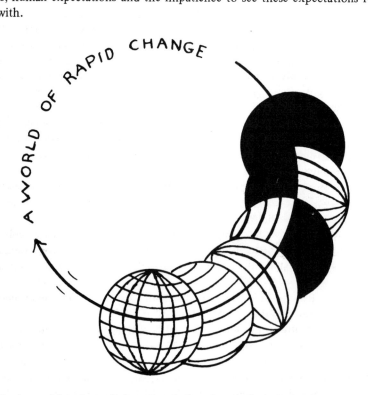

A WORLD OF RAPID CHANGE

With the acceleration of change and the advent of modern communication devices has come a human urge, a desire, indeed a demand to fulfill expectations far beyond those with which mankind seemingly is able to keep pace. Mankind is experiencing difficulties in coping with change and learning to live in his world. At the very time that we need greater understanding among individuals than ever before and greater cooperation among nations, human beings seem to be less able to solve their problems and keep up with the rapid pace which is required.

Creativity is the key to the adjustment to today's demanding and ever changing world. Creativity can help us to learn how to cope with new problems; how to make the best of each day. Men and women of today and tomorrow need this third dimension to their activity. Yesterday's upbringing of professionals, with the stress on knowledge and orderly processes, with the emphasis on book learning and straight mathematical solutions, is not adequate to cope with today's world of change.

Creativity is the source of our human ability to go beyond the orderly, to go beyond knowledge. It shows how to go beyond the straight and expected ways of putting the past together in an obvious and expected order. It is creativity which allows the human being to cope with change. Stimulated, stressed and cultivated, it enables modern man and professional to cope with this ever changing world.

So you have graduated from college! You have learned the latest analytical techniques. You have had good grades. You know how to answer Professor Brown's questions to his satisfaction. You have completed the requirements for a degree. PhD.! MBA. BA. BS! You have studied physics, chemistry, accounting, sociology, history! You are ready to face the real world, to make your contributions, to solve problems that will move mankind forward. You are ready to do your best!

Are you really?

Or you have worked at your bank, in your laboratory, in the production department, in the law office for the last five years, eight years, ten years. You are daily solving problems to move mankind forward. You are doing your best.

Are you really?

Beginner, or experienced practitioner, fledgling professional or successful engineer, scientist, businessman, banker, lawyer, or housewife. We are not doing our best in this changing world of today.

We are using only a fraction of our potential! Surroundings, society, culture and education have conspired to cage us in restrictions. They submerge, subdue, and inhibit our greatest talent, the exercise of our inborn, glorious and powerful creative talent.

This need not be so. This cannot be tolerated. Superman is just an ordinary man who has learned the fullest use of his potential.

We go through life utilizing only the smallest portion of our human potential. We can live a much fuller life. We can fully exert the superiority of humanity by learning how to utilize a large part of our almost inexhaustible capabilities.

This is what makes us superior to the machine. Machines can add, subtract, quickly carry out complex computations; but machines cannot create.

CREATIVITY: THE PUZZLE

What is creativity? Something intensely human. It is the essence of human superiority over machines and over animals. You can live, work, act at a much higher level of human potential than you are presently exercising.

Your Potential
is a
Giant

In the words of Theodore Roethke, the famous contemporary teacher of creative writing, "You are here to find out about your life. That will be the purpose. It may be necessary to change some of your ways of acting and thinking in the process. Well, here we are at the beginning. There's nothing like ignorance to engender wild enthusiasm."

Start at the beginning. What is creativity? "Creativity" has been a much misused word. People still cannot agree as to its origin, source, motivation, even the definition of the word itself. However, one thing all are agreed upon — more creativity, greater creativity is needed and vital to human progress.

Webster defines creation, "to bring something into existence, to make something out of nothing, to cause, to produce by some sort of action whether it be mental, physical, artistic, or scientific."

In a lighter vein, we might consider defining the word this way: a dress: $8.75; a frock: $36.00; a gown: $99.00; but a creation: $345.00!

It is not important that we agree on a definition of creativity. What is needed is an understanding of the nature and the importance of the creative process. What is vital is the ability to strengthen to reawaken, to cultivate our creative talents and facilities, to increase use of our human potential. Rather than attempting to define the creative process let us describe it in terms of human action, originality, and value.

Let us agree that creativity is something uniquely human. It is an attribute or characteristic foreign to animals and machines. It belongs to men and women and it especially belongs to children. It is a capability, a talent. It plays a major role in all our lives.

But what is it? Something inside of us? A part of our unconscious mind? Ideas, thoughts, instincts, an inner urge? No, it is more than that. It is a human talent, an inner drive, an unconscious combination translated into action.

There are three major aspects of human potential.

The first is knowledge. We are all familiar with and usually stress learning and knowledge. This is the receiving and storing of information. Most of our school years stress the importance of blocks of information. Education is made up of storing knowledge which you will use in your future lives. In simple terms, you might compare this aspect of human potential, the acquisition of knowledge to piling up numbers inside you: 1, 2, 3, 4, 5, 6 and so on.

There is no doubt that the accumulation of information, the gaining of knowledge is important. To live and cope with this complex time we must know a great deal. We must have many facts at our disposal to deal with the problems of the real world.

Without tools, without skills there can be only limited action. We need the knowledge, the learning to be able to translate it into intelligent, creative action.

It has been said that nothing is really new in this world. Even the original, the newest, flows from the past. Therefore, we must learn, we must know what is in the past. The elements from the past are required to put the new, original combinations together.

This is why knowledge is vital. Being human and thus fortunate enough to have language, we are able to pass knowledge on from one to another. We can even pass it on from the past to the future, bridging time. Knowledge provides the base for creative and intelligent action.

The second aspect is intelligent action, which flows out of knowledge.

We train our thought processes, our intellect. We use the knowledge in a straight forward, logical way. We are taught that $2 + 2 = 4$. We stress the orderly arrangement of the universe. To cope with reality we impress order on chaos. We emphasize rules and regulations. Whether it be chemistry, physics, or accounting, we try to impose order on the tasks we perform in this seemingly chaotic world.

Two plus two equals four. Hydrochloric acid and sodium hydroxide give sodium chloride and water. $E = mc^2$. Orderly thought and action is our way to cope with reality.

Intelligence is the computer part of our talents. We collect, we store, we select and reproduce, we program our knowledge for action. We reason in an orderly fashion according to well established principles and rules.

We organize our society according to orderly laws, entrust the police force with the task of protecting us from disorder. Thus from the early beginnings of childhood we stress law and order. We learn our multiplication tables or modern mathematics. But do we leave any room for imagination? For creativity?

The third and most important aspect, not sufficiently stressed in the educational processes that we are using, is our imagination, our creativity!

Creativity is the still somewhat mysterious ability of the human to be original, to come up with something new and useful in a way impossible to the machine. This is our ability to add $2 + 2$ and come up with 5 instead of 4.

In contrast to the pre-set, mental capabilities involved in logic, in reasoning, in remembering, in using stored information in the obvious way, this is a different activity, a selection of unusual pieces and their recombination in an original way to produce new and unexpected results.

CREATIVITY: THE TALENT

Creativity is an exercise of the senses.

The artist feels the right shading of colors, the right composition. He doesn't really think, "I need a little more blue on the mountain," he sees it, he feels it. Creativity is a functioning of the senses.

Creativity is intensely human, it is a talent, a universal human capability, a potential to be practiced and exercised. Creativity is also a process, the daily problem-solving activity of each one of us. It is a shortcut, the enjoyable way to live up to challenges and get results in an unusual and original fashion. Creativity is also the product, the new organizational structure that blends and reinforces the talents of many unique individuals. As an example: It is the latest invention that can be a new and useful product for the company. It is the brilliant and original legal defense strategy that frees an innocent man. It is not only the artist's creation of a new painting, but also the creative result of manifold human activities. Creativity is all three: Human talent, problem solving, and novel and original results.

Synergism, that is the unexpected results $- 2 + 2 = 5 -$ describes the creative product. You get more than you had a right to expect. The creative act is the surpassed expectation. However, this only describes the result.

In the words of Gyorgy Kepes, "Creative activity is not a super imposed extraneous task against which the body, heart or brain protest, but an orchestration of all these in one free act of joyful doing."

The sculptor who brings into being a new beautiful statue uses his senses, not just his thoughts. He accomplishes more than putting together block on block like the stone mason. Yes, there is synergism. Three stone blocks are combined not just to produce a stone column, but a statue, an original, a creation. But the process involves more than thinking, more than action. The originality, the creation is a result of the functioning of all his senses: vision, touch, hearing, even smell. While he shapes the stones with his tools, he visualizes the result. He may not see the finished creation in all its details. He follows his creative urge, he gropes and feels for the final image that will satisfy his senses. He listens to the sound of his chisel, he smells the dust of the stone, he attempts to shape reality, the block of stone in his creative image.

Many years ago I heard Homer Adkins, the great organic chemist, state that every organic chemist must be an artist. The same total creative sensatory experience is required to work out a complex original organic synthesis as is needed in producing a work of sculpture. It is what has enabled us to define the complicated structure of natural products.

Not only organic chemists, but all scientists and engineers, bankers, lawyers and especially physicians need this creative ability, the total functioning of the senses to fulfill their calling.

Regardless of whether we are dealing with the talent, the process, or the product. creativity can be recognized, can be understood in the terms of three vital components: action, originality, value. Independent of our distinctions between the creative talent, the process or the product, we can achieve an understanding of "creativity" in terms of these separate and distinct characteristics.

Whether we discuss human potential, problem solving or creative results, creativity requires these basic elements. Creativity = Action + Originality + Value.

CREATIVITY: ACTION!

Creativity is not just something in our mind. Creativity means action.

Something is happening, human accomplishment is of the essence. Many years ago in college I and one of my best friends, a man who today is recognized as a well-known scientist, were traveling on a vacation trip. As usual we got into a hot argument. This one related to the way air was flowing around the outside of our speeding car. He insisted that we stop and paste streamers to the windshield of our car to prove his theory. Only a couple of nuts like ourselves would take the time to stop and paste streamers on a convertible to prove a point. However, even then in his early years my friend showed his burning desire for action in relation to ideas. This does not mean that all nuts are creative. A person who has the willingness and drive to act on the unusual may often, however, be considered that way.

Creativity then means action. What is action? Action is bringing about a change. Human action means: I, you, we change something. Whether it is walking up a stairway or designing a bridge, action means change. Action is positive, something is changed, something is being acted upon. It is not observation nor just thinking. Action goes beyond hearing or feeling, it is change, of human origin.

You do something. You do not just see the oncoming car, you act, you jump out of its path. You do not just see the child in the river, you jump in to save it.

It is not necessarily our nature to act. We show a certain amount of inertia. We

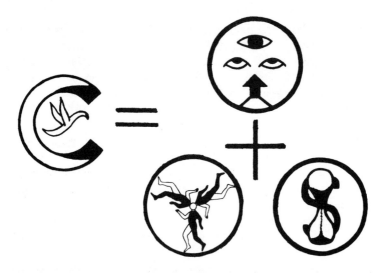

are slow to move. We do not necessarily react to all observations. We are often stuck in a groove, set upon a certain course and unable to react as may be required.

We must overcome our resistence, our inner unwillingness to act. We must break through the inertia barrier. We must train ourselves to be willing to move, to do something to overcome our natural shyness, hesistancy, our unwillingness to do something different. Our inertia barrier must be broken.

Some years ago there was a bad accident at one of our plants. The operator was trained to watch an instrument showing the temperature of the reactor. If the temperature got beyond 35°, he was to carry out a certain emergency procedure to prevent things from getting out of hand. You might say he was conditioned to act upon the image of the gauge above 35°.

One day the gauge was out of order. The kettle overheated. He burned his hand on the kettle, but he did not act. He was not trained to use all of his senses. His inertia barrier was to be breached only by the picture, the image of the gauge. Touch did not trigger the necessary action.

We all have our inertia barriers. We walk along the street and see a tripping hazard, maybe a banana peel. Do we pick it up to protect those who come after us? Most likely we leave it for the street cleaning crew.

Creativity means action, a willingness to cross the inertia barrier. It means an attitude of "do", not just observe or think about it. Act on it.

It pays to be in motion. Action, energy and health are watchwords of the creative individual. It is true that many creative individuals have overcome severe handicaps. Beethoven composed some of his master works even though his hearing was gone. But action is the key. Energy, therefore is vital. You cannot create without doing, therefore, health, strength and vitality are important. They are the basis of the action component of creativity. As Boss Kettering said, "Lucky accidents do not happen to dead cows".

8

Break Through The Inertia Barrier

Motion does not necessarily mean we are going in the right direction. We may not even yet know the right direction, but it is better to roam than to stand still. You may have heard the term "dither". A little dither goes a long way. This goes back to the old mechanical computers first used to control anti-aircraft guns. Their complex machinery was constantly kept in motion by the dither. They could react faster this way than if all the gears and wheels had been standing still.

Thus we must not ever fully stand still. It is so hard to get moving when you are not already slightly in motion. Mentally the creative individual should be in motion in some way at all times. He should be alert. He should be ready to fully utilize his senses. The urge to search, to look, to move must be encouraged. It makes creative action easier. Even when you are standing still, be ready to pounce.

Last but not least, do not think any action too small. Act, pass over that inertia barrier. The observation you bother to report may save a life. That paper you picked up might have tripped the man behind you. No positive action is ever too small. Many blades of hay are required to make a beautiful haystack. Each contribution counts.

Many times we have avoided action because we shyed away from the size of the effort required, the size of the action deemed necessary. One vital rule to encourage creativity is: to "take the first step".

Larger actions have always been facilitated by taking the first step. Before spending millions, check on the feasibility; take that first step. Before turning down major projects which might be a vital contribution, because you think you do not have the resources, take that first step. Most problems can be facilitated by approaching them in a cautious, in a step-wise fashion. Nothing will happen unless you tackle it in some small, slight way, unless you take that first step.

Thus action is a vital and major aspect of all creative endeavors. However, action may be routine. Not all action is creative. Cutting wood or closing the books in the usual routine fashion may be very active, but it is routine, it is obviously not likely to involve the exercise of all our creative talent.

CREATIVITY: ORIGINALITY!

Creativity is more than action. Laying railroad tracks is action but not necessarily a creative act in the terms commonly used in the scientific or artistic fields. Learning the multiplication tables or walking across the street involves action but normally very little creativity.

This leads us to the second and most significant characteristic of creative endeavor: originality.

Creativity means human action in a new and original way. Innovation, change, discovery, some new idea, something different which has not been thought of or done before. Here is where we get into the mysterious, the not fully explained area of the description of creativity.

What is the difference between new and original? A bridge built from prefabricated sections in a way that has been done many times before is not likely to be original. However, the first time man put rocks together to shape an arch, this was not just new, it was original. It was a creative act. It was a surprise. It was a one time first. It was an original combination of the components. Here 2 + 2 did make 5.

That is the essential, the core, the heart of creativity. The human ability to break new ground, to come up with the solutions to problems, with creations which go beyond the expected which are new and unique. That is originality.

In science, as elsewhere, newness in itself does not necessarily imply originality. Original exploratory research for example, must involve a new concept rather than just doing something that hasn't been done before in just this way but may have been done before in a similar fashion. We will discuss and hopefully shed more light on originality and how to foster it in your life later in this book. This is part and parcel of stimulating your creativity.

The creative human is original. Originality is an elusive thing. This mysterious component of creativity needs further study. Originality means being different, having the courage to depart from the norm, the courage to be laughed at. Be unique! Be a free spirit! Approach your problems with laughing enthusiasm, and originality will be just around the corner.

Thus we have examined the two vital elements of creativity: action and originality. We have introduced the concept that creativity — the talent, the process and the product — is tied to human action. It is not just an idea or a philosophical concept, it is an individual human being in action. To be creative, action has to be more than novel. It has to be original, unique, unobvious. The secret of understanding creativity lies in the practice of originality.

CREATIVITY: VALUE!

But action and originality are not enough. Creativity is not yet fully characterized in our terms by the concepts of action and originality. Creativity also requires a positive, constructive element. Creativity also means: value.

Creativity also requires a contribution, a positive act, something of value to you and others. I may be a contribution to science, humanity or the general welfare. We live in a densely populated world full of human beings. We are social animals. We need each other. Creativity requires original action of value to mankind.

If I jump off a high mountain or a newly constructed bridge, this may be action, it may even be original in content, but it is not creativity.

It is true that constructive elements are not always recognized at the time of the creative act; however, they constitute a vital necessity, a must in the description, the understanding of the creative act as a whole. There is no creativity without some value.

The value may not be immediately evident. The opera "Carmen" was booed when it was first performed but it is much beloved today by opera audiences. In fact, since radical changes are seldom readily accepted by a majority, the value of many creative acts may not be recognized for some time. It is a sad but true commentary that paintings usually increase greatly in value with the death of the artist who brought them into our world.

When considering and understanding creativity our value yardsticks are of particular significance. We are used to measuring value in strictly material ways, we practically equate value with money. However, there is an equally and possibly more important measure of value: "time".

Have you ever figured what your time is worth? Take what you are being payed at work and figure out how much it cost your employer for each hour of your time. Do not forget to add in the money you do not see, there are a lot of fringe benefits he pays for your work. Think, also, of the capital invested in relation to your work. You are worth a lot more than you think.

Possibly a little closer to home, you might figure the cost of a repair job you recently payed for. What could you have saved if you had done it yourself?

In more significant terms, time is irreplaceable. It cannot be recaptured. Lost time cannot be made up.

It is important for the creative individual to realize and to make clear to himself that time is not a linear function. The value of time increases the closer we come to an approaching deadline. Time passes more quickly with age. The last few minutes of a football game often prove decisive. Time's value, its importance is closely related to, and vitally influenced by human goals. In creative action, use of human potential, generating the contribution to mankind, the creative product, time as a value scale plays an important role. Do not waste your time, focus it on creative endeavors. It is irreplaceable and its value keeps increasing with every day, every month, every year of your life.

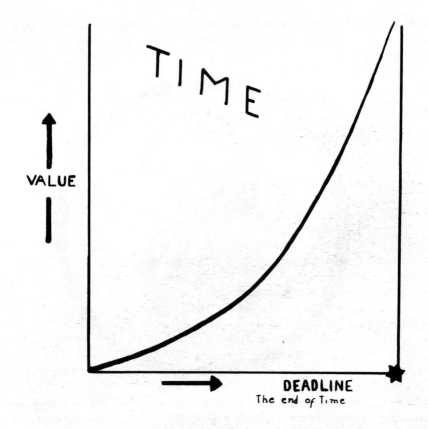

CREATIVITY: THE PERSON.

Creativity is a uniquely human quality. While it may be related to our thought processes, it is a distinct and separate talent, a functioning of our senses which requires action, originality and value for its materialization.

Every healthy human being has this quality to a certain degree. Just like a normal human being is brought into the world to see, talk and walk, so he is born to create. Why then is it that this common human attribute is so little used? Why is it, that we single out some individuals as creative people? Why don't all of us fully employ our God-given talent of creativity?

Many people hold the belief that creativity is reserved to the arts. This is not so. Creativity is required for all problem solving. It is the very essence of a successful life not only for the artists, but also for engineers, scientists, bankers, lawyers, or housewives. We all need to use our creative talents to the fullest to live in this changing and complex world, to have a successful, happy and constructive existence.

How then can we all become more creative persons? What are creative persons like? Let me quote Mark Twain: "the man with a new idea is a crank until the idea succeeds". Or James Bryant Conant: "behold the turtle, he makes progress only when he sticks his neck out". Or Boss Kettering: "it is man's destiny to ponder on the riddle of existence and as a byproduct of his wonderment, to create a new life on this earth".

How do we recognize a creative person? What are the distinguishing characteristics, the common traits of unusually creative people? By studying successful creative individuals, we can learn valuable lessons, applicable to the improvement, the enhancement of the creative talents of each one of us. We can gain new insights into the ways of making all of us more creative.

Psychologists have examined large numbers of creative people to discover common traits as well as keys to their creativity. First of all, while it is true that in large groups of creative people, intelligence is usually high, no true correlation has been found in all these studies between intelligence and creativity. On the other hand, the creative person is apt to be an independent, freedom loving thinker and nonconformist. He is apt to show originality in his approach to life. He is apt to show flexibility and openness in his thinking and discussions. If you could evaluate it, you might find him somewhat playful in his approach to problems, intuitive in his assessments, and last but not least, you will find him energetic, active, a doer.

In the many excellent books which have been written about creative persons and the process of creativity, there are long lists of some of the most important qualities that you can find in creative people. You find the words flexibility, curiosity, restlessness, intense motivation, and many others. They stress alertness, energy, openness and a willingness to be different.

How can we bring order into all these various aspects? Let me repeat again. Creativity is not unique to "creative" persons. Creativity is a "universal" talent. It is a question of developing it, cultivating it, and in some cases stimulating and re-awakening it in the human individual. Let us emphasize, there are not just a few creative individuals in this world. Creative people are not in the minority. Not at all! The vast amount of research that has been done on creativity, especially in the last twenty years, has definitely shown that creativity is a universal trait of man.

Creative potential is possessed by all people in varying degrees. It is not a question of the creative person, the artist, the genius, against the rest of the individuals, but a question of getting the most, the highest degree of creativity from all of us. Most important, and that is the purpose of this book, we have a substantial degree of control over this question of "more or less" creativity in the individual. We can make it "more". We can increase the potential, enhance the creative talents of every human being. Unfortunately, it can also be stifled.

The fallacy is frequently repeated that creativity declines past the age of forty. Some years ago a group of research psychologists working on this problem decided to investigate this generally held belief. In testing a large number of individuals in that age group, they found indeed a slight decrease in the average creativity as measured by their yardsticks between the ages of forty and fifty. Then they decided to look back and extend their studies to an earlier age group. Lo and behold, they found the same slight decrease in the thirties and even in the twenties. When they tested all age groups they found the steepest decline of creativity in the years in which we are most exposed to education. Creativity was at its highest with young people of the ages of 8 to 14, and declined most markedly between the ages of 14 and 23.

The conclusion is that our social and educational system as it is constituted today not only does very little to develop the inherent creative potential which is given to most of us. On the contrary, it does a great deal to suppress and confine and stifle our natural creative talents. No inherent reason exists for substantial declines in creativity, in potential as age proceeds. In fact, with the necessary training, there is no reason whatsoever why overall utilization of your human potential should not greatly increase as the years progress. This is true for both quality and quantity of creative potential. While sometimes a modest decline of imaginative powers might occur, it is easily compensated for by experience, better judgment, motivation, and more highly refined intuition.

With creativity training, there is no reason why your imagination shouldn't play it's major role throughout your entire life. Practice will increase creative productivity as you add increased knowledge, judgment and experience to a high level of continuing and imaginative talent.

To accomplish this, we must give the realm of creativity, the world of imagination its rightful place in our life, next to the stark realities of the world we are facing every day. We must stress the creative attitude, the attitude which says "can do", everything is possible. Human beings can accomplish anything one way or another. It is not surprising that in a world filled with problems and crime, we are so attuned to realities, that we give little space to imagination.

Richard de Mille in his lovely book of imagination games entitled, "Put Your Mother on the Ceiling", talks about the constant war that is going on between reality and imagination.

It is natural for parents and teachers to try to protect young people by stressing the realities of everyday life. It is natural to ban the imaginary friend from the dinner table; natural to smile at things we do not understand. It is natural to ridicule mental telepathy and relegate the divining rod to the realm of magic. But let's not forget that yesterday's science fiction stories are reality today. Jules Verne, over a hundred years ago, described moon rockets and atomic submarines. These are part of everyday life in this century.

To increase our creative potential, to stimulate creativity, to cultivate it at all ages, we must give a greater place in our lives to imagination, to art, to all the many facets of fantasy. We must open our minds to the unreal, to toys, to imaginative games, to fantasy and daydreaming. This does not mean an invitation to chaos. This does not mean to ban the orderly processes of engineering, but it means an open mind, to allow the introduction of a new order, a new creative way to solve

16

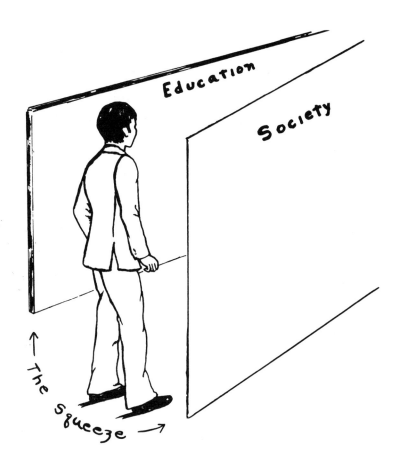

problems of work and life.

We must find a balance between the realities of the world "as it is" and the imaginative world we dream "it can be". We must master the machine world of $2 + 2 = 4$, but we must add the human equation to the computer operation. Only the imagination sees the impossible and makes it come true, thus proving $2 + 2$ can be 5.

CREATIVITY: THE ATTITUDE!

The open, the creative mind sees reality in fantasy and can translate the dream of perfect human beings into a world of tomorrow which will come close to meeting our ideals.

Let us foster the creative attitude, the willingness to do and try. Its strengthening, its encouragement makes for increased creativity in human beings. This attitude stresses that things can be done, there are ways of finding the solution. It stresses

17

the positive, the accomplishment, the "act" of creativity.

This does not eliminate the normal, the analytical or the orderly. Judgment is needed, but it can and must exist side by side with the imagination. Judgment must not be allowed to interfere with imaginative ways, prematurely or excessively.

We are so ready to see the negative side of any proposal. We all come up with so many reasons why our new idea is not workable. This cannot be tolerated. Creative attitude means an open mind. Let's try. Let's try again. Let's keep on trying even if our first reaction may be negative. Let's withhold judgment. Let us let ideas grow freely.

Foster a positive attitude. Believe in your ability to carry through. Let the enthusiastic, the gay and happy part of your personality gain the upper hand. What can you loose?

An open mindedness towards the realm of imagination and fantasy and a positive attitude towards accomplishment, this is what creativity is all about. We have described it in terms of action, originality and value. We will study it, we will cultivate it, we will stimulate it.

This book aims not so much to assist you with the understanding, the recognition of creativity, but mostly to encourage creativity in yourself and others. Creativity can be stimulated. If you're young and free spirited, you can continue to combine imagination and knowledge for a successful life. You can strive for the fullest development and use of your human potential.

If, over the years, your creative talents have been submerged by the influences of society or if stifling harm has been done through education to your inherent abilities, it is never too late for creativity. You can reawaken and bring forth your full potential. Much is known and a great deal of work has been done to develop means for stimulating, training, and developing creative skills, not only in the young, but at all ages.

What can we do to stimulate, to provide the atmosphere to remove all obstacles to the free and unhindered working of the process called creativity? Possibly one of the most important factors is an atmosphere of freedom.

Freedom is at one time the single most important, as well as the single most misused word in connection with creativity. First, I believe when we talk about freedom, we must be sure at all times to talk about responsible freedom. Freedom does not mean license — just as freedom of the press does not include pornography — so freedom of creativity must be a responsible self-disciplined freedom.

Secondly, the creative individual, just as any human being, and sometimes more so, wants to be needed and appreciated. Thus, interest in his work, his creative activity, and sincere appreciation is not only a great help, but in many cases, a vital requirement, a motivation. Thus, freedom means responsibility, interest and faith.

Temptations are great in our society with the ever-increasing centralization to create conditions in which the rules are supreme. As pointed out so well by Gardner, in his inspiring works on "Excellence" and "Self-renewal", when organizations and societies are young, they are flexible and willing to try anything once.

When the society grows old, vitality is apt to diminish, and flexibility gives way to rigidity, thus impairing creativity.

Thus, to improve creativity, we must encourage a willingness to critically examine rules and to do things in a new and better way. We must not stress the "how", but the "what". We must look at the results, at goals, at achievements, rather than at only the road to get there. The rules, I am talking about, are not only written rules, but often are unwritten rules, shared attitudes and values that accumulate in any society. The danger is that little by little, "how it is done", becomes more important than "whether it is done". Let us never forget in our work that the job's goal comes first, that if we can find a new, better, faster, a more creative way to do it, this may well be the best one. Creative results are our contribution.

There is still another hazard to creativity, another drag on the innovating capacity of our society, this is the vested interests of its inhabitants. The vested interests may be found wherever man acquires a shirt for his back or like privileges he would be reluctant to loose. The vested interests may be the prerogatives of a certain group, the prerogatives of the scientist or the engineer, the prerogatives of the student or the administrator. Certain rules and customs remain unchanged for the simple reason that changing them would put in hazard the rights, privileges or advantages of specific individuals.

If we want to truly be creative and foster creativity to its utmost, we must reconcile the safe-guarding of these vested interests with the accomplishment of creative goals. Where the two cannot be reconciled, creative goals must not be impaired, creativity must not be held down for the holy cow of the vested interests. As Gardner puts it: "No one vested interest seems very hazardous to the nation. Taken all together they form a tough and leathery web that may slowly immobilize our society."

But let's not look at the negative side of creativity — those conditions which are apt to impair it. Let's look more on the positive side — how do we encourage creativity? How do we fertilize the soil from which creativity arises? Much has been said about ideas, the germs of new things, the germs which arise in our minds, which lead forth to creative action. Ideas are the center of the creative process. Ideas are the expression of the creative talent. Ideas are the seeds from which creative products grow. As one scientist in a group whose actions were investigated stated it, "people have good ideas by having lots of ideas, but the way to have them is to start thinking. I make discoveries and have new ideas by training myself to have them or by getting myself in the proper condition."

Scientists have many methods of probing the unknown. They recognize that the story of science is the story of neither the completely predictable nor the absolutely controllable. As one theoretical physicist expressed it: "We have to understand what we do. We take a flying guess at something and then we check whether it is like the experiment." This determines whether the theoretical idea or viewpoint is correct or not correct, but the real question is: On what viewpoint to try to experiment. That's the creative aspect of inventing a new concept.

No two scientists work and think in just the same way. We proceed by common sense and ingenuity. There are no rules — only the principles of integrity and objectivity with the complete rejection of all authority except that of fact.

However, if you never chase side lines, you never find anything new. if you chase all side lines you never find anything either because you're running down too many blind alleys. The better intuition a person has, the more you find out he is full of facts. Facts of all kinds, often from unrelated fields, stimulate the mind.

Thus, we can cultivate a state of readiness for the unexpected. If we read a great deal, even possibly on subjects that seem unrelated to what we are doing at the present time, or if we read in related fields, this is apt to assist the process of creativity. As Kettering put it, "unintelligent motion is a great deal more important than intelligent standing still".

Most important is a willness to risk failure and a freedom from fear. No creative man can always be right or successful. You must be willing to take a batting average of less than 1000; if you want to be creative, you must be unafraid to do something wrong. You must be willing to try to acquire new skills regardless of whether you think that it is within you to do so. Nobody can do everything right at all times.

Finally, you must have sufficient self-discipline to take advantage of your creative periods through documentation. It is not enough to have the good idea while shaving or while driving your car to work. You must sit down and write it down as soon as you can. It is not enough to have a new solution formative in your head, you must perform the experiment, which will prove whether your theory is really the step forward, that you thought it might be.

Thus, we can encourage creativity through an atmosphere of freedom, through stimulation by other creative people, through willingness to put innovation before the rule book, and before vested interests, through willingness to learn new skills, through willingness to risk failure as well as excuse failure, when honestly come by, and through encouragement of drive and conviction.

Creativity is a tool to contribute productively to the complex world we live in. Creativity is a human talent, a potential, largely unused and unexploited. Creativity is the process for solving problems of the day, problems of the month and problems of the future. Creativity is the product, the novel and original contribution to mankind. It is our imprint on human progress.

Creativity is action, originality and value. It is not just a philosophical concept, not just an idea, a theory, it is action, change, movement. It is dynamic, non-static. It makes its impact on us and the world.

To understand creativity we must comprehend originality, the new and the unusual. Originality is the "surprise" step beyond the obvious, the difficult but immensely valuable capability of synergism, of achieving a whole greater than the sum of the components. That is the mysterious, the essential, the vital core of creativity.

Creativity is value. Value not only means money, but value must be thought of in terms of the irreplaceable commodity, the ever more valuable, nonlinear time function.

Every healthy human being is creative. It is not age, but social and educational pressures that tend to reduce creativity as we get along in years. This is not a natural or inherent necessity. These factors can be overcome.

Creativity can be taught. It can be cultivated, enhanced stimulated. It can be reawakened, nurtured, reinforced. Creativity training is worthwhile. As with other human talents, practice makes perfect. The potential of each individual can be developed to a degree seldom thought possible.

EMPHASIS
CREATIVITY: YOUR POTENTIAL

What can we do about it?

Creativity is a functioning of the senses.
Train your senses: vision, listening, feeling, touching, smelling.
Sharpen your sensitivity.
Increase your awareness.

Creativity is action.
Move.
Jump the inertia barrier.
Develop an attitude of "do", not "observe".
Bring yourself to be ready to pounce.

Creativity is originality.
Have an open mind at all times.
Practice a creative attitude.
Hold your judgments.
Use your imagination.
Yesterday's fantasy is today's reality.

Creativity means value.
Contribute to your life and that of others.
Add on, build, create something for others.
You are part of this world, society, the human race, culture.
It is not recognition, but contribution that counts.

EXERCISES

It is vitally important that you get in the act. Only through action can you practice creativity. You can train your potential. You can sharpen your senses.

1. Now that you have read Chapter 1, walk around the block four times and do nothing but think about the chapter.

2. What has changed in your world? What significant changes have you observed? Or have impinged on your life in the last week, the last month, the last year? How does the world compare between today and ten years ago? Write down specific

answers to these questions.

3. Make a list of things, areas, fields, activities you believe you are good at and those you believe are difficult for you. Take one, that you think you cannot do, and find a way of doing something about it.

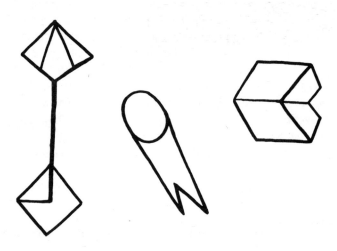

4. Creativity is an activity of the senses. The illustration shows three pictures of varying degrees of sensitivity. Look at them carefully. Write down descriptions that might enable you to reproduce them a number of times and then put the illustration away in a drawer. Then put a bare piece of paper on your night table and the next morning and three days later reproduce the drawing. Compare with the original. Do this during several weeks to see how much you can improve your capability of seeing the drawings and reproducing them from memory.

5. It pays to be in motion. Go for a fifteen minute jogging trip and see how much better you feel. Jump in one spot for three minutes. Stand still for three minutes, but try to cultivate the same feeling of motion which you experienced when jogging or when jumping up and down.

6. Spend a day looking for litter. Wherever you are, if you see a cigarette butt, a piece of paper, if you see a broken bottle, pick up the litter, collect it and discard it. Sharpen your eyes looking out for litter and act on it.

7. What actions have you put off in recent weeks? Make a list of anything you have put off in recent weeks or months. Examine each item that you have put off and take a first step toward accomplishing, what you wanted to do.

8. Lay down on a couch with a minimum of noise, no television, no radio, no

music and play an imagination game with yourself. First, try to think about a scene, about an image of the recent past or further back. Then try to think of an image which is novel, which is new, an imagination, a fantasy, a dream. Practice day dreaming for five minutes every day for one week. See what it does for you.

RECOMMENDED READING

The book can only serve as a guide to the vast and interesting literature on creativity. Many of the ideas have been expressed in one form or another by the competent and brilliant contributors to the more important fields of creativity training. Therefore, additional reading and acquisition of a library on creativity is vitally important as a contribution to the enhancement of your creative potential.

Richard de Mille, "Put Your Mother on the Ceiling: Children's Imagination Games", Walker and Company, New York.

John W. Gardner, "Self-Renewal, the Individual and the Innovative Society", Harper & Row, New York.

E. Paul Torrence, "Education and the Creative Potential", University of Minnesota Press.

E. Paul Torrence and R. E. Meyers, "Creative Learning and Teaching", Don Meade and Company, New York.

Arthur Koestler, "The Act of Creation", The MacMillan Co.

George F. Kneller, "The Art and Science of Creativity", Holt, Rinehart and Winslow, Inc., New York.

Stanley Rosner and Lawrence Fabt (Editors), "The Creative Experience: Why and How do We Create", Data Publishing Co, New York.

John R. Platt, "The Excitement of Science", The Riverside Press, Cambridge Press, 1962.

Sidney G. Parnes and Harold F. Harding, "The Source Book for Creative Thinking", Charles Scribners and Sons, New York, 1962.

Richard de Mille's book can be highly recommended as an excellent means to gather perspective concerning the role of imagination in the lives of children and adults. It is especially recommended for action in conjunction with young people. Paul Torrence's book is of great value, especially to teachers and anybody who is interested in helping to balance the nurturing of creativity with the gathering of knowledge. "Creative Learning and Teaching" is of particular value to the elementary school teacher, but would be helpful to anybody interested in furthering the creativity of the young. Koestler's book is the classic on creativity. It is most stimulating and fascinating. While somewhat difficult to read as a whole, it contains many interesting and inspiring concepts and should be on the library shelf of anybody interested in this subject. "The Creative Experience" is an interesting collection of brilliant conversations with brilliant people. It throws light on the subject of creativity from many sides and in many fields. – A must reading. – "The

Excitement of Science" is an excellent book to serve as an introduction to the science student or to stimulate and encourage the professional who feels that his work has become routine. Parnes and Harding's book is an excellent compilation of vital and classical research on the subject of creativity.

CHAPTER 2
ORIGINALITY

Effective surprise
Newness and relevance
Perceptive humans
Finding the unexpected
Seeing the undiscovered
Synergism 2 + 2 = 5
Images and imagination

Bisociation and humor
Change of direction
Creative displacement
Gates to fantasy
Charged with creative energy
To be different, to be different
Unconscious play

The magic ingredient in creativity is "originality".

Now, you might rightly say that we are just substituting one abstract word for another. Not so. We are looking at an interesting key and relating it to the other two components of creativity: action and value.

We are creatures of habit. Many of our actions every day are done routinely with little variation, without change, without thinking or even the slightest application of creativity. We get out of bed, shower, brush our teeth, breakfast, drive to work. Habit! Routine!

We have learned these routines well. From childhood we have established a pattern. It takes only one day of illness, such as a case of vertigo to really appreciate the habit of daily balance. The natural equilibrium, popping out of bed and standing upright without giving it a thought is a delightful routine.

The transition from sleep and dreams, where all these habits have been suspended, comes easy for us. We thrive on routine, on repetition, on order. In fact, our very process of learning stresses the orderly grouping of impressions, perceptions and concept. To learn, to acquire knowledge, we arrange, we sort, we file, we establish habits. This knowledge, all in its file drawers, allows us to deal with life's many routine situations. We are good at handling the common repetitive problems from day to day in quick, successive, easy fashion. Get up, shower, brush your teeth, breakfast, go to work, and now what?????

Can we live our entire day in this habitual, routine fashion? When does habit give out and when do we need something more? Where does routine end and originality begin?

We have little difficulty recognizing originality in the theories of an Albert Einstein or the paintings of a Picasso, a Dali, or a Matisse. No doubt the music of Aaron Copeland is original, but what of our daily lives? A routine life uses only a small fraction of human capabilities.

Brushing our teeth does not require much originality. Electric toothbrush or

$$E = mc^2$$

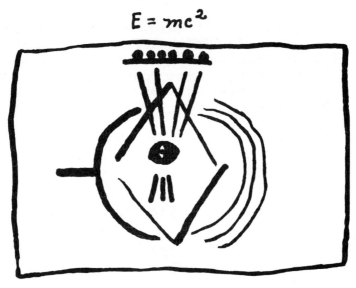

EINSTEIN OR PICASSO

manual operation, once we have established an efficient procedure it may actually be better to use it the same routine way every day.

So when does originality come into play? What is originality?

Originality is "newness with a plus". It isn't just newness, doing something the first time, it's more than new, it's original. If we can understand this plus factor, we will have come a long way in laying the foundation toward increasing our ability at being original. "Newness with a plus."

If I lay steel sheets up in stacks, I may be starting new piles every so often, but I am not being original or creative. If I write fairly standard business letters, I may write new letters to new customers. If I design a bolt for a specific job, I may be generating a new design. However, the shifting of steel, the letter writing, the design, are routine jobs for me. They may be new jobs; however, I have established a matrix, I have learned a routine way of doing these jobs. I do them according to a learned and established pattern. I follow a well established map.

Now, if I thought of a way of breaking that pattern, that might be original. A way of avoiding the drudgery of stacking those steel sheets, that could be newness with a plus, originality. A new kind of letter with a special twist might be original. If it was capable of an unusual result, if it offered special novel insights to the reader, it might be "newness with a plus". A significantly different fastener, maybe not a bolt, capable of doing the job in a uniquely different way might be original. A design getting an unexpected result might be "newness with a plus", originality.

What then is originality? What do we mean by it? How do we get "newness with a plus"?

26

Scientists and engineers are used to thinking in terms of extrapolations. We draw lines through the points we know and expect these lines to be valid in unknown areas. We assume that nothing unusual will happen or is present to upset our lines of extrapolation. We expect the unknown, the new to fall in line, to follow the rules we have learned and established. If the unexpected happens and we are off the line, we are surprised.

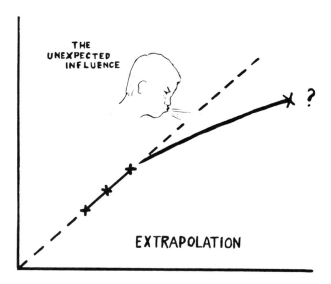

J. S. Bruner explains originality and creativity in excellent fashion by the concept of "effective surprise". He talks of "effective surprise as a hallmark of a creative enterprise".

Surprise, the unexpected happens. Surprise is nothing new to us, we experience it every day. Your son comes home unexpectedly. You have a raise in salary. A new and interesting coworker, an unusual observation or report was experienced during the day. We experience many surprises.

The unexpected that impinges on us, whether physically like an unexpected collision, or mentally like an unusual view or insight, you encounter it frequently in your daily, your weekly, your monthly activities.

But some surprises really matter. You are part of them. They are truly significant. Whether it be a sudden shock of recognition or a slow dawning, this surprise really counts.

To be an "effective surprise" an unexpected event must be related to something that counts, that matters, that is important.

"A painting lives only through him that looks at it." Pablo Picasso.

"The artist must speak to the human condition of the beholder if there is to be effective surprise." J. S. Bruner.

Originality is "newness with a plus", "effective surprise". Much that is new is not creative, not original. Accidents are not creative acts, neither are routine plans.

Bruner's "effective surprise", originality is the extra new, the significant and unexpected. "Oops! I never thought of that! I would have expected something else!" Even more embarrassing: "How obvious!" How simple and natural it seems now! Surprise! Eureka! Aha! "I've got it! Why did I not do that in the first place?! I should have seen that months ago! Oops! Now I see the light!"

That is originality, the "hallmark of creativity".

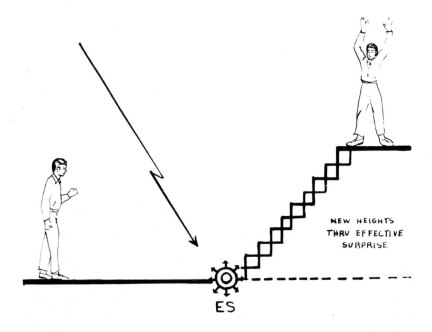

NEW HEIGHTS
THRU EFFECTIVE
SURPRISE

ES

Let's look at another model for the understanding of originality and its practice. Arthur Koestler in his magnificent book, "The Act of Creation", explains creativity, and originality in terms of our reactions to humor. He opens his book with a chapter entitled, "The Magic of Laughter".

What makes us laugh? What is humor? Under certain circumstances we laugh, we cannot help it. We do not really think, we want to laugh, in fact, we cannot force or control spontaneous laughter. Laughter is a reflex, a reaction to humor. Laughter is our spontaneous, almost automatic reaction to something that is funny.

No doubt the generation of humor, the writing of a joke, the creating of a humorous play or essay is a creative act. However, this does not concern us here, the question is: Why is something funny? The question is: Why do we laugh?

Possibly it would be easier to understand if we use the image of a train which goes merrily along on its established track. This is our normal routine way of following doggedly the line of extrapolation through the known and the unknown. Suddenly, there is another track, another train, an intersection of the two tracks, and a collision. Koestler calls this bisociation. We are all familiar with the term association which operates in the frame of one reference or matrix; a single plane relationship. Bisociation operates in two planes, two self consistent but normally incompatible frames of reference. However, this is an unusual, a surprising derailment. A rocket rises from the wreckage. Two tracks resulting in a new, an original, a very surprising change.

Let's look at some humorous examples. A woman bought a horse. She had it delivered to her apartment on the 34th floor in the city. After much commotion, the horse was safely inside the apartment. The delivery man could not contain himself any longer. "Lady", he asked, "why do you want your horse up here?"

"Well, for 40 years my husband has come through this door every evening asking, 'What's new dear?' I want to see his face tonight."

We are going along the well-known track, the usual: "What is the horse for?" A horse cannot fulfill its normal extrapolated function in an apartment building. Then suddenly the track of the routine husband. Bisociation, humor, or by now the explanation dawns on us. We see a connection, we experience bisociation, and we laugh, we react to the humor.

Another example is the battle of wits between Winston Churchill and Lady Astor.

Lady Astor: "If I were your wife, Winston, I would put poison in your coffee."

Churchill: "If I were your husband, Nancy, I would take it."

Bisociation looks at the plus factor in humor. It's "effective surprise", the second plane colliding with habit, the first plane which causes the explosion: "Laughter."

The theory of bisociation, explaining originality, is even easier to understand if we see it in the light of Bruner's concept of "effective surprise". We identify, we care, we move along with the story line of the joke. We "are" Winston or the delivery man. We put ourselves in their places, we are part of it. We are visualizing the scene. Suddenly, there comes a surprise, the unexpected, the other track, an insight. We get the point of the joke. We enjoy the sudden collision. We "see" the joke.

The result: "Laughter." Koestler calls laughter a "luxury reflex". It seems to serve no apparent biological purpose. When pricked with a pin, it is reasonable that we should have a reflex and move away. When suddenly exposed to a bright light, we blink our eyes. It's much harder to fathom your laughter, when Buddy fell down. "Shouldn't you have cried?"

Unexpectedness is not enough. Collision alone does not make for originality.

In Koestler's words: "There is a distinction between the routine skills of thinking on a single 'plane', as it were, and the creative act, which, as I shall try to show, always operates on more than one plane. The former may be called single minded, the latter a double minded, transitory state of unstable equilibrium where the balance of both emotion and thought is disturbed."

To laugh we need bisociation. We need "effective surprise". We must care about the joke. We must identify with it. We must see it or else it isn't funny. That is why humor ages so quickly. That is also why we have such difficulty enjoying a British joke. We are not part and parcel of the condition. We cannot identify if it is an "old joke" or if it is that "British humor".

The saying "Beef prices are so high, they no longer brand cattle, they engrave them," may not strike us as funny as soon as we have gotten used to the high cost of meat. However, it is a good example of bisociation, since we normally group branding with beef, engraving with money, and both leave their mark, collide in this simple, though not timeless joke.

Originality and humor both involve bisociation. But there is a difference. Laughter comes spontaneously as a reflex. Originality requires action, involvement. The creative act requires that we must do something consciously. In the element of action as against reflex, the enjoyment of humor, is different from creativity, but they share the concept of bisociation. They both are "effective surprise".

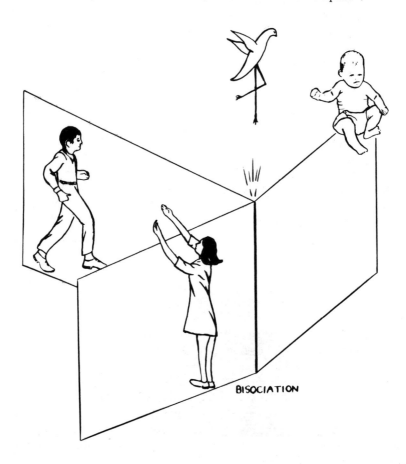

BISOCIATION

Our attention, our expectation, our concentration, our senses are well-established processes. We are focused in one direction. As Koestler puts it, "we are operating with one matrix". Now either suddenly or gradually, another set, another matrix, another focus combines with the first one, leading to the unusual, the funny, the humorous: laughter.

It is only a short step from laughter to creative originality. The same intersection of two processes, the same departure from the usual is evident. In both something happens to upset the line of extrapolation.

Koestler's concept of bisociation moves us from the normal plane, the plane in which extrapolations are always valid. The interference, that extra element, the flash of lightning, that extra track, joins with the normal elements to steer us in a new and original direction, to move us into a different plane, which has its own new paths.

The story teller carefully leads us up the primrose path only to surprise us with his punch line. We involve ourselves by listening, by reading the story to the degree that we experience a special kind of "effective surprise" when the departure comes. The result is spontaneous laughter, a reflex.

In the case of creative originality, we have the same pressures to come to the normal point. It is easy for us to follow the ordinary straight line, to stay in the established pattern, to see the expected image. Then, when we see it in the other, better way, we have a creative insight. The "original" has been generated. Whether this comes slowly or fast, whether an insight dawns upon us gradually, or whether we experience a sudden recognition, originality is not a reflex. Therefore, it is vital that we have the initiative, that we be trained to act. We must exploit the bisociation, the original, new paths.

The excellent writings of Donald A. Schon, offer another model, to the understanding of originality. It is the concept of "creative displacement".

We go along the normal, expected path. We progress along a well-established line, according to an imposed and accepted pattern. If we continued, we would be able

to go on, but we would be unable to achieve a higher level. To get up, to get out, we must make a "quantum jump", to the new level.

An outside influence may have helped us to achieve "creative displacement" or we may have built up the tension, the energy necessary for displacement within ourselves. We have collected all of the necessary pieces, found the one and unique idea to get that new and original insight. We have left the level of the obvious and are suddenly traveling on an original road.

Displacement originality illustrates even better than "effective surprise", that we are not just dealing with accidental change. Whether accident, incident, or plan, none has a monopoly on originality. Originality is not reserved to the stroke of genius, or to the fortunes of chance. Originality can be cultivated, facilitated, influenced, brought about, even almost controlled.

The "creative displacement" can be made to occur by overcoming our stability, our balance, our captivity in the normal groove. To generate the "quantum jump" we can learn to build up energies. We can try to minimize both our inertia, and build up the internal oscillations which suddenly will generate originality, leading us to a new and creative road.

We all believe we know how to "think". Our "thought processes" are rather familiar to us. Logic, reasoning are the concepts we are used to. Not so with originality, or imaginative creative activity.

It may be helpful to draw a parallel to our normal, everyday logical thought processes. Even though our brain is infinitely more powerful, we can compare it to a modern computer. Let us use the machine to assist our understanding of the relationship and the differences between originality and imagination and the logical, reasoning thought processes, stressed by mankind.

Our human computer can handle three types of input: language, numbers and images. It can manipulate these inputs logically to get the "expected results".

Language is the divine gift which elevates humans above the animal world and makes progress possible. The human computer begins with letters, words, and meanings, uses them in an agreed upon way, to reach the desired goal of communication. How to handle words is one of the first things we all learn.

Then there is the world of numbers: "1, 2, 3, $x = a + b$, $E = MC^2$ ...". We are good at numbers. We know how to manipulate them and put them to use in a thousand ways.

Most importantly, there is visual input. We do not always consciously consider it, but our mind, our human computer is excellently equipped to work with images. We practice "visual thinking". We are good at handling pictures of all kinds. "Circle, square, box, eggs, apples, clouds, trees . . ." We can see them in our minds and work with these images, "visual thinking".

Our brain combines and works with these inputs interchangeably. When we reason, think, we do not stop to consider whether we are using language, numbers, or images. We are working with all of them.

Now a computer works in an orderly fashion. It may work very fast, but it goes through thousands of gates in a predetermined orderly way. That is how it arrives at the desired result. So it is with our normal thought processes of reasoning. We go through the right gates. We go through the streets according to plan. We use a map made or learned for this purpose.

We select our gates in an orderly fashion. This may require much knowledge, much learning, and great skill, but it is the orderly, the logical, the predetermined way. Just as its mode of operation has been built and programmed into the machine computer, so our logical thought processes have been trained into our brain structure.

What role then does originality play? What about imagination, creativity? What about the "plus" function of the brain? What about this beautiful human talent that so far we have not been able to build into the machine? It is like a "pixie" let loose in all that intricate machinery. There is a free spirit there. It can bypass, shortcut, or leap over a thousand gates and come up with a superior, an unexpected, a "surprise" result. The input is the same, language, numbers or visions, but the result is unique: an original, a surprise. "Oops! I never thought of that!" It is like walking the streets with the map to get to our loved ones' house; however, suddenly we pull out the magic pogo stick and get there in one jump. Normally we "think". We are pedestrians looking for the gate. If we want to, we can fly. We can be creative.

We might look at originality in terms of the familiar "gate" of the science-fiction stories. In many we find the link between the world of today and the world of the past or the future. A "gate", the time tunnel that makes time travel possible is the opening to an original world. The "gate" allows the transition, it opens the door to a new and fantastic world.

Originality is the gate to creativity. Understanding the functioning of this gate, we can freely travel from the humdrum life of routine to the inspired existence of creative humans. We can achieve original results again and again. We can move freely onto original levels of greater human potential. Originality is the proof that the human computer is beyond the capabilities of mechanical or electronic computers, as we know them today. We have added the gate of originality to the machine gates. We have moved from the realistic, everyday world to the world of human creativity.

Effective surprise, bisociation, creative displacement, originality are our gates to greater contributions, greater fulfillment.

The normal thought processes of the average human are language oriented. Many professionals, especially lawyers, politicians and teachers, are most conscious of the language input, the language fabric of their activities. Mathematicians, bankers, and accountants, on the other hand are particularly adept at numbers.

To foster originality, most of us could greatly profit by training and developing further our abilities to handle visual input. The artist and the physician do a good job at this. To practice their professions, they have undergone extensive training in perception and working with images.

Whatever we do, training of the visual texture of our mind, visualization can make a particularly significant contribution to originality. Visualization can be the key to improved understanding in all professions. It can set off the bisociation, it can bring about the creative displacement. Adeptness at imagery, the ability to visualize, to see and to work with images contributes to originality in a major way.

To become more original, let us have a gay heart, let's be playful, let's be open minded, let's be receptive to the unexpected, but above all let us give the widest possible latitude to imagination. Imagination, images, seeing with our eyes closed, visualization: those are the roads to originality. Visualization is an excellent means to open the doors to bisociation. Our normal matrix, our abilities, our thought processes collide and bisect the inner image.

It is amazing how limited we are in our ability to solve problems with images in our minds. I have used the following brain teaser, related in Koestler's book in many creativity classes without finding students able to solve it quickly or easily. We are the slaves of our culture, our education, unable to free ourselves, even when we are told to use our imagination, our ability to see pictures, images in our minds.

"One morning, exactly at sunrise, a Buddhist monk begins to climb a tall mountain. The narrow path, no more than a foot or two wide, spiraled around the mountain to a glimmering temple at the summit.

The monk ascended the path at varying rates of speed, stopping many times along the way to rest, and to eat the dried fruit he carried with him. He reached the temple shortly before sunset. After several days of fasting and meditation he began his journey back along the same path, starting at sunrise and again walking at variable speeds, with many pauses along the way. His average speed descending was of course, greater than his average climbing speed.

Prove that there is a spot along the path, that the monk will occupy on both trips at precisely the same time of day."

We are likely to try a mathematical approach at solving the problem, or we think about speed, distance, data which we are not given. Few of us will quickly visualize a super imposed picture of the monk traveling up and the monk traveling down, a doubling of the monk so to say. If we visualize that, the solution is obvious: they must meet somewhere, sometime.

Imagination is more than bringing images into consciousness, imagination is an act of the mind that contributes the most, and helps us most to produce new ideas or insights. Out of chaos, imagination forms a thing of beauty or of truth. It is imagination more than reason which helps us to create, to generate the original.

Regardless of where we seek originality, whether it be in our private lives or our profession, whether it be in artistic expression, play, entertainment or work, originality comes most readily if we maintain a relaxed attitude, allowing the "pixie" to work. We must encourage and favor a shift to those tracks which are not the normal ones. We must see those images that have not been stressed or observed in our past, regular exposures.

Jerome B. Wiesner in reviewing creative performance in the sciences, emphasizes that the creative phases of the research process appear to be loose and informal and very personal. They are very different from the highly structured and formal way in which scientists report their results. Wiesner states: "it seems clear that it is this private, relatively unstructured, perhaps only partly conscious process that results in the creation of new ideas and insights."

He stresses: "although analogy and metaphor are techniques definitely pre-scribed for formal reasoning, they may turn out to be dominant in the intuitive, sometimes illogical and initially random process of scanning and searching for new connections and clues. To be creatively efficient, such scanning and searching might well need an uninhibited, habitually exercised capability to consider, and explore, ideas in true contradiction to accepted fact: obviously, the larger the universe of relevant data, the greater the efficiency of the process."

Here we have one of the greatest scientists of our times exhorting us to let the pixie have free rein. He tells us to explore in contradiction, to hunt for that second track, to fly instead of walk.

With an understanding of originality, with the concept of "effective surprise; the image of Koestler's "bisociation process", and the possibilities of "creative displace-ment" we have gained vital clues and a basis for stimulating and developing our originality.

We can now make thinking easier. We can go beyond logic. We can generate the environment and the attitude which will allow us to find the unexpected and see the undiscovered. Effective surprise happens to those who are really looking for it to occur. Only those who are prepared, will experience the creative displacement. We must generate the energy, fill the vessel to the brim for originality to erupt.

We have stressed before that creativity does not originate in a vacuum. We combine elements not previously combined in an original fashion. These original combinations, that produce effective surprise require valid input. They almost always require craftsmanship. They require work, and they require skills. Bruner recounts his daughter's conversation with the famous figure skater, Dick Button. She asked him how to achieve his creative perception of skating performance. His answer was: "practice, practice, practice!"

Thus, the striving for originality cannot be an excuse from the need of develop-ing skills. We must have craftsmanship. Admittedly, this can be very arduous, it can even be a very long routine and tedious job. It will be insistence on hard work: "practice, practice, practice!"

Another vitally needed attitude that follows from our understanding of original-ity is a *willingness to be different*. If you will not deviate from habit, if you won't depart from tradition, effective surprise will be hard to come by. You must cul-tivate an open mind. You must develop a high degree of tolerance for new influ-ences. You must be ready to do anything other than the obvious. In fact, for the development of your originality, you should exercise being intentionally different. Avoid the obvious, the commonplace.

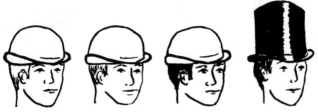

Dare To Be Different

The action drive must carry over into the stimulation, the exercising of your originality. You must not only act, you must want to act. There must be passion. There must be commitment, there must be a will to go a different route. The creative individual, whether engineer, scientist, banker, lawyer, or poet, finds his individualistic, his nonconventional, his original role through an inner drive. This inner drive can be encouraged, it can be cultivated. We must not only see, act or think originally, we must believe in being "original". In fact, it helps to be "*an original*". Original people do not have to be nuts, but being a bit nutty in the eyes of the routine plodders should be welcome.

To foster originality, we must be receptive humans. This alertness can be cultivated. We can be ready for the "effective surprise", we can be oscillating for "creative displacement".

We can practice action to foster originality. Moving will get us there. This means opening the door to play and games, to random thoughts and random pieces of information. Standing still in the midst of old rules and conventions cannot engender originality. Keep on jogging. Move around mentally or let your senses, even your unconscious hunt around and effective surprise will strike.

Koestler's concept of "bisociation" is particularly helpful in understanding why so many significant acts are the results of combinations of widely different areas of human endeavor. *Gutenberg's bible*, the revolutionary invention of the printing press was an original combination of the wine press and wooden block letters. Both were known widely at that time. However they originated from two widely different arenas of activity. To foster originality then, to facilitate the bisociation process, to encourage creativity, we have to counter today's specialization with broadening efforts.

Creativity will be fostered and originality stimulated by jumping out of the narrow boxes of over-specialization. We greatly increase the chances of bisociation to occur by studying, playing, and exposing ourselves to perceptions outside our normal area of activity.

It is true, that in our complicated world of today, specialization is unavoidable. But narrow focus, full concentration in a fenced in field can easily inhibit originality. Therefore, read outside your specialty. Engineers should study anthropology, ancient history or biology. Maybe they should pick up daVinci's books, such as his fine work on anatomy.

36

Bankers, how about a course on modern communications? Or a lesson in painting?! Scientists, read any book, "but any book" as far removed as possible from what you are most keenly interested in at this moment. Lawyers! Science can be interesting! You do live in a scientific world. Science can help you towards an original solution for your next case.

The skills learned in one field of specialization can be applied to another. Changing fields, can be highly beneficial. At the point of change you may at first think that every specialized piece of knowledge is wasted. However, it may be just this input which may serve as the basis for instant solutions, never thought of by the practitioner who has spent many years in the field you have just entered. True, stability and craftsmanship are vital in many fields of specialization. However, transfer and change can lead to cross-fertilization and blossoming of originality not otherwise attainable.

In that connection a warning is in order. Creativity is mainly synthesis, putting building blocks together to yield effective surprise. While analysis is vital to problem definition, which is the beginning of many creative processes, analysis must be followed by synthesis. We must not take things apart without putting something new back together.

There are human beings who are endowed with a particularly strong analytical sense. They are used to allowing their analytical attitude to dominate. They can take things apart beautifully. They have the knack to see the flaws. These people do not always have the ability to be open to effective surprise. In an oversimplified fashion we might say, there are positive and negative people. Originality requires positive people, people who can see beyond the flaws. What we are trying to do is to convert both positive and negative people into "unusual people". That is, what it is all about.

Originality can get a particular boost from the study and enjoyment of the arts. Not only professionals, but all of us underestimate the stimulation we can get from various art experiences. There is a natural association of "art" with a sense of "implied spontaneity". When we think of art we almost automatically think of enjoyment. This can be carried into our personal activities of all kinds. It will make a real contribution to originality. Art in all its forms can contribute much to the nonartistic specializations. We should go back to the playful, spontaneous, to the artistic, original, creative approach which we first encountered in our early years of kindergarten and schooling. We can regain the simplicity of those first images, sandcastles, or that first look at sand grains under the magnifier. We can strive to visualize our difficult complex problems with the simplicity and beauty of the colored picture of that first drop of food coloring billowing out in the water.

All art forms from poetry to sculpture can make an important contribution to the stimulation of our personal style, our personal ability to be original. Poul Anderson's intriguing science-fiction story, "By Worlder", describes the Sigman, a strange creature from a distant world. The Sigman circles earth in a superb space ship, obviously for some purpose. Humanity tries to solve the riddle. Establishing language contact proves to be extremely difficult. All attempts at discovering the wishes of the Sigman, all attempts of communicating with it seem doomed to failure.

It remains to the artist to determine its desires. The Sigman visits earth in search of artistic, creative stimulation. It is only the artist through the use of art forms who can establish contact and fulfill the Sigman's wishes.

Imagination, fantasy. Are we in the real or the dream world? There's much discussion of whether we can create in our dreams. A dreamlike state, a fully relaxed mind is certainly more open, more receptive to effective surprise than a mind engaged in a routine procedure. Dreams and displacement are natural combinations. We have left the real world for the dream world.

Imagination is our unconscious at play. It is the paddle with which we can stir around in those recesses of our minds that are hard to get at. Imagination allows us to put our subconscious to work side by side with our conscious efforts. We may not be able to create in our dreams, but dreams contribute to our creativity.

Gordon Parks, a highly creative renaissance type of man, known for his photography and films, as well as his musical compositions, describes how he traces his love for music back to a daydream he had when he was seven years old.

"The Kansas day was hot and I was hunting June bugs in our cornfield when I heard a murmuring in the corn stalks. The murmuring grew into music and I stood there with my mouth full of mulberries, puzzled, looking up at the slow drifting clouds — wondering if there was a music source. The violins, horns and drums were as true to me as the sunlight, and I had a feeling the music was trapped inside my head, that it would have been there even if I had no ears. I covered them with my hands, and the sounds were still there and they continued until all the clouds had moved away and there was nothing but pale sky. Then it was gone as mysteriously as it had come, and I ran towards the house a little frightened, a little joyful. Then in a frenzy I started banging on our old Kimball upright, trying to reproduce the sounds I had heard."

Gordon Parks ascribes his initial desire to compose music to this beautiful dream.

Gene Houston, Director of the Foundation for Mind Research in Pomono, N.Y., has experimented with trances and their relationship to creative work. Subjects were put in a trance in a number of traditional ways such as hypnosis; no drugs were used. One of the subjects, an author who could not finish a novel, was instructed to "watch and listen to the characters in his book as they finished the story".

After three trances during which the characters played out the three remaining chapters, he was able to finish his book.

In Houston's laboratory, a pianist claimed he condensed eight hours of practice into 10 minutes and thus elucidated a Bach toccata. Even more remarkable was an entranced lady songwriter who during the trance imagined listening to a cabaret singer singing three songs. She was able to sing the songs complete with lyrics. She had, in fact, composed them.

These experiments do not rule out that they just set up the creative conditions for originality in a concentrated fashion after the subjects came out of the trance. However, they are an intriguing addition to our knowledge of imagination and the subconscious and the fostering of originality.

Imagination leads us to another door to originality, the striving for synergism. Synergism is the ability to get more for our money, to get the extra out of using our resources. Synergism is to add up the components and obtain a result which is more than the usual, obvious combination. The artist combines three stones into a work of art, a monument. To us, they were just three stones. We might have made them into a pile of stones. He made them into a work of art.

Thus striving for more, for excellence, for the special *effect*, for the unusual result, aiming at the plus leads to originality. If we aim for novelty, we aim for getting more than the normal result. If we expect $2 + 2$ to give us more than 4, we are likely to achieve originality.

Creative people have the knack for getting results with simple tools. They are usually masters at the art of improvisation. In practicing originality, in striving for synergism, we must foster an attitude of "everything is possible with the means at hand". The tools we have can do the trick. They may have been made for a totally different purpose. A scissors or a string may serve as a pendulum. A shoelace makes a good string. A shoe a good hammer. $2 + 2 = 5$. Get results with the means at hand.

To foster originality we must not readily be satisfied, we must keep on trying for the better, the best, the unusual, the unobvious. Only excellence is good enough to the creative individual.

Gordon Parks in his advice to young people, urged them not only to excel, but to learn their craft well, so that it becomes a natural extension of their personality. He urged experimentation, through it we can discover unpredictable things. We can use the tools in an unpredictable way. To quote him, "and there are the things hiding, waiting to be flushed out and exposed, that makes a difference.

The late Vivian Rivkin, who performed three of my piano sonatas, used to threaten to slit my throat because I insisted that she strike a particular cluster of notes with her fists instead of a more pianistic way with her fingers. She told me, 'I would not dare to do that before an audience'. I worked with her for one full afternoon on this passage, which was a rather violent one. Finally after pounding her fingers swollen trying again, and again to gain the effect, she shouted, 'to hell with that stupid chord'! And she banged it with her fist and then she grinned, and to my pleasure, she banged it the same way during the concert that evening."

Finally, if you want to encounter effective surprise or meet yourself at the bisociation corner, do not be afraid. Be ready, willing and able to experience displacement from the road you are on, to change paths, to jump to an original or more challenging surrounding. Feel free to go down the less worn path. Do not be afraid. Explore, experiment, play around. Detours can be fun. The seldom used road may lead us there. We must want to get off the ground and learn to fly.

You must learn to practice "Serendipity".

We owe this term to a lovely tale by the late Horace Walpole who revived an ancient Persian story of the Princes of Serendip. In the fairy tale the three Princes of Serendip traveled far and wide. They were always making discoveries by accident, of things that they were not really searching for.

Serendipity is not just an act of luck. It is a mental attitude of "travel with open eyes". Have open eyes ready to go. Carry your magic pogo stick. All humans are individualistic. No two of us are alike. So be a Prince of Serendip. Maybe for you it's reading certain types of books. Maybe it's visiting museums. Maybe you should talk more to strangers. Maybe you should take courses in a new field. To practice serendipity, we must search, we must hunt, we must play around, we must look for new ways to add ammunition, to add components which will contribute to our originality. Go out and travel. Go out in search of new impressions, new perceptions, new food for your imagination. You will find originality on the way.

Whether it be in your private life, your profession, your job or during your leisure hours, your life need not be dull. Originality is there for the taking. You can make happy headway with a string of surprises. You can discover and unleash your hidden potential and even surprise yourself.

ACTION PAGE

ORIGINALITY

"Understand Originality"

Get away from the daily routine of extrapolation. The obvious may be avoided. Practice effective surprise!

Unexpected, significant and relevant. Practice "bisociation"!

Humor, laughter, originality, break through to an original plane. Practice creative displacement!

Increase that charge, intensify the pressures. Favor the receptivity to enable the quantum jump.

Words, numbers and images.
Visualization favors originality.
Maintain a relaxed attitude, explore and play around.
Originality does not thrive in a vacuum.
Practice, practice, practice.
Willingness to be different counts.
Jump out of the narrow box of over-specialization. Changing fields can foster effective surprise.
Enjoy, appreciate, practice an art form or two.
Learn to see with your eyes closed.
Fantasy and dreams, a playful road to originality.
Strive for unusual results, look for synergisms.
Only excellence is satisfactory.
Serendipity! Be a happy Prince. Be ready for the unexpected.

EXERCISES

Write down ten humorous captions for the picture of the kangaroo.

Have a friend cut out twenty cartoons from magazines for you without the captions and write your own original captions, try and try again. Do not give up too easily.

Get six of the best jokes (surprise effect) from books, papers or from friends. Memorize them. Try them on your friends and watch for the surprise effect.

Take a blank sheet of typewriter paper, heavy felt pen and copy on each separate sheet the marks which are shown on the following page.

Now complete the most original sketch you can, using what is already on the paper. Close your eyes and try to visualize it before you start drawing.

Try to write a short composition using all the words listed, adding only verbs, prepositions and articles:

Beauty queen, front door, trumpet, elevator, president, clothes, bear, eskimo, jogging, transparent, space ship, friend, wheel chair, men, stork.

Write a short story to the following titles:

The Upsidedown Belly Dancer
Flying Fish of Glass
Turning a Round Corner
The Man Who Spit in the Ocean
The Last Ride on the Orient Express
The Computer Went Wild

RECOMMENDED READING

Jerome S. Bruner, "The Conditions of Creativity and Contemporary Approaches to Creative Thinking: A Symposium at the University of Colorado", Atherton Press, New York, 1967.

Gordon Parks, "Creativity to Me: Creativity, A Discussion at the Nobel Conference", North Holland Publishing Company, Fleet Academic Editions, New York, 1970.

Arthur Koestler, "The Art of Creation", Chapters 1 through 6.

Donald A. Schon, "Inventions and the Revolution of Ideas", Tavistock Publications, 1963. "Displacement of Concepts", Tavistock Publications, 1963.

Frank Baron, "Creativity and Personal Freedom", Northstrand Insight Series. Northstrand Company Inc., Princeton, NJ, 1968. See especially Chapter 16, page 200.

Jerome B. Wiesner, "Education for Creativity in the Sciences", "Daedulus Creativity and Learning, Summer, 1965", Journal of the American Academy of Arts and Sciences.

Ernest Dichter, "Motivating Human Behavior", McGrawHill Book Company, New York, 1971.

Poul Anderson, "The By Worlder", Signet Book, New American Library, 1971.

"We never really come into direct contact with reality."

> William V. Haney
> Communicational and
> Organizational Behavior

"What we call seeing
Is the interpretative imagining in the brain
Of the significance and meaning
Of the nervous system reports
Of an assumed outsideness of self."

> Buckminister Fuller,
> Intuition.

"A technologically explosive society needs the integrating reward of art experience."

> Duane Preble,
> Man creates Art creates Man

"A work of art is a statement about the nature of reality. From an infinite number of possible configurations of forces, it picks and presents one."

> Rudolph Arnheim,
> Art and Visual Perception.

CHAPTER 3
PERCEPTION: DOORS TO AWARENESS

Sleepwalkers awake	Preconceived notions
Fill your memory banks	Television and other barriers
Use all your senses	Removing the blinders
Your perceptive potential	Vision and visualization
Open your eyes and see	Total sensitivity
"Feel" the world	Perception creates fertile soil
Eyes in the back of your head	Output is based on input

Perception. Doors to awareness!

Did you know that you see the left side of the stage first when the curtain opens in the theater?

Did you know that a bright spot in a painting out of balance with the whole looks to you like a hole in the canvas?

Did you know that you perceive only a very small portion of what you see, that you see what you want to see?

Did you know that the talented artist can coordinate the sound of the music he generates with the desire of his expression and the touch of his hands?

Did you know that you can learn to develop your ability to taste wine to the fine point of recognizing vintage and origin?

Did you know that a talented machinist can develop his sense of touch to compete with the most accurate instruments?

Perception is the basis of performance. It has been said that eyesight is insight. Eyesight, hearing, touch, taste, smell, our senses determine our innermost capability of perception. They are our tools, our contact with the world around us. They form the bridge between the creative self and reality. More than a bridge, perception shapes our creative self. We perceive the real world as we recreate it within us.

Do you face each day with open eyes? Do you know how to see, what to look for? Do you truly hear what he is saying? How fast can you perceive something? Do you notice the important things in your life?

Sleepwalker! Awake! Forsake the dormant stage. Open your eyes, and unplug your ears. Alert your mind. Taste life and smell your surroundings. You will not only live a more successful and happier life, but you will also open and reopen the doors to your creative abilities.

Have you had adequate instruction in the use of your senses since kindergarten? Once you started grade school were your senses taken for granted? You were taught the 3 R's, reading, 'riting and 'rithmetic. But were you expected to see, hear, taste, smell, without training or assistance?

The arts are uniquely suited to help develop our vision, our musical perception, leading to improved hearing and listening and shaping our sense of feel and touch. Did art education play only a secondary role in your life?

Do you believe that the training, the conditioning of our senses is taken seriously in our society? Many career failures can be directly traced to a lack of sufficient and well-developed perceptive skills. One of my best friends, a brilliant chemist, was unable to progress at one point in his career. After much soul searching and investigation, it was determined that he had an abnormally low reading speed. That can be fatal for a scientist. An intense course in speed reading, an excellent example of our capabilities in modern perception training, put him back on the road, and opened the doors to a highly successful future.

Ability to perceive, skills of visualization, total image forming, and use of all of the senses is vital to creativity for two reasons.

First, creativity, especially the originality portion of the creative process, is the non-obvious way of putting things together. The better your perception, the more pieces, the more ammunition you will have to work your creative will.

The more colors you have seen the more you can paint them. The more you are used to seeing tell-tale signs of a chemical reaction in a flask, whether they be smell, color, pressure, temperature, or viscosity, the more you may guide it creatively to the desired goal.

The more you are used to seeing the faint unconscious signals in a man's face or in the movement of his hands, or the reaction of his body, the more you may reach an understanding of his true motivations and values.

The new, the original, the creative act is based on past perceptions. Tomorrow's past is today. The more we can truly perceive, fully absorb, joyfully live for today, the more creative can we be tomorrow.

But there is a second reason why perception is so important to creativity. There is another reason why perception training is key to the improvement; the full use of your creative abilities. There is a close relationship between the creative process and the process of perception. We've discussed the close ties of thought and reasoning to the creative act. Both are intimately linked to perception and memory. You may think of a triangle with creativity and imagination on the left, thought and reasoning on the right and perception and memory at the base. Thus, interrelated and working together, they establish our unique human performance. Understanding, cultivating perception can not help but contribute greatly to the development of your creativity.

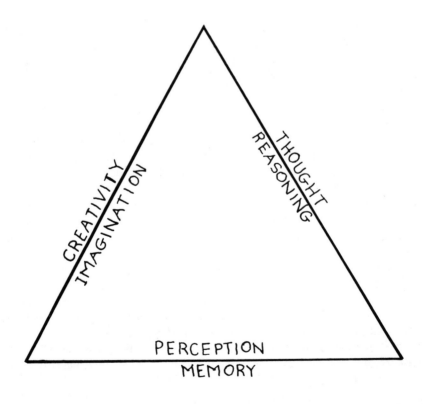

Except for the specialist in a certain branch of psychology, or the artist philosopher, most professionals think of perception in terms of its mechanics, its physical working. The camera comes to mind. The microphone. But human vision is not like photography, and the process of hearing is not like the operation of a recording studio. Human perception is a highly complex and interesting systems operation. It uses and combines the senses in a unique way. It is not as most of us might think, an addition of many different pieces. It is not a puzzle to be fitted together. On the contrary, we perceive a large picture as a whole and select from it meaningful portions or segments to notice and remember.

Let us choose reading as an example of perception. Do you know your reading speed? The average skilled reader can perceive between 300 and 600 words per minute. Now to do this he doesn't go about it step by step identifying 10 to 20 words per second, or even 40 to 80 individual letters. His reading speed, his perception is only possible because he takes in the entire system, the total reading image, the text. He could not handle that many isolated words or letters; however, since our perception works on a total system basis, he can read at this speed.

A good glass of wine, the open window or the strains of a beautiful melody, these are complex systems made up of large numbers of stimuli to the eyes, the nose, the ears, the total of our senses. What we perceive, how much we perceive depends on us.

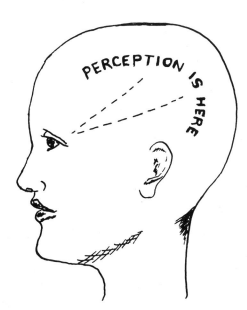

Perception is in us, in our mind, not out there. It is not even in our eyes, our ears nor in the total human apparatus of vision, hearing, tasting or smelling. Perception is more than that. It is the ability to take in, to work with the senses, and, most important, to absorb and to select from the multifold stimuli of the complex and wonderful outside world. Selection of the significant is the key to better perception. It is also the basis of improved retention, since obviously it is more difficult to remember that which has not been properly perceived.

There is much "out there" but our attention span is limited. We pay attention to certain parts of the whole, and only vaguely take in the rest. We focus on certain aspects of the available total. How much, how fast, which part? What is the extent of our ability to perceive? What do we hear, see, perceive? Which signals do penetrate to our mind? How well are they received, digested, and interpreted? This depends on the whole environment, the context in which they are perceived.

Ambiguous stimuli are interpreted in a straightforward way once we put them in context. The message we had such a difficult time seeing, now seems obvious. The hidden animal in the landscape, which we had such trouble finding, now is readily identified and clearly visible. "Oops! Why didn't I see that in the first place?"

Our perception, whether it be recognition of a figure, a pattern, the understanding of a phrase in a foreign language, or the recognition of the taste of a California wine is adaptable, dynamic, flexible. It can be sharpened and trained. We tune in on the picture, the melody, the voice to perceive better.

If you want to prove to yourself that you can train your perception readily, take a simple child's book and try reading it upside down. Practice for a while. At first you will find no dramatic increase in your skills. You will have trouble seeing letters, words, and making sense out of it. But as you continue you will find yourself reading sentences more and more rapidly. You will put words in context. You will begin to see the system even in this unusual position. Similarly, when you listen to a speaker with an accent, or a speaker with a particular habit of addressing you, you will find that initially you have some difficulty of hearing, of understanding him, of putting his words in context. Soon, however, you will get used to his mode of presentation and you will be perceiving the content of his presentation. Finally you will not notice the strangeness, that first made perception so difficult for you.

Our perception depends on our state of mind, our conditioning. There are many facets to the interesting and complex processes of perception. The human ability to perceive has several dimensions. Maybe it will be easier to understand if we once again use the computer for comparison.

When we think of the computer, first we must consider its design and its construction. If it is well put together and well-designed it may do many complex operations at high speed. But only if it is in good order can it perform all we might expect of it. Similarly, a blind man cannot see, and color blindness is a substantial handicap to many people. We must make sure our perception apparatus is in good working condition. While we are used to having our eyes examined, much greater stress needs to be put on assuring that all of our senses are in the best possible working order. It is vital to determine the ability of our senses to function. Testing should go beyond the normal medical examination and include some of the modern measurements of sensing: speed, range and threshold. The last is our ability to detect differences. Finding our limitations can be significant to the improvement and training which is so vital for our further development. Every means at our disposal should be used to put the perception equipment in the best possible shape, whether this be vitamins or eyeglasses, eye training, hearing aids, or just jogging or playing tennis to improve our health and to sharpen our reflexes.

The computer can also store information. If we put more and more into the computer memory and set it up with a program to solve our problem, it has a greater ability to assist us in our work. Similarly in perception if we have once seen a cow, we are able to identify other cows even though they may be very different in size, color, and other particulars. This is called grouping by the psychologist. It is a vital part of our perceptive capabilities. Just as the computer stores up information and uses it through an effective program, so does our ability to perceive. This can be trained, sharpened and improved by exercising it. If you exercise your taste, you will be able to recognize fine differences and enjoy pleasures that you were unable to experience before. You can be trained through continuous seeing to recognize many types of airplanes, as the plane spotters were trained during the last world war. Their ability to group, to categorize various visual impressions was carefully increased. You are able to sharpen your sense of seeing to an extent, you might have believed impossible.

It is no accident that the blind man's sense of touch is so highly developed. Necessity is a great stimulus for training. But even without such dire motivation it is possible to improve storage and program, that relates to our perception.

In Rudyard Kipling's classic adventure story, Kim, the boy is taught the "jewel game."

In the jewel game Kim was shown a copper tray full of objects. He was told to count them, to handle them, to look at them. Then after the tray was removed, he was asked to remember the items and to describe them in detail. The object was to take one look and recount them all in great detail. Kim first was totally unable to even remember all of the objects on the tray, but with consistent training he sharpened his perceptive skills and was able to become a master at the "jewel game."

We must all learn the "jewel game." It will greatly contribute to our lives and especially to our creative performance. Modern speed reading is just one excellent example of how we can systematically sharpen our perception.

Finally, let us complete our comparison to the machine. The computer, as necessary as it may be to modern civilization, is in essence still a glorified adding machine. It is only a very weak shadow of that marvelous human brain with its almost unlimited abilities for perception, imagination and reasoning. If we feed the computer a wrong number, a wrong input, the end result, the output cannot be right. The computer may be programmed not to accept my wrong number, but then everything stops. In the words of the computer programmer, "garbage in — garbage out."

We can draw an interesting parallel to perception. It is obvious that I cannot hear Beethoven's symphony at a rock and roll concert. Now you might say, that I will stay away from a rock and roll concert if I like Beethoven, or, conversely, I will stay away from symphony hall if I like rock and roll. This however we seldom do. We are the slave of our surroundings, of fashion, and of inertia. We listen to whatever is handy on the radio or television and see whatever is conveniently available. Therefore, an intentional effort to expose our senses to what is worthwhile, to open our perceptive eye to the beautiful, the excellent, to reach out to unique stimuli is called for.

This also has a bearing on the influence, discussed earlier, of prior information, the storage of past impressions in relation to our perceptive ability. The experiences which I have today, affect my ability to perceive tomorrow. Thus, children brought up on good art are more likely to see and appreciate good art than those primarily exposed to ordinary magazine advertisements. The perceptions stored, when we are young, have a great bearing on what we perceive as we grow up. If you have been brought up in the country you may have a greater ability to enjoy its beauty, but your perception of the city's features will be limited.

Even more important is mental conditioning. Conditioning which is not truly related to a specific perception can never-the-less influence it in a major way. We see what we are conditioned to look for. In the illustration on the next page the sailor will see the ship, the priest the church and the engineer the bridge.

There are clouds in the sky every day. Engineers or lawyers are not apt to see them. But the artist who has to write about them or paint them, knows what clouds look like.

What do clouds look like? What are their colors? Most of us think of clouds in terms of our high school science experience, where we may have learned about the different types of clouds. We think of big balls and feathers, and most likely we think of clouds as white. But there our visualization ends. In creativity classes I have asked the question: "What do you notice, that most clouds have in common, as you look at them up in the sky?" Usually a vacant stare greets me. Very few people other than artists have noticed that clouds are usually dark at the bottom. This is not too surprising since the light during most of the day comes from the top. When you go out, look at the clouds. Notice their shape and fine shading, the many colors other than gray and white that you might see. Confirm that they are usually darker on the underside.

What we perceive does not depend just on prior input, but on our attitudes, our desires, our orientation. What do we select? What do we put in?

For example, how do you look at people? Look at your loved ones, or the man or woman sitting next to you, or your boss. Now go out of the room, or if you can not do that, close your eyes. What kind of a nose does he or she have? Unless you are a portrait painter, you normally don't include noses as part of your perception of human beings. Yes, there may be someone with a very unusual nose. But that is the exception. We may look at some certain parts of the anatomy of a pretty woman, we may look at eyes, hair, hands, legs, but rarely noses.

HARBOR

AS SEEN BY SAILOR

AS SEEN BY MINISTER

AS SEEN BY ENGINEER

Our mental attitude then, our willingness to see, our desire to experience the specific something, our interest in the information has a bearing on the process of perception. This does not always work to our advantage. We can so completely succumb to conditioning that we bias our perception.

The interrogator listens and watches for tell-tale signs of discrepancies and lies. The negotiator hears key words indicating possible agreement and consensus. The student looks for understanding and for significant items worth memorizing. We see the red warning light in the control room. We see that one beautifully colored tree in the forest. Are we looking for the right things?

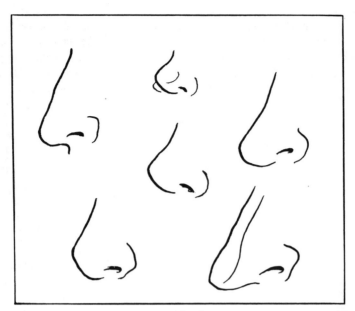

NOSES

Do You See Only The Smoke?

Pollution is much on our minds these days. Have you caught yourself looking at a beautiful landscape and singling out that lonesome smoke stack and its plume, the most noticeable and ugly feature? Only a few years ago you might have perceived that smoke stack and its plume as a pleasant and picturesque accent to the beautiful landscape. Yesterday's factory image as a source of employment and wealth and progress is gone. We only see the smoke, not the building, the plant, the real undertaking.

Most recently I caught myself focusing on three plastic cups and one discarded bottle at a beautiful California beach that I had never seen before. How much better to be conditioned to see the flowers, the birds, the rocks, and the shape of the waves. Surely the trained bird watcher is seeing birds before he sees litter.

Perception is what we take in. The total system. It is the portion that we pay attention to, that we absorb with our mind. It is strongly influenced by the contexts in which we experience it. It is also strongly influenced by our attitudes and conditioning.

Our ability to perceive is a function of our health, the state of our sensing organs, and our total alertness. It is the result of past perceptions and learning, since they are part of the context in our mind. The greater the storage and the better the program, the more we are perceptive. Conditioning plays a great role. We perceive what we look for. The search for taste is rewarded by good wine, the search for beauty by a lovely sunset. Whether we perceive the beauty of the soul or the deformity of a cripple, it is up to us. Most important of all we can do much about our perceptive skills. Perception can be trained and developed.

We have many senses — touch, smell and taste require almost direct contact. Hearing and vision can bridge larger distances — they are "distance senses". Vision more than any other sense is the key to our creative performance. Music is most purely creative since it is not tied to human language. Having a language all of its own, it has an almost direct impact. Not only composing a melody but also listening to music is truly a creative act. Except for the highly trained professional musician, this is direct sensual experience. There can be no mistaking between reasoning, logic, thinking, and creative perception here.

How do we truly and effectively use our perceptive potential? Can we improve it? We have mentioned that practice makes perfect. How do we "practice" seeing, hearing, or tasting? What should we look for? What is there to hear? How do we go about it? Can we develop our taste buds? Are we afraid to touch? Can smelling be pleasant? Most important how do I see, what is worthwhile, what I want to see?

Vision has a unique and important role. Improvement of vision, that is, conscious and effective seeing, can be of great help to us. In his stimulating book, "Visual Thinking", Rudolph Arnheim talks about "essential ingredients of perception itself".

He lists:

active exploration	correction
selection	comparison

grouping essentials	problem solving
simplification	combining
abstractions	separating
analysis and synthesis	putting in context
completion	

We professionals can learn much from the artist. The artist, whether in a film, on canvas, or in a book of poems gives us his "packaged perception". He hopes that he has chosen and reproduced for us a worthwhile experience. He has preselected a system for us.

A scientist friend and I were window shopping in Santa Barbara admiring beautiful paintings on exhibit in the many galleries that cater to the visitors. It was a relevation to him, that you could more than glance at, or just see a painting. I suggested that he let his eyes wander from point to point on the canvasses. I pointed out to him, how good composition held your eye within the frame, rather than leading you away, out of the painting. We looked for essentials, the focal point, the attraction of the art work. We saw the simplicity, that was inherent in the beauty of some of them. We took apart, analyzed, and put together again the ingredients of those we liked. We compared the various coastal scenes of one artist, determining why we liked one presentation more than another. I still remember some of those pictures today. Would I have been able to, without this intense and enjoyable, conscious effort to perceive? We used more than our normal perceptive potential. Years ago, before I took up painting in a modest way, I would have been unable to perceive in this way. I could not have helped my friend to see, if I had not been trained to do so myself.

The professional of today needs extensive training in vision and visualization. It will allow earlier spotting of a new and valuable technical possibility. It will permit seeing an essential feature or a physical phenomenon that might otherwise be overlooked. It will sharpen perception in the conference room, when weighty decisions affect the fate of many people. It may even allow us to quickly spot something that could not be right, even though the mighty computer has told us that it is! Vision is a creative process. This process can be practiced, we can improve our skills of vision. Seeing, the process of vision, has many ingredients. We must learn how to go about it. Knowledge of the ingredients and craftsmanship in their use is the road to increased perceptive potential. This will hold true whether we perceive directly, as in the observation of an experiment, or the explanation of an art work, or whether we create for ourselves our own work of art, from nature's beautiful scenery around us. This will even hold true for the images we perceive with our eyes closed. We can not only see better what is today, but better visualize what was, what will, or what could be.

Let us actively exercise the process of vision, this creative undertaking of our every waking hour. Let us explore every view that is worthwhile. Let us learn to taste, smell, feel, and touch. Let us actively exercise our senses. To explore, we must be aware, alert, ever watchful, roving and searching. We must go down the new road to see. Take those extra steps into the museum, visit your friend's office, go to see the open house at the neighboring plant. Take advantage of every opportunity for perceptual experience. Let your eyes wander and explore the sights. If you have a camera, take many pictures. Film is cheap, and the opportunity for this picture may never come again.

Addition and selection are the keys. Our senses are overwhelmed with material. This dynamic world has so much to offer. We must exercise our right of selection. We must make the right choice. Look for the beautiful, the worthwhile, look for the important. Look for things that are interesting to you, that concern you. Remember, what is of interest to you, what concerns you. Remember to be creative is to keep an open mind. There are always new things to like, new things to see and taste, new things to select. Be open to effective surprise.

To improve your visual potential some mental arranging, some grouping of essentials will help. The trees in front of the open window are not only interesting and beautiful in themselves, they form an attractive grouping. Work with, play with your impressions, your perceptions. One pipe, one wheel does not make the essential image. Group them together. Put several essential items together to tell a story. This will complete your visualization.

Simplification is also vital. The human mind yearns for simplification. We live in an all too complex world. We can not grasp it in all its complex details. Simplification is an aid to improve vision and visualization. Key objects stand out of a complexity of impressions. Key objects combine into a simple arrangement. Simplify your perceptions as much as you can, and you're likely to enjoy them more and remember them better.

Abstraction is another concern. Viewing the colors in abstract shapes is a vital means of seeing more. The windows, the markings of the airplane may be unessential. We perceive a landing jet at an airport as the abstraction of its impact, sounds, the plume of its exhaust, and the changed noises of its reversing engines. A water skier is a spray of light. An audience is the roundness of a multitude of shadowy heads. Abstractions are helpful for better perception.

Analysis and synthesis are another valuable way of perceiving with increased awareness. A landscape is composed of fields, houses, trees, animals, skies and clouds. Now we put them back together again in our mind. You enter the office of the new boss. His face, his hands, the items on his desk, you notice his smile. Now put them back together again. What is your visual impression? What clues does it offer for a favorable opening?

Completion of the image in your mind is another tool. You could see only clues. You could see only parts. Still, you formed the whole picture. You can give your imagination free rein to complete the perception in your mind. Your completed inner image, your personal visualization may be better than reality. It is proof of our creativity that we have an uncanny ability to complete images from the most minute bits of information. Watch out — you may be "seeing" a deer instead of a cow! We are excellent at interpreting visual clues. Try it. Look at a part of a picture and complete it in your mind. Doing picture puzzles is an excellent way to strengthen this important ability.

Correction is another degree of freedom at your disposal. Unlike the photographer, you and the painter can manipulate reality. You can eliminate the ugly telephone pole from the picture in your mind. The photographer has a difficult time leaving anything out. Retouching is not always possible. Not so for the artist and the viewer. You don't like that hedge? Well, don't see it! Do away with it! I see the trees, the flower, the birds in my yard but I long ago stopped noticing the ugly power wiring. We have not only the ability, but a right and duty to correct images to suit us. We must not see the ugly, the distorted, the negative, unless we have a specific reason to do so. The power of "correction" is ours to exercise.

Equally helpful to better vision is our ability to compare. Comparison is a useful aid to other forms of improved perception. This wine tastes better than the previous one. I like this melody better than that of the other song. This man looks like his father. The new salesman is better dressed than his predecessor. His sales literature is more attractive than that of his competitor. Comparison increases perception by offering a yardstick where no absolute measure is available. Comparison introduces measurement, converting the merely qualitative to more quantitative perception.

Visual images can relate directly to problem solving in our minds. We see how the column holds up the bridge. We see how the champion tennis player can field the impossible return shot. Problem solving can guide our seeing, and seeing can solve problems. We see the meaningful, the real, the problem solving, the worthwhile image.

There are three further ways to visually explore, feel, and experience images. These are combination, separation, and putting everything in context.

We observe the golf swing, the tee, the impact, the fairway, the green, the flight of the ball. The combination gives us our image: the champion's drive. On the other hand we might separate. We may follow the caddy around. We might separate out the story of the caddy. A different visual impression, a separate alternate image, not the champion but the caddy will result. Finally, context, the ball in the air has little visual impact, it is almost lost against the sky, but what image, what meaning in the context of a surprising "hole-in-one".

Combining, separating, putting in context, how much better can we exercise our senses that way.

Let us exercise our senses actively, seek those impressions. Let us see, hear, smell, touch, feel, taste. What wonderful sensations! Let's practice them!

To practice effectively we must seek for perfection, for enjoyment, for oneness with our experience. There are many ways to go about this effectively. Let us examine our active perception, and especially the all important act of vision in terms of what is significant, vital and creative. Specifics are important, such as shape, space, light, movement. However, more important creatively, are the human windows through which we select worthwhile perception. These are balance, simplicity and truth.

We can gain a true insight from the perception and recreation of the artist. Just as we enjoy, get strength and inspiration from certain art objects, so we can create our perceptions to give us enjoyment, strength and inspiration. The images we perceive can be works of art.

The answer to this lies in ourself. What art object, what perceptual composition, what visual selection is in harmony with us? Even more likely, and most important, how can "we" be in harmony with what we perceive? Can we train ourselves to benefit? Can we train ourselves to choose a system to benefit from?

A great deal is known about the psychology of art. Much of this equally applies to the psychology of our perceptions. There are many facets to which a large number of observers react alike, independent of individual taste. Art appreciation can be increased by a study of some of these factors. Perceptive skills can equally derive great benefit from this knowledge.

What then do we look for? First, there is balance. When we look at a simple figure, such as, a round black disc upon a white square, we first of all visually and immediately locate that disc in relation to the total surface. Most of us have a strong sense of symmetry. The disc will seem more stable and most balanced if it's located in the center of the square. At any other location we have a feeling, a desire, an urge to do something about it. As psychologists put it "there is a tension aimed at achieving balance".

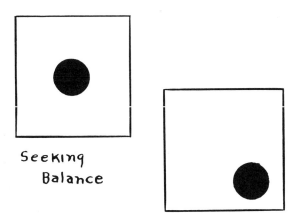

Seeking
Balance

Maybe this is easier to picture if we think of the image of a leaning pole or tree. It is off balance. We want to see it straight, upright. We have an urge, a tension to see it in a correct position. We might even be satisfied with a brace. An object in our visual field may be propped up, balanced with another. Balance is "on" our mind. Balance is "in" our mind. The artist may achieve it by a variety of means, color, composition, arrangement. But only if we see it that way will he be successful. In seeing, we strive for balance. We are more apt to enjoy a picture in which the artist has tried and succeeded in achieving balance. Most importantly if we learn to see balance, to strive for it, we will perceive it. We will construct balance from the complexities of the images facing us. We will be developing our talent to select from the material available, to give us the balanced image. We will not see only the red dial with the main readout on the left side of the machine, we will balance it with the perception of an important secondary readout on the right side. We will not just see the tree in the back of our yard dominating the view from our window, we will balance it with the view of the little boy playing in the foreground. We will balance it with the tiny red bird, who so nicely completes the balanced image.

Rudolph Arnheim in his stimulating book, "Arts and Visual Perception", states that balance is indispensable because in our perception as well as in the work of art, everything has come to a standstill. As dynamic as our overall perception may be, as much as we explore, move our senses around, the creative selection and addition of the components is a frozen image. Only a balanced image looks natural, satisfies our sense of completeness, our need.

Art teaches how to achieve balance. The main factors determining it in a painting are weight and direction. Weight depends on where the object is, the more off center, usually the more weight. Interestingly enough, an object in the upper part of the composition is heavier than in the lower. We just normally look straight, look forward and do not look up.

This happens with sound, too. I heard my name called in a concert hall. I looked all around me several times, before I finally lifted my eyes to the balcony where the call came from.

Obviously the weight also depends on the size. The larger machine will be more impressive, catch the eye more quickly. Also, if an object stands alone by itself, it will be more noticeable, have more weight.

Direction and shape, the character of the object have an influence. Something that points may take our eyes along a path. A triangle may be showing us a new way. Compactness alone makes for weight. A chunky object may be noticeable.

Finally, our predisposition will have a substantial influence on balance. Even though we know that it has been standing that way for a long time, the leaning tower of Pisa is off-balance to us. Direction itself, independent of shape and weight, has an influence on balance. It is impossible to feel balance when we are falling.

We are part and parcel of this question of balance. We follow a tennis ball from side to side. We follow an auto during a race from the appearance of the car in our field of vision until it is around the turn. With a strong dominance of direction, with a one-sidedness, such as in an auto race we may actually experience unsettling effects.

Balance and direction are not only visual. Noises, speech, motion, in an otherwise motionless scene can have major effects. However, never forget you are the determining factor. It is you who will perceive more weight below than above. Most people if asked to cut a perpendicular line in half without a measurement put the cut to high. Also, most people, and this is very likely to include you, see an image, a picture, whether on canvas or on stage, in a factory or in an office from left to right. This lack of equivalence of up and down and left and right is in us and has a bearing on our ability to perceive. It is significant in relation to our desire for balanced perception. Whatever we see on the left assumes greater importance. If you want something to attract attention, put it on the left. If you want to perceive balance, beware of the left. Be aware of your natural tendencies.

In putting the system of perception together, in forming the image, we strive for balance, knowing that a balanced perception will be more satisfying. We are more likely to be in harmony with balanced images. Since they are less jarring, there is less tension. It is not only easier and more enjoyable for us to see them, but retention, memory may be benefited. Balance, order, unity are more readily absorbed. We are not putting up a defense mechanism. We are not fighting it, we are taking it in.

Equally as important as balance is simplicity. Perceiving is not a passive act. It is an aggressive act, dynamic, pointed and directed. We explore, we select, we strive for the image that is essential, significant, and meaningful. This hunt for clues, this completion of impressions ends with simplicity. We're uniquely skilled in creating that simple, that valuable, that significant perception from the clues, the snatches, the hints we are given. This ability to find the truly valuable, the meaningful, the simple perception can be trained and improved. Simplicity does not mean the opposite of complexity. In the sense that we are seeking perceptual simplicity, we are not just seeing a little, we are not just seeing a few things, we are conceiving the essential, the fundamental. We are perceiving the vital stripped of unnecessary frills. We are seeing the significant without the distorting, covering fringes and excesses. A simple image is one that shows us the essence of perception. It contains the vital essentials without distracting side effects. We look to the heart of things, we can see right through to what is important. We can tell the quality of an engineering solution, the caliber of a new machine or device based on its simplicity. We can perceive, whether it solves the problem in a straightforward, direct, essential and therefore simple fashion. Detecting simplicity is seeing the most important in a direct way.

Perception forms the basis for creativity. Perception is closely related in its functioning to human creative skills and potential. Perception determines the condition of our storehouse of creative ammunition. Our perceptive abilities not only determine the way, but also the extent to which we can perform creatively. Perception, like creativity, means action. Contrary to common concepts, it is an active process. There is nothing passive about it. We do not just perceive with our senses. We do not just passively hear sounds and noises. We do not just passively receive images. On the contrary we actively seek out sounds, find words, melodies, separate them from noise, chatter, background. We actively identify sentences, place them in context, compare them to stored patterns to get their meaning. In the same fashion we actively see contours, and distinguish the shape of objects from the ground and identify groupings in a meaningful way.

We can improve and perfect our perceptive skills. First, they must be mechanically in order. Good health, corrective measures for the functioning of the eyes, and the ears, if required, are a must. The mechanical ability to see, and to hear is only part of the total system. We perceive with all of our senses. We literally may "hear" with our eyes, as we see a person's lips move. To train our perceptive skills, we must not only be conscious of the skills within us, we must practice, we must strengthen them.

For training, and practice, the systems approach is vital. Feedback is of the essence. We must not just read. We must underline, take notes, review, abstract, and so on. We must consciously reproduce our visions, sketch them, describe them.

To improve our vision we must practice seeing, perceiving. We must look at many machines, at their details, at their drawings, take in the total picture, the concept, the perception of its working, if machines is what interests us and makes up our livelihood. But if we are machine oriented, we must also feel them, touch them, take them apart, and put them back together again. We need to draw or sketch what we see. Ask an operator to sketch the instrument panel that you want him to watch and you will find, only when asked for feedback, does he really begin to see it.

If you want to live a successful life, a beautiful life, select your exercises well. If you are a ballplayer, diagrams and trick plays are important to you. As a lawyer you may prefer elegantly written decisions by a famous judge. A chemist may profit from studying a unique synthesis. We all will profit if we choose our perception, our practices wisely. Excellence breeds excellence. Beauty begets beauty. Expose yourself. Practice perception on worthwhile objects. See, feel, taste the desirable, the valuable, the honest, the beautiful and you will develop the skills of perceiving the positive, the worthwhile, wherever it may be found. Your perceptive skills will condition you to creative performance and serve you well as a fountain, the origin, the supply house for the components of your creative compositions.

ACTION PAGE

PERCEPTION

Perception:	Attention
	Awareness
	Action
Perception:	The outside world inside you
	Source of strength and joy
	Your creation of reality
Perception:	A vision at your fingertips
	Platforms for performance
	Building blocks of creativity
Perception:	Balance
	Simplicity
	Beauty

EXERCISES

1. Cut a frame out of a piece of cardboard. Practice picture taking by looking through the frame. Look for the picture. Look for focus. Look for interest. Look for composition. Look for balance. Look for simplicity.

2. Get a camera, any camera and take pictures. Make your own choices of what you want to take pictures of. Select your topic. Examine your product. Collect worthwhile pictures. Put them together in a worthwhile fashion, in an original type of collection.

3. Select a "watching topic" and practice. You can be a bird watcher, a tree watcher, a plane watcher, a girl watcher. Excell in the kind of watcher you want to be. Practice feedback. Sketch. Describe what you saw and collect your records.

4. Smell a number of household items, soaps, cleaning fluids, perfumes. Describe the odors. Try to identify odors blindfolded.

5. Practice your feel, your sense of touch. Assemble a variety of shapes and textures. Brushes, felts, cloths, wood. Blindfold yourself and experience the isolated sensation of feeling by touch. Record your impressions.

6. Play the "jewel game". Assemble a tray of objects and using a stopwatch, determine how you can gradually describe the items and remember them in more and more detail, even though you look at the tray and handle it for shorter periods of time.

7. Visualize and sketch:
   Example:
   Large, small, forward, back, near, far away, male, female, old, soft, hard, warm, cold, dry, wet, narrow, wide, alert, love, hate.

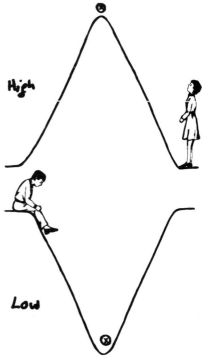

8. Draw the shape or structure of 10 different trees, 10 different cars, 10 different trucks, 10 different boats. Visualize. Sketch. Do not try to be an artist.

9. Taste beer, ginger ale, coke, cold duck, wine. Write a comparison evaluation. Try to detail each experience. Do the same thing for dishes such as hamburger, hot dogs, eggs.

10. Look for something you have not seen before in your living room, your office, a city street, and other locations.

RECOMMENDED READING

Rudolf Arnheim, "Art and Visual Perception", University of Calif., Berkeley, 1969.
Rudolf Arnheim, "Visual Thinking", University of Calif., Berkeley, 1969.
Paul Baken (Editor), "Attention", D. VanNostrand, 1966.
Jozef Cohen, "Sensation and Perception", Rand McNally and Co., 1969.
R. H. Day, "Human Perception", John Wiley and Sons, 1969.
R. L. Gregory, "Eye and Brain", McGraw-Hill, 1955.
R. L. Gregory, "The Intelligent Eye", McGraw-Hill, 1970.
Julian E. Hochberg, "Perception", Prentice Hall, Inc., 1964.
Gyorgy Kepes (Editor), "Education of Vision", George Braziller, New York.
Duane Preble, "Man Creates Art Creates Man", McCutchan, Berkeley, 1973.
Herbert Read, "Education Through Art", Pentheon, Third Edition, 1956.

Arnheim's and Gregory's book are highly recommended for further study. Kepes book will serve well for in-depth study.

CHAPTER 4
PROBLEMS HAVE MANY ANSWERS

Problem solver, conqueror
Problems, an endless string
People problems, machine problems
Solutions, need and reward
The creative challenge

Recognition and definition
Understanding is half the battle
Tackling the right problem
On the time axis
Many, many solutions

Action! The problem solver conquers the world. Engineers, statesmen, bankers, businessmen, housewives, or teenagers, life is an endless string of problems. There are people problems and machine problems. Solution of problems is what we live by. It is what most of us are paid for. Every problem is a creative challenge. There are few prefabricated solutions.

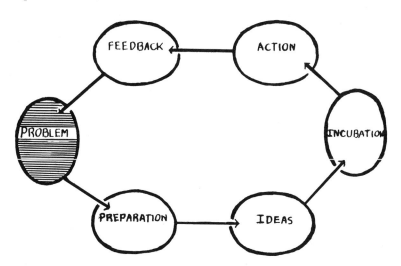

Neither robot nor God, we are humans. Robots are built to perform tasks, to repeat, to solve over and over again what once may have been a problem. A machine may be also called upon to assist us humans in solving problems. Gods have no problems. Humans love, live for and thrive on problems.

Tasks are deeds, actions that require the same prefabricated solutions. We can build a machine to lift, to turn, or to shake a tree limb so that the fruit will fall on a moving belt. Machines will perform many tasks; they will do it well again and again. In these days of automation, robots can perform even complicated and difficult tasks. The computer-controlled machine tool, for example, may shape a piece of steel in a sequence of many individual, intricate steps. It may repeat these steps and generate the final metallic shape hundreds of times with amazing accuracy. However, it does not solve problems. It does not confront a new situation. It only performs a difficult, but repetitive task. The real problem solving, i.e., the creative element, is in the conception of the tool and the imaginative program required to use the tool for a required task. The tool must be set up, it requires a human input to solve a problem.

Problem solving is the creative human endeavor that has brought us from the life of the primitive cave dwellers to the heights of modern civilization. Our creative skills at solving problems will keep us moving forward. Without this talent, without the application of creativity we would slip quickly back to the Stone Age. Creative problem solving is the key to human success, to a happy life, and to a functioning society.

We must strengthen and cultivate our problem solving skills. We must insist that our educational system, which has traditionally been geared so much to repetitive tasks and the routine accumulation of knowledge, the stale storing of information, be turned around. Too many of our professionals, our most highly educated citizens, have not been encouraged to cultivate their imagination, to sharpen their perception, and to insist on originality. They need help to redevelop, to exercise, to hone, and bring forth their innate creative abilities.

Over the years I often had occasion to interview young scientists and engineers seeking employment in industry. One of the recruiting questions I frequently employed to illustrate the gap between the academic and the real world was,

"Imagine you have been working in industry for a short time and you were assigned to set up for the manufacture of aniline. What would you do?"

Sadly enough, the majority of those questioned would start digging in their memories for some remnant of an organic chemistry class long forgotten. A few would talk about nitrating benzene followed by reduction. One or two might remember an alternate, chlorination of benzene, as a starting point.

The exceptional few would talk about attacking the problem in a systematic, creative fashion. Very few would realize that the days of closed book examinations were over. Very few would talk about determining the specific needs of the company first. Very few would talk about consulting other people, consulting the library, getting updated on the state of the art first. Very few were aware of the preparation required to tackle an assignment creatively in the real world.

Usually as expected I would end up explaining to the candidate that the facts he had learned in his classes were only background and might already be badly out of date. Now, in industry, in the real world, he had to think in terms of solving problems with "all" the possible resources at his disposal. The emphasis during his schooling was usually to test his memory. Now he was not to rely on his memory alone, but he was to add to it and check it by referring to the literature and the knowledge and experience of his colleagues.

The artificial barriers of the classroom are not permissible in industry. They interfere with problem solving in the real world. Restrictions may well be helpful for training purposes, but there is no place for them when tackling real problems in real life.

Another vital distinction of real life problems is that most of them have many answers. The teacher needs, for testing and grading, problems where he can determine whether the student has paid attention, whether he learned what he has been told. This teaches many that problems generally have only one solution. They are given multiple choice questions, and asked to choose one answer. They are rewarded for repeating what the teacher presented. They choose from true or false, right or wrong.

While there are some of what I call "one line problems", most problems of the real world are not "one line". They are "many lines". Most real problems have many solutions. It is our task not only to generate and consider the many solutions, but to select a suitable one from the many. Notice we are not saying a right or wrong solution, because the selection process could lead to different, "suitable" solutions at different times or under different circumstances. Choice of a solution may be a matter of degree, not black or white, right or wrong. The appropriate solution need not always be the best solution.

The creative human, the active professional in particular, faces innumerable problems day by day. To achieve his goals and those of society, he must successfully navigate in, on and under an ocean of problems.

What do we understand by a problem? Some people think only of situations when something has gone wrong. To them a problem is a deviation from the norm. In the broader sense, however, a problem is "a situation, a set of circumstances susceptible to positive change by creative human endeavor." In contrast to a *task* which might be handled by a machine, a *problem* requires more than automatic, more than predetermined or routine action. A problem requires creativity in its solution.

There are "positive" and "negative" problems. It is certainly helpful to realize which side of the scale we are on. Negative problems are those where something has gone wrong. Events were happening normally as expected, everything was going along evenly. Then, surprise, something happened. Some change caused new, unexpected, abnormal, undesirable circumstances. We say: "we have a problem." Often analysis, finding the nature of the problem by discovery of the change, or what brought it about, is the key to its soluiton. In these cases, problem definition itself requires the application of the creative process. Here, problem recognition may lead us most of the way towards an acceptable solution. It is for these "negative" problems that problem analysis, recognition and determination of the origin of the problem, is important.

You operate a business. Sales have dropped off materially. What is your problem? Is your merchandise defective? Is your price noncompetitive? Is your sales force incompetent? You know that not so long ago your business was successful.

Problem analysis is required. What changes caused the present situation? Where did your problem originate? This is likely to be the key to finding creative solutions to put you back on the desired track.

You operate a power plant, or a lathe. You operate your car. The machinery breaks down. Problem analysis is likely to be the activity most required to find solutions to these problems. You have to define, recognize, nail down, and investigate the origin of the problem before you can tackle the choice of a suitable solution.

Negative problems of this kind take up much of our energies. In fact, many professionals engaged in maintenance and services devote most of their time to solving negative problems. Some excellent creative problem solving process techniques have been specifically designed for negative problems.

One is the widely taught Kepner-Tregoe method of management training. It stresses that: "a problem cannot be solved unless its cause is known." A well-defined, systematic, step wise process is then prescribed to find the cause of the problem. The method stresses the need for identifying the deviation from the norm or standard which is at the root of the problem. It also offers a step wise procedure for finding the cause of the deviation, thus hopefully leading to a full analysis, a full recognition of the "real" problem.

However, there is really no basic difference between these negative problems and finding solutions aimed at problem solving in the positive arena. How to land on the moon and bring the astronauts back is a good example of a positive problem. It was solved by applying a high degree of creativity. Whether we have a change from the usual or expected in the minus direction or want to achieve a change from the usual or expected in the plus direction, both negative and positive problems are basically alike. In both cases, we want to bridge the gap between reality and our goal. In the case of the negative problem, a solution has to overcome the gap between what "should be" and what "is".

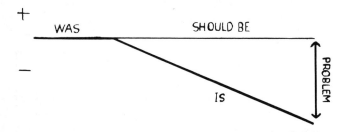

In the case of the positive problem, the solution has to fill the gap between what "is" or "will be" and what we would "like" to have. We want to go from reality or the state of the art to a desired goal, a breakthrough.

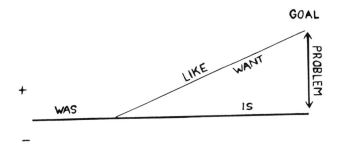

Possibly the most difficult positive problem of our times was, as noted above, how to get astronauts safely to the moon and back. Of the many solutions possible, the one chosen, the moonlander, was a particularly ingenious and creative one.

The positive problem of getting man to the moon and back was a difficult one. Basically, however, it was no different than the negative problem of arresting the cholora epidemic in Naples. Both were vital to mankind. The first was aimed at a positive, new and desirable goal: knowledge and information from the moon. The second was aimed at offsetting a negative change that affected and could impair the continued life and existence of that human community. Both were problems or situations that required the best talents available to devise solutions. Both problems required the same creative technique.

We have thus defined a problem as a gap between two sets of circumstances, the desirable, the wanted situation and the undesirable, the real situation, which will prevail without application of the creative problem solving process. Action bridges the gap. Originality facilitates and makes it possible. And in an ethical society, in a human world, the desirable situation will be that of greater value. Thus, we equate problem solving with our definition of the creative act or the creative process.

To recognize this gap and define the problem, we need to consider the desirable situation, the real situation, and the origin of deviation.

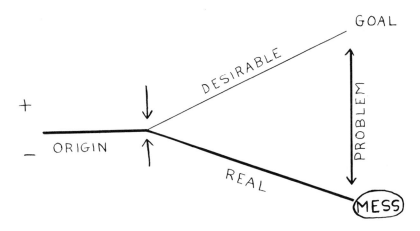

67

What is the real problem? Often we have great difficulty in recognizing it. We have usually not the slightest idea where things went wrong and we have to be very clever or work very hard to trace things back to the origin. It is a natural tendency for us not to look beyond the immediate reality, the "mess" we are facing. We have a difficult time looking beyond what we experience at the moment. We are very hesitant to look beyond immediate circumstances. This is where a creative attitude, an open mind, and intent to be original are very helpful.

An aviation engineer, a student in one of my creativity classes, was helped in solving a problem which had been around for some time by being urged to apply careful problem analysis. For some time his group had wrestled with the problem of coating the sight glasses on aircraft instruments to eliminate reflections and thus improve visibility. The problem to them was, "how do we make a coating for our sight glasses to improve visibility?"

Creative problem analysis shifted the focus. The real problem was identified as, "how do I make the information more visible without major changes and without sacrificing the protection of the instruments?"

Once the problem was properly recognized, the solution almost offered itself: An all plastic covering material. Improper problem definition, asking for "a coating", had interferred with the selection of a suitable and effective solution to the real problem.

If we want to apply the creative process, if we want to develop creative ideas towards the effective solution of the problem, we must fully understand and recognize the problem first. It is important that it be the real problem, not the apparent problem. The genuine problem, not the mess that normally faces us must be recognized.

Often this means spelling out the problem in the broadest possible terms, free from any unnecessary restrictions of incumberances. In problem definition, we want to find an umbrella large enough to cover the entire "mess". Broad problem definition makes it easier to conceive or find many "solutions" from which to select.

It is our nature to include a lot of detail in the problem definition process. If we have an idea for a solution, as in the sight-glass example, we include it. We include the coating in our problem definition. This is going the wrong way. Every problem has many solutions. Let's define the problem in the broadest sense, first. This means the simplest, the broadest possible statement, the most general concept possible which describes the gap between the real and the desired circumstances.

Let me illustrate this by comparison to a patent claim or a mining claim. The simplest, the shortest patent claim is usually the most valuable because it covers the largest territory.

The more words, the longer the description, the smaller usually the territory. This is equally or even more evident when you compare which is the biggest of two pieces of land claimed. Is it "Smith Valley" or is it the "last third of the northeast section of Smith Valley"? To define the problem, remain as simple as possible. Go

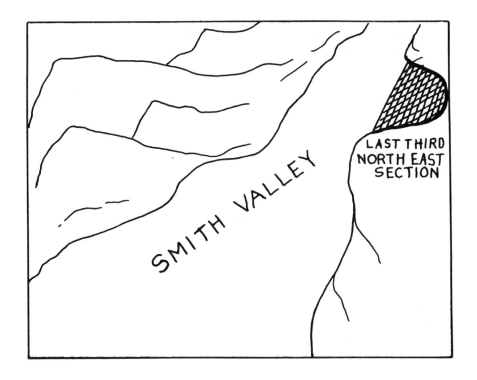

behind the apparent problem and ask questions to find the real, the genuine problem.

In "Synectics", a highly developed and effective group method of creative problem solving, the creative process starts with the PAG. PAG is short for the "Problem As Given". This is a general statement of the problem to be solved. It may have been given to the group members by an outside source, or they may have generated the statement themselves. The problem as given is first subjected to careful analysis. In fact, an expert may be employed to explain the problem, give background history. The problem is examined in detail. Questions are asked to gain an understanding of the problem. Since the expert is usually a participant in the problem solving process, as a member of the group, he doesn't have to make everyone as knowledgable as he is himself. The goal is to gain a real understanding of the problem. One of the very ingenious tricks used in the Synectics method to loosen up the participants and to encourage originality, is to make the strange familiar. For example, a simple analog may be used as illustration. This is applied to the problem analysis as well as to the remainder of the problem solving process. A purge is also used by airing a few solutions which seem most obvious, most immediate. Such potential solutions, if considered carefully and without allowing them to narrow the problem definition, can greatly contribute to the understanding of the problem. This familiarization with the problem as given (PAG) and purging by consideration of most immediate solutions leads to the PAU. PAU is short for the "Problem As Understood".

How many hours of fruitless searching, of frustrating disappointments, could we avoid, if we always took the time to fully understand our problems, to recognize the real problems. It is essential that we always initially progress from the PAG, the "Problem As Given" to the PAU, the "Problem As Understood".

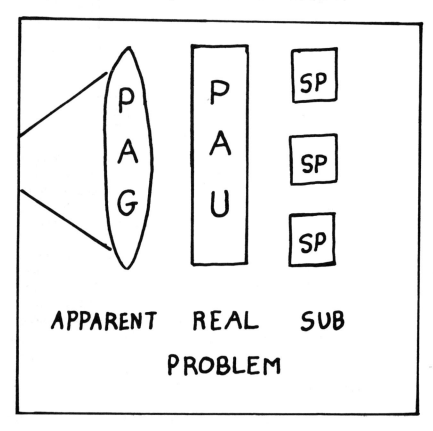

In problem analysis the question "why" is most helpful for leading us from the "mess" to the recognition of the real problem. It is vital that we ask "why" not only once but often, to lead us from the hazy, obscure, confused, or the imagined problem to the genuine problem. Careful consideration of the "why" question leads us from the "mess" back to the origin of the problem. It helps us recognize what we really want to accomplish. Consider our coatings problem:

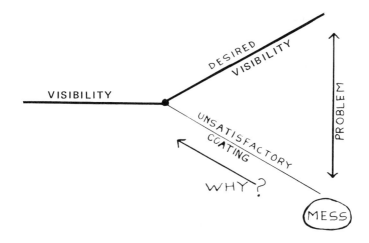

We have to work our way back from the improper visibility situation through the question "why", along the answer "unsatisfactory coating" to what we really want, better visibility. We recognize that the real problem is not an unsatisfactory coating, but the gap between the existing and the desired visibility. Thus, through asking "why we have improper visibility", we work our way back to the origin and finally to a proper definition of the real problem.

I had lunch with a friend whose responsibilities include a continuing education school. He said he was wrestling with a problem of what title to choose for his diplomas. He asked me to tell him what I thought of the title, "Fellow of the Institute" for people who had successfully passed a number of courses. The question "why" brought out the real problem quickly. His problem was, how to motivate students to take a series of evening courses rather than just one.

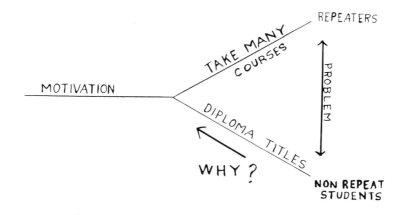

Thus, working our way from the "diploma title" problem (PAG) to "how to motivate" (PAU) we go back to the origin of the problem. We then see that the problem is really the gap between the desired and the actual motivation of the evening students. This opens the way to a much larger number of potential solutions than the question of the diploma title.

Another help in finding the real problem beyond the apparent or given problem is suggested in Sidney J. Parnes excellent creative behavior guide book. He suggests changing the verb in a given problem statement. One of his examples suggests that instead of how to "park cars" you might ask how do we "store cars". The change in statement can be helpful in freeing the mind from a preconceived notion. We are used to parking cars side by side in a horizontal lot or on multiple floors of large garages. A recent creative solution which some of you may have seen on television or in pictures, stores the cars in a vertical structure or elevator-like storage bin. Many cars can be stored vertically in the parking space normally reserved for two or three cars.

A worker in a crowded downtown area consistently arrived late for work. The usual statement of the problem as given is: "How could he avoid arriving "late" at work?" We might better ask: "How could he get eight effective hours of working time? This opens the door to other solutions. It may be to stagger working hours, arrive and leave at a different time, work extra hours on a busy day and many other possible solutions. Note the key change from the phrase "arriving on time" to "working effectively".

Try to change the verb in the statement of the apparent problem, the problem as given. It may help you recognize the real problem.

Baker illustrates the need for recognizing the real problem with the excellent example of the moles.

The gardner was outraged that the moles were damaging his lawn, so he tried to poison the moles. He had little success. He saw his problem: "how to kill the moles".

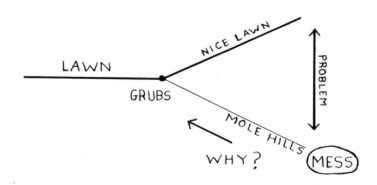

In this case we can arrive at the real problem most readily by asking the question "why". The answer in this case would be "he had a desire for a beautiful lawn". Examining the lawn showed that it was diseased, a condition caused by underground grubs. The moles fed on the grubs. So the origin of the real problem was the grubs. He got rid of the grubs by treating the lawn with insecticide and the moles went elsewhere.

You might approach this same problem definition with verb changes. The word "killing" might be replaced by "moving away" or "scaring off". This will lead you to examine why the moles are in your lawn and thus discover the solution of removing their food, the grubs.

Find the real problem. Unscramble the mess. Ask the right questions to get at the heart of it. Many problems come wrapped in preconceived notions. Problems come hidden by details and distractions. Problems come to us distorted in time and colored by recent events. To find the real problem, we have to probe. We have to ask "why". We have to find our way back to the origin, to clearly see the gap. As we have emphasized, most problems have many solutions, some more palatable than others. We must define the problem to allow widest possible application of the creative approach to its solution. We must take all the wrappings off and remove the barriers that we ourselves have erected. We must attack the problem from all sides.

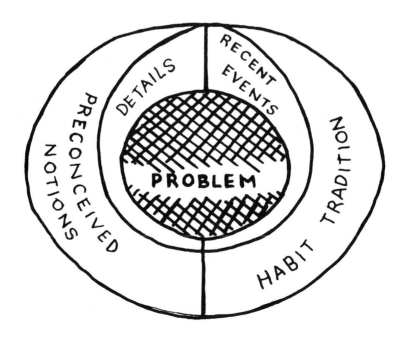

Determining the real problem will allow us to analyze it further. As we have already discussed, it is helpful to realize whether we are dealing with a positive or negative problem. Another very helpful distinction is whether we are dealing with a "people" problem or "machine" problem. Is the key to filling the gap something that involves human behavior or human interaction, your own or that of others? Often early recognition that we are dealing with the "human factor", that our problem primarily is a people problem can be extremely helpful. In fact while we may commonly think of our problems as machine problems, on careful analysis we will find that a large number, many more than we normally think of, are people problems. The people problems are commonly much harder to solve than the machine problems.

The construction of the Alaskan Pipeline may be a significant and a complicated technical problem. But initially, it has been a people problem. It was a people problem that held up its construction for two years or more. As professionals we have a strong tendency to forget or under estimate people problems. We readily recognize and tackle machine problems. We have difficulties to recognize problems that are primarily problems of human interaction. Many a seemingly technical or totally business-type problem turns out, on careful analysis, to be a people problem. People problems not only require the most creative problem solving activity, but they also lend themselves most readily to creative and original solutions.

We must often subdivide our problem as understood into a number of subproblems. It is usually much easier to solve subproblems than to solve the overall problem. Wherever it is possible to identify and analyze a problem in terms of a number of specific subproblems, the overall solution will eventually be arrived at in a better and more creative fashion. All discussions concerning problems naturally apply equally to the larger overall problem as they do to specific subproblems.

We have discussed problems, positive and negative, one-line and those that have many solutions, machine problems and people problems, general problems and subproblems. We have discussed specific goals, the specification of a desirable situation. What then about objectives?

Objectives and goals are usually a set of desired circumstances wanted in the future. They differ only in scope and timing.

To live a positive, valuable, contributing existence, all humans need goals and objectives. We need to specify what we want to accomplish. The emphasis, especially for the successful professional, is on specificity.

If I say my objective is to be happy or successful, this has very little meaning or value. To be useful, objectives have to be specific. Much has been written about management by objectives. Objectives are broad descriptions of those wider, desireable circumstances we want to attain. An objective may encompass an entire hierarchy of subobjectives. It may require the attainment of many goals. Achieving an objective and attaining of the necessary intermediate goals will force us to find appropriate solutions to a multitude of problems. Only in this fashion can we ultimately accomplish our objectives.

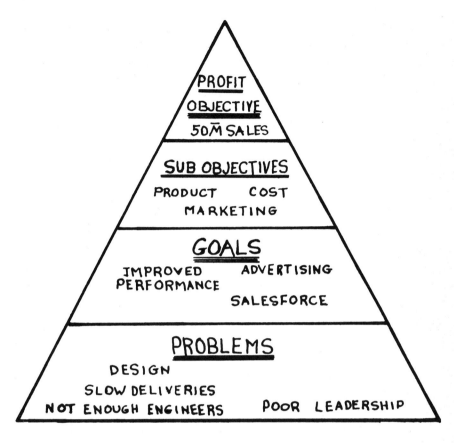

We Can Only Start at The Bottom

Thus, in a growing new business, our overall objective may be to attain $50 million in sales. However, this becomes meaningful only when you look at the subobjectives required to achieve the main objective. They may be a superb product. They may require marketing skills of high caliber. They may be based on low production costs allowing good pricing. Ample financing may be required as a basis for the other three subobjectives. In each case we may have to reach certain goals related to these subobjectives. There is little doubt that many problems require proper solution on the way to the achievement of these goals. Thus, many solutions are needed to lead to the overall accomplishment of the $50 million sales objective.

Thus, our problem solving existence is an intricate one. Objectives, subobjectives, goals, problems and subproblems.

The creative approach to life requires a recognition of the problems and creative action to tackle them. Action, however, is possible only on the bottom of the

75

pyramid. We cannot act broadly to be happy. In fact, there is not a single general action that can be taken to achieve the $50 million sales goal.

Creative problem solving action, is required on each specific problem to achieve the goals, the subobjectives that combine to let us reach our main major objective. No problem and no subproblem is unimportant. Creative problem solving, a creative life with valuable major objectives starts with the specifics. We have to solve the first problem, then each of the next ones in turn, if we are to reach our objectives.

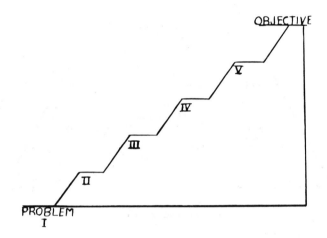

If we want to get an important order from a European technical company, we may have to visit them. The first problem may be how to arrange our present activities to find the time. We may also first have to acquire some technical information. The order in which to tackle specific problems may thus be of significant importance.

Another vital consideration in creative problem solving is the importance of the seemingly little problems. How often do we catch ourselves thinking that to solve this problem is really not important. It is too small to be worthy of our creative activity. However, a haystack is made up of countless blades of grass. A major objective or large problem is solved only by tackling and properly choosing solutions for even the littlest component of the large problem. How to get to the moon and back is a major objective worthy of mankind, but it is composed of a seemingly endless number of detailed problems. One simple problem can effect the entire system.

We have a tendency to throw our hands up and be discouraged by seemingly huge problems. We shy away from the magnitude of a major change. To overcome this tendency the creative problem solver must recognize, define and tackle the specifics. He must not be discouraged by the number of subproblems or the magnitude of the major objective he faces.

76

In analyzing the major problem, the system, we find we have interrelated sub-problems. As noted earlier, the order in which we tackle them is often significant, but first these subproblems must be recognized and defined. This makes it possible to plan either a logical step-wise, "one-at-a-time" approach, or determine the one or two subproblems that are the keys to achieving the objective and attack them first.

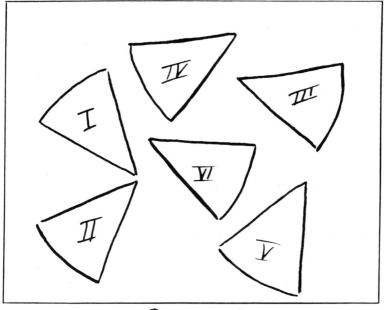

Fitting Problems Together

The illustrations depict these two situations. In the first step-wise case, we have a road to the objective. Each hurdle has to be jumped one at a time to get there. As in going up a ladder, each step must be taken before the next one can be approached. In the second case, we may have an objective which, like a jigsaw puzzle, requires many pieces. So this objective requires a solution of many problems to put it all together. Unlike the first case, however, they may not be time-related. There are many objectives requiring a combination of both these approaches.

The problem solver conquers the world. Engineers, statesmen, bankers, business-men, housewives, teenagers, professionals, or non-professionals, our life is an endless string of problems. A problem is a hurdle that must be jumped to get to the next problem. Life is full of problems, big ones and little ones. There are problems standing by themselves, unique problems and problems interwoven and inter-connected. The solving of one problem may lead to the solution of another or it may open the doors to many new problems. Solutions are what we are paid for.

Every problem is a creative challenge. There are few prefabricated problems just as there are no prefabricated solutions.

Robots can perform tasks. Automated machines can repeat and multiply the solutions to our problems. It is the creative human who first has to solve the initial, the key problem. He has to build the machine, develop the program for its repetitive actions.

The creative human thrives on problems. It is what he is needed for. Professionals are trained to solve problems. The lawyer is hired and paid to solve his clients problems or to prevent his client from having new problems. The scientist delves into the problems of the universe whether it be to recognize the makeup of moon rock or the interrelations of our earthly ecology. The engineer tackles the problems of survival whether it be opening the arctic, bridging a river or coping with urban transportation. Most important, we daily face the problems of human interactions, of living with ourselves and with others in a complex and crowded society.

There are not only negative, but also positive problems. Problems are gaps between the desired and the real. These can only be filled by human creative action. There are machine problems and human problems. Most problems have many solutions. In fact, all human problems have more than one solution. Machine problems may equally have a multitude of answers.

Proper problem analysis, which results in recognition of the real problem, is vitally needed to allow us to develop the many solutions from which we can choose a suitable one.

Modern education and testing stress a false image of problems. We are taught to select one answer from several multiple choices. This puts the emphasis on "always right" or "always wrong" answers. This is not the real world. In the real world, what is right today may be wrong tomorrow. Problems have their solutions on a time axis and the selection of the appropriate solution may depend on time and circumstances. In the real world, there may be many choice solutions. The optimum solution may be unattainable and therefore, may not be the creative choice. There may be five right answers. To act on one answer may be infinitely preferable over continuous inaction. Waiting to find the one and only supposedly true answer does not solve anything.

Problems do not stand by themselves; they are interrelated, interwoven. They may be ordered in a sequence like a road or a ladder. They may fit together like a jigsaw puzzle. Most important, even the smallest problem may be a vital key to the solution of major overall human objectives and a successful, creative life.

EXERCISES

1. Choose a specific current problem, whether related to your job, your family or your city or state government. Write down the problem as given, the situation. Write down ten specific questions aimed at defining the real problem.

2. Choose the same or another problem. Relate it to five similar problems. List those and other related problems.

3. List twenty unsolved problems, which are in one way or another important to you. Resolve for each problem whether it is a people problem or a machine problem.

4. Take the three most significant problems from the previous list and analyze your initial statement. Ask questions to arrive at the real problem. Compare your statement of the real problem with the problem as given. You should have a simpler statement, you should be using fewer words.

5. Identify your three most pressing problems:

At work	Your town or county
In the home	Your state
At your club	The nation
Your church	

RECOMMENDED READING

Samm S. Baker, "Your Key to Creative Thinking", Bantam Books, 1964.

W. I. B. Beveridge, "The Art of Scientific Investigation", W. W. Norton and Company, 1957.

Edward de Bono, "The Five Day Course in Thinking", Basic Books, New York, 1967.

Carl E. Gregory, "The Management of Intelligence", McGraw-Hill, New York, 1967.

Charles H. Kepner and Benjamin B. Tregoe, "The Rational Manager", McGraw-Hill, New York, 1965.

Lewis E. Lloyd, "Techniques for Efficient Research", Chemical Publishing Company, New York, 1966.

Alex F. Osborn, "Applied Imagination", Charles Scribner and Sons, New York, 1963.

Sidney J. Parnes, "Creative Behavior Guidebook", Charles Scribner and Sons, New York, 1967.

The Kepner-Tregoe method is particularly to be recommended for problem identification of readers engaged in the business world. However, the book may have to be supplemented with actual K-T training. Samm S. Baker's book "Your Key to Creative Thinking" is available in pocketbook edition and while somewhat simplistic, is of great help to young and old alike. Lewis E. Lloyd's book "Techniques for Efficient Research" is particularly to be recommended to the practicing engineer and scientist.

CHAPTER 5
BUILDING BLOCKS FOR CREATIVITY

Hard work and craftmanship	Accessibility for your needs
Ammunition for the battle	Unconscious storage
Bricks and mortar for creativity	53 years to paint a masterpiece
Learning can be fun	Help from others
Man and machine	Preparation for creative progress

Fact finding, data collection, and the accumulation of ideas of the past, supply the creative individual with the raw material for the creative act. Nothing comes from nothing. Past knowledge supplies the building blocks for future problem solving. Facts are needed to generate new ideas. Old ideas may stimulate new solutions.

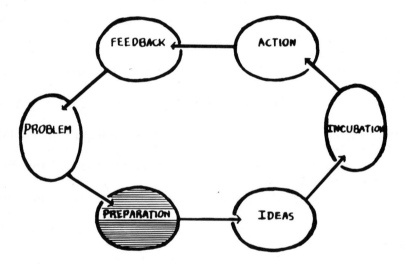

Originality springs from the unusual combination of prior knowledge used in new and constructive ways; in a surprising synthesis from what went before. Without the raw material, without the building blocks, originality cannot blossom; cannot generate the ideas that lead to creative problem solving. An important activity for the creative individual is generating facts intelligently. He must sort and assemble worthwhile data conscientiously and store them for use in creative problem solving throughout his life.

It has been argued that preparation just confuses us. Some say that by learning what has gone on before, that by excessive library study, we clutter our minds. They believe that the new idea, the new and creative solution, may be blotted out by the old.

It has also been argued, that many great men were not trained in the field in which they made their most brilliant discoveries. However, in all those cases, it can be shown that limited knowledge and freedom from established patterns of thought in the field in which they contributed were joined with knowledge and training in other fields. In fact, it was usually the knowledge and training, the preparation in these other fields, applied to a new field, that allowed these outsiders to make their substantial contribution.

There is no real question that preparation is vital to any kind of human success, especially to creative problem solving and the creative process. However, the right kind of preparation is vital. Preparation is needed that is orderly, that is geared to allow the creative process to function, rather than foreclosing it. Preparation must open doors rather than close them. Knowledge is like a lake behind a dam. We need its powerful stored waters to generate power. However, that stored treasure must also be contained, controlled, ordered, available for our needs. To use it we must open the sluice gates properly. Creative problem solving is an activity, which requires the right ammunition at the right place and at the right time. The process cannot function without lifelong preparation; without always gathering supplies, components, tools, suitable for use in the execution of the creative act.

The ignorant — those who lack knowledge — cannot provide creative solutions. The expert who has a closed mind may be equally handicapped. Preparation is not only a process of storage, not just a filling of a warehouse with information and facts and knowledge of data. It is also a state of mind. We do not just store knowledge or data. We, as creative human individuals, also absorb feelings, sights, and sounds. We are more than just a computer memory bank. We are a finely tuned, living instrument in which learning, feelings, perceptions, unique human talents combine to generate a uniquely human result. Thus, preparation for creativity is not only an intellectual process but it is also a question of attitude; of readiness of the mind to function in an unusual effective, productive human way. We can prepare for creativity. Creativity training, which involves focusing, understanding, and striving for the creative attitude, is part of this preparative activity.

What is our capacity? What are our skills for this act of collecting and storing in available form the needed impressions, feelings, and information for creative problem solving? With few exceptions we all have the capacity to gather, to accumulate, to store facts. We can remember concepts and ideas. However, how skilled are we at choosing what to collect? How well are we able to retain the significant? Most importantly, how can we encourage availability of the stored facts and concepts for future creative use?

We differ greatly in storage profiles. First, as a base for most professionals, there is general education. Next there is specialized training. Finally, there is specific preparation. Some of our institutions of higher learning stress a liberal education as a base for creative problem solving. We value a broad collection of knowledge, facts, and concepts.

In our discussion of human skills of perception we stressed how important this broad base of preparation is to the creative individual.

Whether you are an engineer, a banker, a lawyer, or a politician, many an idea for creative problem solving, even in your specialty, will draw upon the broad preparation base of a general liberal education. You can benefit greatly from such broad cultural preparation. But your store of ideas requires continued updating, not

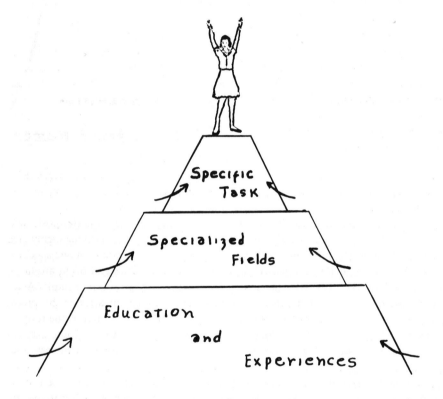

just in electronics, your specialty, but also, perhaps, in the latest developments of astronomy or astrology. A book on the mating habits of the dolphin or an account of the most recent findings concerning excavations in South America may sow the seeds for your next creative breakthrough.

Today's professional, to be creative, needs a lifelong, continuing source of preparation. He needs to be well equipped broadly, culturally, and in depth in his field of specialization. It is in the latter arena where most of us are often called upon to perform the creative problem solving process. As a result, we find many specialists

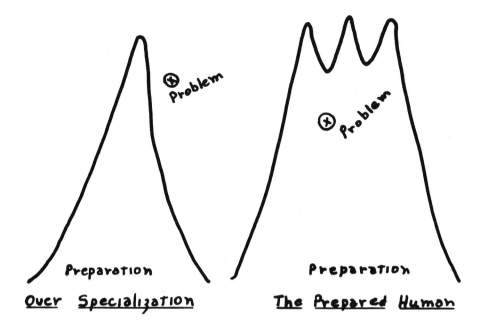

Over Specialization   **The Prepared Human**

today who are extremely well prepared in their narrow field but have neglected to prepare themselves broadly. Often they continue to neglect preparation in areas outside their specialty. Over-specialization can inhibit creativity.

The well-rounded, culturally well prepared specialist is in a far better position to draw upon his stock of knowledge for a creative solution. In studying highly creative people, we usually find that they prepare in and stress more than one specialty; they have accumulated knowledge in a variety of disciplines and often are highly active and motivated in fields far removed from their specialty. For example, Albert Einstein, the great mathematician and physicist, was a patent attorney by profession. He was also an ardent violinist by avocation. Originality often is the result of applying knowledge and concepts from one specialty to another. Therefore, it is not surprising that so many creative individuals have broad interdisciplinary interests.

Preparation can be fun. Preparation can be a game. Preparation can be routine. Preparation can be hard work. Most important, the principles of creativity and originality, the willingness to be different must be applied to our methods of preparation. First of all, and very importantly we must record. Since human memory is very limited, since we are apt to forget 25% of what we want to remember within 24 hours and 85% of what we want to remember within one week, the key ground rule is to keep a notebook. Writing it down is the most essential of the simple aids for preparation. No professional, in fact no creative human being, should be without a notebook and a writing tool at all times. We must show the initiative and motivation to write things down as they occur to us.

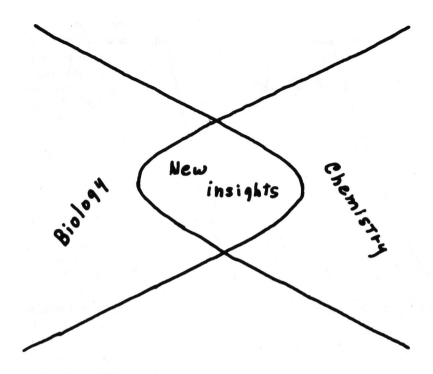

This is an essential habit for the creative individual to acquire. From time to time, we can transfer the notes and items that we have recorded into more permanent, better organized records. Preparation then becomes a fulltime affair, as it should be.

But it is not the mechanics, it is the spirit in which we store the ammunition for creativity that counts. We may collect from many sources. We may store many pictures, we may store books, we may store films, we may store audio cartridges, articles, jokes, interviews, personal impressions — it isn't what we store, but the spirit in which we store, the way in which we select for storage, that is all important.

Why do we collect? Why do we build up, and how do we go about building up our store of impressions, knowledge and experience? Most generally, the first answer that would come to our mind is: we do it to accumulate knowledge. But pleasures should not be excluded. Living a full life, accumulating impressions, sensations, is a pleasurable experience. We can enjoy the preparation for creativity! We can enjoy building and growing professionally. Hopefully, we also build this store so that we are able to contribute to others. Our advance, our growth should not be solely a selfish endeavor. We want to add new values and balance to a specialization that we are greatly devoted to.

Motivation for collection and building of our experience reservoir has a great deal of meaning in relation to how we should go about it.

If we feel that knowledge alone is the motivating force we can go about it in highly systematic and routine fashion. I think all of us have encountered people who are walking dictionaries. You may remember the television programs in the fifties. We were highly impressed by people who had practically memorized the encyclopedia. Interestingly enough, many of these people who had acquired such a great deal of information did not necessarily know how to use it. In some instances they were totally unable to apply this information in a creative way.

I strongly urge that the "how" of preparation include the pleasurable way. Make things interesting for yourself. Make studying a pleasure. Make it easy on yourself to acquire the tools for creativity. Preparation can be fun; preparation should be fun; preparation must be fun.

Two major recommendations concerning this fun attitude may be helpful. First of all, preparation is a "human" activity. It is an individualistic activity. You should exercise your originality in the preparation phase the same as in the other phases of the creative process. Follow your individual preferences, use your personal style, be willing to be different. Preparation for originality requires originality.

On the other hand, don't be proud. Just as you are willing to help others, ask and accept the help of others. Good preparation does not prejudice the sources of information. In fact, quite generally, good preparation, original preparation, human preparation requires an open mind. Now an open mind means not having any strong prejudicial opinions. We must be free in the choice of what material to accept, what material to store. We must be open-minded as to the sources we are willing to use. However, there must also be a willingness to be skeptical about the information that we do find, to test and prove its validity.

The textbook may be wrong. A young friend of mine was particularly open-minded, which greatly helped his creativity. At one time, he suggested an idea for a synthesis of a type of organic phosphorous compound. This was contradicted fully and completely by a statement in the standard textbook. But he felt strongly enough that he went ahead with the experiments anyway. His skepticism was borne out. His creative stubbornness resulted in a fine discovery and two patents. The textbook was just plain wrong. He added enough of a slightly different twist to the state of the art to succeed, where people who had tried many years before and upon whose works the textbook statement was based, had been unsuccessful.

Thus, an open mind is vital for good preparation. The professional must display an open mind which accepts information, accepts impressions, accepts experiences from many, even possibly strange and different sources. He must exercise an open mind which is willing to explore and look for preparation in widely divergent fields. Lastly, there must also be an open mind which does not foreclose or decide based on supposedly authoritative information.

An open mind should also regulate our relationships with the all important machine preparation of today. How far should we go in utilizing the computer? Can computer storage take care or replace some of the drudgery, some of the detailed storage effort that is required for specific preparation?

It must be remembered that it takes human effort to select the information for a computer to store. It takes human effort to code the information for retrieval and it takes human ingenuity to retrieve the desired information. Once this information is retrieved, it must be digested, it must be absorbed by the human worker to be of value in the creative process.

Proper use of computer storage and retrieval can be a time-saver, provided that the open mind is applied to this exercise. The open mind means the recognition that computerizing the information does not make it infallible. Computer-generated data may be just as wrong as human-generated data. It really and truly is human generated data, speeded up or made more accessible with the help of the marvelous machine. Thus, machine preparation can be of great assistance provided we expand and emphasize the doctrine of the open mind for machine preparation just as we did for textbook preparation. In fact, in considering how to improve our ability to prepare, it is rather helpful to think of the human mind in terms of a computer model. Just like the computer, we have to consider that the human mind has to undergo acquisition of information or experiences, retention of the information, and then retrieval when it is required.

Let us consider the human as a processor of information, especially as a processor of information which may come to us through our senses; something we have seen or heard.

Our limitations begin in the aquisition process with the very difficult to understand problem of attention. Our ability to perceive, to conceive, to distinguish, and so to acquire information in such a fashion that it can be stored and remembered is not unlimited. The process of human memory is a magnificent, difficult to understand phenomenon which makes us so unique in the animal world.

There are two types of memory: distinct and specific. They explain some of the processes that take place in the complicated, difficult act of perception and storage. The so-called short-term memory makes it possible for us to perceive. Without the ability to inter-relate immediate impressions, the original acquisition would be impossible.

Attention is a phenomenon which augments the clarity of all that we perceive or conceive. By clearness we mean the distinction of those things we want to focus on and their internal analysis, their relationship, their subdivision. As we discussed in the chapter on perception, we select information from the many possible worlds around us. We see the world in our own image, we digest it. With the help of our short term memory, we have our own specific way of seeing, of perceiving, of acquiring experiences, impressions and information. Therefore, our memory of the present, our immediate memory, has a great influence on what we perceive. And certainly, unless we perceive and acquire, we cannot store for long term memory.

This is where craftsmanship, expertise, and skills acquired and developed play such a great role. The music critic, because of his background, his craftsmanship, and the many times he has heard a piece of music, has the ability to pick up fine nuances. He can perceive, and acquire information in a way that a less skilled person would have great difficulty to accomplish. Craftsmanship, acquired talents in the medium of your choice, are of great importance for the acquisition process. It is the basis of all new preparation. Thus, preparation of the past, skills and craftsmanship, talent, play a role in deciding the level at which you can presently acquire. In today's preparation process, the various experiences of the past, the information, the data you can bring to the table, will serve you to be creatively successful in the acquisition of new sensations.

This craftsmanship can be developed, honed, and improved. Thus, you have the possibility through intentional activity to improve your ability for preparation. You can develop the skills to draw on. You can practice the enjoyment of fine literature through extensive reading. You can sharpen your talents of appreciation of outstanding performances in the arts, music, painting, sculpture through extensive exposure to a given art form. Your craftsmanship can be exercised through regular concert or opera attendance, frequent visits to museums and art shows, or actual personal performance in a given art medium.

Preparation in the creative medium of choice is of such importance because prolonged preparation honing of your skills, craftsmanship, improves your future and continuing acquisition of skills.

A chemical engineer must know and acquire a feel and an understanding for the chemical behavior of the many materials that he works with. He must understand and develop the expertise in the strengths and weaknesses of the processes used in the chemical industry.

A banker must be familiar with the influences that shape the money market, the beneficial and constructive things that money can do. He must practice an understanding of interest, profit, and the many forces that play such a key role in his profession. A lawyer must understand the motivation of humans, the rules of the adversary process and the power and limitations of the written and unwritten law.

Thus, in all professions, the training, the development of the skills of the medium is a necessity. Training and development of skills determine our ability to acquire new knowledge and new capabilities.

Next there is the significant problem of storage. How do we store information, sensations, experiences in our minds. How can we facilitate, encourage, improve retention? Only if we can store and retain, will there be a chance for retrieval at the time that we want the information to serve us. To be useful in creative endeavor, information that is stored must be meaningful and accessible. Stored knowledge, feelings, sensations must be meaningful to the human creator and accessible at the time of the creative act.

With the large number of sensations we experience, with the immense amount of data that might be significant for a future creative act, with the limitations of the human senses and the human mind, proper choice is extremely difficult. Especially in the area of general preparation, but even when preparing for a specific problem, there is usually so much available information that selection and storage becomes a difficult task.

Not only must we store information in a meaningful way, but we must also retain it in an accessible way. That means various items of information, various impressions, sensations must be related. They must be stored in an orderly, systematic way. They must be keyed, through out mind, in such a fashion that they can be recalled. Even though this task is difficult, we perform it exceedingly well. We can do much to make the task easier for ourselves if we fully understand what is going on. We can learn how to go about attaining optimum meaningful and accessible storage of information.

First we must realize that there are at least two major systems involved in all data collection and accumulation, the internal and the external. The external system may be a collection of facts in a book, in an encyclopedia, or a machine collection of data of a scientific investigation. There are many other ways in which facts and impressions are accumulated, collected and made permanent. Equally important and susceptible to our improved efforts is the internal system, the human memory. How do we remember, store in our mind the information for future use?

Just as in warehouse storage, storage of data and information, impressions and images can be most successful if we realize that two things are vital — order and relationships. In terms of the modern data retrieval systems, two things are required — storage capability and the program. We readily understand that we can get books from the bookcase better if they are stacked in orderly rows than if we randomly throw them in the same space. We are used to arranging books in an orderly fashion whether by subject, by authors, or in a volume or time sequence. Thus, we are used to relating, to orderly storing of our external information such as books, both in a physical way of orderly stacking and a programmed way of relationship by a certain type of key. The same basic principals apply to successful internal storage of data and information for creative use in all human activities.

Storage requires order for successful accessibility. It requires relationships. We require a key to regain access to the stored information. The external system is certainly the easier one, and most of the professionals have been trained in one way or another to know the ins and outs of a variety of external systems. In the library, we use the Library of Congress system, or use an author or subject index. In a law library there are special systems developed for finding applicable case law and prior decisions. A number of well developed systems are familiar to each professional.

Interestingly enough, the chemical professional who may do an excellent job in using a system such as Chemical Abstracts, or Beilstein in his profession, may fail to develop a suitable and effective system for his internal storage and retrieval.

The human mind and the human senses have very significant limitations. We mentioned that most people forget 25% even of what they *want* to remember within 24 hours and 85% of what they *want* to remember within a week. This certainly underlines the importance of the external system since our internal system has great difficulty in terms of retention and total storage capacity. Much of what we want to retain or what we may consider valuable for future use, must be stored in an external system.

Hopefully we can learn to couple the external system to our internal system in such a way that when we combine the two, we have access to a large and varied store of information. If I own an excellent book on brain surgery, I do not have to remember and store in my mind all the details of that book. At the time the information is required for a creative act, all I have to remember is the existence of the book and where to find it. I can then retrieve the necessary information by going through the book and reaquainting myself with the data available there in accessible form.

Thus, the data in order to be accessible to storage must be digested, it must be ordered, it must be related and valued, it must be abstracted, it must be carefully selected. First, it must be stored in an external system, but also ultimately it must be keyed to the internal, human system. Thus, it becomes accessible through an orderly mechanism for future creative use.

As we have stressed, the creative act is entirely human and, therefore, all preparation must funnel in one way or another to the creative human. It must be part of his conscious or unconcious storage. Certainly the more our mind is loaded with a wealth of material, the more we have to draw on, and the better our chances at making those novel, original combinations that characterize the creative human.

Thus, we need to evolve, use, and get used to a good external system of data storage. We may want to accumulate a library in our specialty. We may want to get familiar with libraries available in our community. We may want to select information of a specific kind that intrigues us.

However, only if we arrange things in an orderly way, if we store pieces in such a way that we can get there again, will recall be true and meaningful.

The most marvelous joke will be lost if we do not write it down, if we do not make it part of our external collection. Without this, the chances of remembering that joke again in a suitable form for use are very slim indeed. Develop your system of external storage. Prepare your personal card file. Accumulate books in areas of interest to you. Know where to find the necessary information.

Most significant, the greatest sources of inspiration, data, information, ideas, and suggestions are other humans. Collect humans, collect humans who have a great deal to offer. One of the most valuable collections of data is a circle of interesting and knowledgeable friends. The modern professional should choose for his friends not only those who have the same interests and the same background. He should collect friends and aquaintances who have a great variety of talents and knowledge. Just as we assemble teams of various disciplines in modern research and engineering so it behooves all of us to assemble our own team of friends. This can and will be one of the most fascinating and enjoyable sources of experience, data and information for a creative existence.

Just a few general rules for developing your own external system. First of all is the permanent record. Write it down, put it on cards, draw pictures, somehow tie it down in a concrete and specific way. Second put it in order. Somehow relate it in a certain way according to a scheme, according to a program or else it will just be an accumulation of dusty files which will seldom be used. You must have a key. Without a key you will not be able to use that data at the right time in the right way.

Many classification systems can be used. Probably the simplest is a chronological system. At least you may remember when you did such and such and thus be able to go back in your personal file system to find the clue to the information. Better are systems based on subjects or interests. You can use systems related to keys whether they be specific indices of interest to you or whether they be outlines of a scheme of a broader nature.

For special preparation it is recommended that you develop a key early. Prepare an outline against which the special preparation can be stored. Thus all your external systems, whether they be tape recordings, pictures, books, articles, notes, whatever, should be arranged in orderly fashion according to an intelligent scheme. This must be keyed in such a way that your mind can connect back to the information in your external storage system. Only in this way can the data be made meaningful, and available.

Think of the statistics for the weather. We are all used to thinking of the weather in terms of dates. The weather is fine and the sun is shining. The temperature is so many degrees today. In terms of weather statistics, we are used to the Farmer's Almanac, we are used to certain statistical information given us on the news. It relates today with weather of tomorrow or with the past. However, the code has to be an intelligent one. It tends to relate to something that is meaningful to us. The temperature at 10:30 everyday is not too meaningful. However, the maximum and minimum temperatures of a given day give us a good idea as to what type of weather we experienced. In comparison with the all time maximum and minimum, it is of increased interest to us.

Data has to be orderly arranged, it has to be recorded, in the Farmer's Almanac or in a computer, somewhere to be accessible. It has to be programmed in such a way that only the meaningful data, the data that relates to our interest, is recalled when we desire it.

The instrument left by the astronaut on the moon designed to measure, record and transmit data on ionizing radiation does receive this data every moment as long as it continues to function and record. That data does not become meaningful until or unless it can be related to more than just the time factor which ties it down at the moment of its gathering. It must be related to the rotation of the moon, to the position of the sun or to other events in space to become significant. It must be put into an orderly context with other events. All this may be done in an external system through intelligent use of computer correlations. However, it requires the human mind to ultimately use this data, explain it, correlate it in a creative way.

This then brings us to the all important internal system. The human system which strangely enough works in somewhat similar ways. We can assist it, train it, and explain its workings, although the full functioning of the strange human capability, that we call memory, still escapes complete scientific elucidation.

It was thought at one time that memory, just like muscles, could be built up by practice alone. This has been scientifically disproven. However, memory can be improved by understanding its functioning. By taking advantage of what we know about memory, we can improve our ability to remember those items that we want to remember in a specific way.

It is certainly possible and desirable to consciously improve our memory. First of all, memory storage will depend on our ability to successfully acquire the information which we want to store. Retention will be tied to acquisition. Not all humans retain the same type of information equally well. For example, many humans have a better ability to retain visual information than information gained through the sense of hearing. In many cases, memory will be assisted by acquisition through more than one of the senses.

Many people can improve their storage capability by using not only vision and hearing but also by involving themselves in an action to improve the likelihood of retention. For example, many of us will remember much more readily if we personally write something down than if we just see it in writing. The mere process of going through the conscious act of writing down the item in question improves acquisition for potential storage.

Thus, it is important that you are conscious of the way in which you personally can best acquire information for the purpose of storage. Are you endowed with a visual memory? Is your greatest strength in hearing something or are you particularly in need of a combination of various inputs to allow you a higher probability of storage and retention.

Many memorizing schemes are available. Some are kept secret by their practitioner who astonishes you with his seemingly amazing skill. Others are published in a variety of interesting books. None of them is totally completely and scientifically understood. However, all of them have those traits in common that we mentioned for the external storage system. They teach us to pay attention. They stress focus, concentration on a given item to be remembered. They stress order, organization, relationship of various items to each other and to something else in order to facilitate storage and retention. Good memory performance is not a question of practice. In fact, practice alone will not do the job. We must know how to go about it. We must know the rules of the game. We must have learned a system for memorizing. We must know how to help ourselves: whether to stress storing images; and what kinds of relationships to select. Most important, we must have confidence, we must be convinced of the power and capability of our memory.

Successful memory schemes relate the material to be memorized to some previously learned organizational device. There are many ways in which this can be done. You may want to choose your own system. The most commonly employed techniques are the use of a rhyme or rhythm and the use of locations. Thus, for example, I remember my home phone number by the rhythm of the number which I have told myself aloud a number of times. In school you have learned the verse, "30 days hath September, April, June, and November". I was taught this same piece of data to memorize when I was a youngster by looking at the knuckles of my hand. Counting from left to right, knuckles show the longer months and the spaces between the knuckles the shorter months. This then brings February between knuckles and has July and August, the two long months, side by side because you go from one hand to the other. These are simple examples of two common ways to assist and develop memory: rhythm and locations.

In his book, "The Art of Memory", the English historian Francis A. Jates relates how the method of locations was first originated by the Greek poet, Simonides, who was called away from a banquet hall just shortly before the roof fell in, crushing the host and all the guests to death beneath the ruins. The corpses were in such an unrecognizable state that the relatives who came to take them away for burial were unable to identify them. But Simonides remembered the places at which they had been sitting at the table. He was thus, able to tell the relatives which were their dead. This experience suggested to the poet the location principle of the art of memory of which he is said to have been the inventor. Noting that it was through his memory of the places at which the guests had been sitting, that he had been able to identify the bodies, he realized that orderly arrangement is essential for good memory.

In many a highly successful memorization, we relate the items that we want to retain and have available and accessible in our memory, to an orderly scheme of location. This may be a speech outline, or it may be the method of the ancient Roman orators, who visualized a building. They stored the introduction of the speech in the entrance hall and took a trip through many rooms, each one serving as a depository of some of the ideas and facts that they wanted to recite. This helps greatly in remembering the various points in the right order since the order is fixed by the sequence of the rooms in the building through which we might travel.

Outlines or other devices for assisting our memory are important to remember large amounts of information. Just as with external information, it is not only significant, what we memorize and the amounts of information we memorize, but also the order in which we memorize and the way in which we key the information to a specific and orderly system of memory locations. To make it more helpful, it is desirable that the locations be as interesting as possible. They must not be too similar to each other to be useful. We are more likely to remember the humorous, the unique. It is easier to remember something unusual, out of the ordinary than an ordinary, common place occurrence. More striking images are more readily remembered.

In essence, all these methods bring us back to the need for organized storage, the necessity for a system of order. Our internal kind of library must be well arranged. If a book is misplaced on a library shelf, it is hard to find. If a piece of information is stored in memory without relationships to others, without a program and a key to retrieve it, it is most likely to get lost. It will not be of value to enhance our creativity.

We have difficulties in storing more than a certain number of items. Psychologists have formalized this into what they call the principle of the magical number of

7. We have difficulty in remembering more than seven at a time. This can be overcome by grouping, by remembering a smaller group than the final complicated system. For example, telephone numbers are grouped. We do not use all the numbers together. We use smaller groups in combinations. Thus we can assist our storage effort by grouping things, by categorizing, by ordering, by clustering and thus breaking down larger items into smaller bits.

Certainly it is easier to store a bunch of keys and the locations of the houses on a piece of paper than it is to store the houses. Thus, in order not to clutter our mind, it is vital to abstract, to reduce large amounts of data to essentials so that you can store the key rather than the entire item. The essence of a good book can be remembered. The same holds for other large systems of information. They can be condensed, abstracted and keyed for better memory utilization.

The total system is an "in and out" mechanism. The data are acquired or fed into the system, eventually they will also have to be processed out again for creative use. They have to be combined with other bits of human memory to allow creative activity.

Preparation involves storage and storage involves order. Interestingly enough, while we forget and forget and forget, much of what we really desire to retain may be available to us in our subconscious mind. The strength of the creative process, as we will discuss in a later chapter, is that it enables us not only to draw on our conscious mind, but also on that larger amount of additional memory storage available in our subconscious mind. Many of the impressions, images and data that are not readily available consciously, can be remembered at least in shadowy form from the subconscious mind. This is the strength of the intentional practice of the creative process. It offers special techniques for encouraging the full participation of our subconscious.

Data, images, impressions, our external real world is unlimited. Our external system, our human memory and especially our retrieval capabilities are greatly limited. How can we reconcile these opposites?

What should we store? What is worth storing? Our culture, our civilization is oriented towards knowledge. Can we go about learning indiscriminately? Do we recognize what is fact and what is fancy? How readily are we fooled? We already stressed the need for skepticism and an open mind, but what about the information itself? Do we know the distinction between fact and nonfact?

Do you know the distinction between reports, inferences and judgments? For selection of data, especially in the intellectual arena, it is desirable that we distinguish between reports, inferences and judgments. We may want to refrain from storing inferences and judgments since they are not clearly as helpful to our future creative acts as reports.

A report is defined as a piece of data which is verifiable. We say this building is 24 stories high. We can check it out or it can be checked out by somebody else. This then is a report. Quite generally we have a whole host of conventions that make it easier for us to believe a report. We can agree on the fact that they are verifiable even though we may not undertake to verify them ourselves. The measurements of science, the conventions of verbal agreements in a great number of areas, are reports. Reports, either singly or put together in an orderly, verifiable form are important. They are worthy of storage if they are unique, interesting, and pertinent to our interests.

We must learn to distinguish reports from inferences.

Inferences are statements about the unknown made on the basis of the known. Needless to say, inferences may be right or wrong. I see a man lying in the gutter. I infer that he is drunk. But he may be sick and not drunk at all. My inference from his appearance may be right or wrong. This distinguishes inferences significantly from reports, which are verifiable.

Third and important to recognize is a judgment. This is a very personal thing. It is an expression of a specific individual's approval or disapproval.

As a general rule, it is more valuable for us to store reports, and less valuable for us to store inferences or judgments. Judgments may be time dependent. Their storage may be a detriment to the creative process, to a new and better solution. We might be impeded by prior judgments.

The process of cumulative storage over the years, the gaining of expertise, skill and craftsmanship does involve the combination of a great number of experiences. The interaction of various items of storage to a final more useful total than the individual items contributes craftsmanship and favors origniality. A famous painter gave a masters class. A student asked him how long it took to paint one of his well known and highly valued watercolors. His answer was, "it takes me 53 years to do one of these". He intended to convey the need for the total preparation over the years. It all culminated in his latest achievement.

What we are, the total human, is important. What to select, in what fashion to accumulate the vast amount of storage needed for successful creative endeavor, this is the unique human skill. Each of us has a unique style of our own. What we do is equally important as how we do it. Put away gold nuggets and discard gravel? This will be a human decision. This will be the part in which the creative personality plays a great role in deciding the success of the preparative growth of each individual.

Thus far we have considered general knowledge, gathering, accumulation, and storage. Preparation is also a specific step to solve a specific problem. It is part of the creative problem solving process. Thus, we must know how to proceed in finding the raw material most suited to a particular task.

Robert Fulton once said "the mechanic should sit among levers, screws, wedges, wheels, and so forth, like a poet among the letters of his alphabet considering them as an exhibition of his thoughts in which a new arrangement transmits a new idea to to the world".

The lawyer works surrounded by his library, the depository of the thousands of cases, problems of similar nature and their solutions in law. The chemists and physicists avail themselves of their technical literature to gather data for the solu-

94

tion of their problems. In our specialty it has been part of our training to know how to go through a specific sequence of preparation in relation to a given problem. Some excellent guides to preparation are available.

We may spend days, weeks, even years, before the material necessary for the final product is all available and ready in our mind at one and the same time.

Edison said that "genius is only 1% inspiration and 99% perspiration". We could rightly paraphrase that to say "99% preparation".

Bertram Russell put it more practically. "For my part I have found that when I wish to write a book on some subject, I must first soak myself in detail. After all the separate parts of the subject matter are familiar, then one day if I am fortunate, I perceive the whole with all its parts properly interrelated. The nearest analogy is like first walking over a mountain in a mist until every path, ridge and valley is separately familiar, and then from a distance seeing the whole mountain in the bright sunshine."

In skiing, to win the slalom, you must not only have practiced for a whole lifetime to acquire the craftsmanship of the champion. You also have to study each gate carefully before you put it all together and come down in record time.

Besides general and specific preparation, we must be aware of the value of direct and indirect preparation. Professionals readily accept the value of and the need for direct preparation. Direct preparation is the accumulation of information and skills that obviously relate to the problem to be solved. Direct preparation for the chemist are his chemical journals, textbooks and related information sources. They may also be specific preparation such as a search of the chemical literature as part of the problem solving process.

Most professionals neglect indirect preparation. This is not surprising. Time is limited and usually our initiative, our interests are centered on our field. We focus our mind on the problem at hand. Indirect preparation, however, is particularly vital to the creative approach. It is a collection of seemingly irrelevant experiences, concepts and factual information. These serve to generate, trigger or supplement an insight. Our normal expectation in problem solving is that all the pieces we need, all the ammunition, all the preparation is that which is directly required by the problem. However, creativity and originality require and favor the "surprise" factor. Digressions favor surprise. Direct preparation is less likely to result in an original idea, an original solution than indirect preparation.

It is in the difficult area of indirect preparation that we can most assist our creativity. Indirect preparation assists originality. This does not mean chasing all the sidelines nor does it mean a chaotic, undisciplined gathering of any kind of fact or experience. The trick is in choosing indirect preparation that will be truly helpful, even though the results as well as the applicability of the indirect preparation are at times almost impossible to predict.

An interview with the executive producer of the highly successful TV science fiction program "Star Trek" illustrates not only broad preparation but also the value of indirect preparation. The first portion of this man's life was spent in a successful career as an airline pilot. He then decided on a writing career and in preparation held a variety of jobs which took him all over the world. He became a policeman. In police work he saw firsthand all the facets of human misery and human suffering. Eventually his preparation led him from writing to the creative career of producing.

How many professionals consider this need, both for broad general preparation and the value of indirect preparation in their job choices? You may look at it from two angles, your own preparation and your own choices. Diversify your skills to increase your own value. This can be broad exposure to cultural experiences. It can be a determined effort to add new and intriguing specialties to your area of expertise.

On the other hand, many of us at one time or another have such decisions to make for others. How often do you consider the value of diversifying skills? How often do you assist in making sure that others as well as you subject themselves to indirect preparation? How often do you consider indirect preparation and diversification of skills in the selection of a man for advancement or training for greater responsibility.

For growth and a greater chance at creative performance, indirect preparation, diversification, broad experience is significant. The creative individual needs that broadening. Switching fields of specialization or a variety of experiences greatly enhances the individual's capability for creative problem solving. The experience of one field may well be applicable to another in an original and novel way.

Plastic foams of many types play a major role in many applications today. The original pumping and metering problems in making such foams were solved by a German submarine engineer who brought his knowledge of diesel equipment to the plastics foam generation field.

Indirect preparation is of particular value to the teaching profession. It is highly desirable that our academicians have extensive, indirect preparation. It is necessary that they be skilled outside their teaching specialty, that they experience a test period of nonacademic training. They must encounter the realities of their profession, of their specialty, outside the academic influence.

We have considered how to prepare, what to prepare, finally we must ask the question of how long do we prepare. While we have stressed that general preparation is a lifelong process, preparation for specific tasks, objectives, goals, and problems must be frozen at a certain stage or else the creative process will never fully function. We must be conscious that if we are to solve a problem, we have to be satisfied with certain limits on our specific preparation. If the preparation process does not end, we do not get around to the idea stage and the solution of our problem. The creative individual must be willing to stop preparation at the right point; to divert his attention to the generation of ideas, the next vital step in the problem solving activity.

Preparation may be resumed on specifics as required by further development of the problem solving process. However, this should be considered with care since the danger always exists that we use the preparation activity as an excuse for putting off the creative idea-generation step. We may use it as an excuse to keep from really coming to grips with the problem, with ideas and action. Thus, while general preparation is a lifelong activity, specific preparation and indirect preparation must be deliberately limited in time.

We must allow the creative steps of the problem solving process, idea generation, followed by action, to be initiated. The creative individual in his driving desire to solve problems, to be original, to move forward, realizes that while he is never fully and ideally prepared, creativity requires movement, requires progress. The preparation phase must be terminated for the sake of the blooming of creative ideas.

ACTION PAGE

BUILDING BLOCKS FOR CREATIVITY

Preparation:	Necessity
	Selection
	Storage
Preparation:	State of Mind
	Life Long
	Never Ending
Preparation:	Interdisciplinary
	Multidisciplinary
Preparation:	Fun and Games
	Routine
	Individual
Preparation:	Open Minded
	Collections
	Memory
Preparation:	Special and General
	Direct and Indirect
	Time Limits

EXERCISES

Collect more than a thousand ideas in one month. This is only fifty ideas each for twenty problems, one each working day.

Example problems: A friend needs a job. How can he best help himself? How can you help him?

You have a hundred dollars for charity, what is the best thing to do with it?

Your office needs rearranging, redecorating. How, why, when?

RECOMMENDED READING

J. Barzun and H. F. Graff, "The Modern Researcher", Harcourt, Brace and Company New York, 1957.

George F. Kneller, "The Art and Science of Creativity", Holt, Rinehart and Winston, New York, 1967.

Don Locke, "Memory", Anchor Books, New York, 1971.

A. L. Logan, "Remembering Made Easy", ARC Books, New York, 1970.

Donald A. Norman, "Memory and Attention", John Wiley and Sons, New York, 1969.

"The Modern Researcher" is a very helpful work, especially for preparation of written material in the humanities. Many other good books are available in the field of "memory". Preparation means: A good library.

Chapter 6

IDEAS, MANY, MANY

Generation and cultivation   The case for quantity
The vital recording   Check listing
The more, the merrier   Attribute listing
Judgments prohibited   The perfect match
Reinforcement requested   Health and emotions

Our world does not stand still, it keeps on building. Culture expressed in the arts, science, law, or banking; all progress springs from what went before. It is from components, impressions of the past, shaped and combined in unique humans to new composites and novel systems that the world moves forward. In preparation, we store components. Our ability to remember and reproduce information enables us to prepare for the idea stage. The idea is a combination formed in the human mind. It is putting components together, they may be old, parts of an old system, or they may be new.

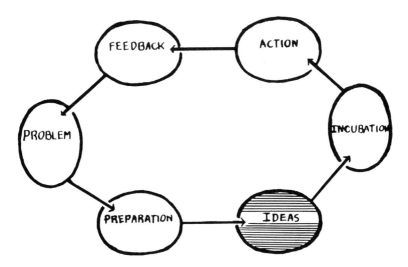

Colors, sounds, thoughts, are the subassemblies of the new system. They are pieces to be fitted into the jigsaw puzzle that is our future. The raw material, the storehouse of preparation, however, is not enough. The simple building blocks of knowledge, images, and impressions deposited in our libraries and memories cannot bring progress by themselves. They cannot lead to the solution of problems without combination, or assembly into an idea. Ideas are the true driving forces of the creative process. Ideas are the flywheel, the energy carrier, the motive power of creativity.

the Last Piece

Ideas are not the monopoly, the prerogative of genius. Ideas are the daily arrangements and rearrangements made by every competent human. Ideas are not the perogative of intelligence, wealth or position either. Ideas are free for the taking. They are available to all. In any field of human endeavor, in any professional activity, ideas are the key to problem solving. Ideas are needed to find solutions, to select the road to progress.

Human existence has become most complex. We are crowded together with ever increasing needs and expectations. Ideas—many, many ideas—are essential to fulfill our desires, to make our dreams come true. Ideas are the building blocks to a future of progress that can live up to the ever more demanding human expectations.

Most problems have many solutions. To find them, to select the best solution in the frame of time and circumstance, we need ideas, a multitude of ideas. Prefabricated solutions can only rarely be used. Things change too rapidly. Yesterday's solution is not the solution for today and tomorrow. We need ideas, many, many ideas, but only a multitude of new ideas can prevent us from trying to make an old solution fit new circumstances.

In these times when it is so easy to oppose progress, where we find detractors in any profession, synergism is a must. Routine forward motion, that is $2 + 2 = 4$, is not enough. To overcome opposition, to avoid that $2 + 2 = 0$, to avoid destruction ($2 + 2 =$ less than 0), we need either a miracle ($2 + 2 = 100$), or synergism ($2 + 2 = 5$).

The miracle ($2 + 2 = 100$) is hard to come by, but ideas, many ideas can provide the creative human consistently with synergism, ($2 + 2 = 5$).

Human beings have the strange, unique and exciting ability to come up with ideas. They have the ability to synergistically add $2 + 2$ and come up with more than 4, with 5. Triggered in all kinds of ways, human synergism, human idea generation, sometimes comes suddenly. But more often it comes as a result of hard work.

The "idea" is an expression of the superiority of the human race, as far as we know, only humans can generate ideas. Ideas flow most readily if we are conscious of this marvelous human ability. We can encourage their flow by generating a "working mood". That is, it helps to be "aware" of the ability of the human to generate ideas. It boosts our self-confidence, stimulates our imagination. Most important, we must be "aware" that we need quantity, that we need many ideas, many, many ideas. Quantity is the watchword. The man who has many ideas, has some good ideas, and a few original ones. The working mood can be fostered. Like in athletics, practice makes perfect. We can build, train, and encourage, the working mood for the generation of ideas. We may not be able to develop idea muscles but we can develop idea attitudes and habits.

What are the characteristics of the right attitude? How can we strengthen our ability to generate ideas? How can we favor the working mood?

First, there is the understanding that to foster ideation there has to be motivation, a vibrating, forward moving desire, a striving which brings forth ideas in quantity. This striving can be motivated by a variety of human urges. First, there is the urge to contribute, which stands most creative individuals in good stead. We enjoy performing a creative act, an act that has meaning to ourself and to others. Then, there is the pride of accomplishment. Most humans want not only to make a contribution, but to make a significant contribution, an accomplishment.

Striving, energetic motion, keeping our imagination stirred is what generates ideas. By general preparation over the years, and through specific preparation, we have accumulated much raw material in our conscious and subconscious minds. It is through the urge to generate ideas, through motivation and desire that we can stir and mix these many impressions. Sensations, memories of the past are collected to generate new combinations, new results, new ideas.

There has to be some discipline. Idea generation is not a chaotic random operation. There has to be a blend of impatience and patience. If we are too impatient, too hurried, the best ideas are likely to escape us. But if we are too patient, we may not sustain enough of the driving force to generate new and original ideas.

The time factor must also be considered. We must be persistent. We must continuously fuel our desire to excel. Idea generations, "a working attitude", means an urge to excel, an urge to accomplish, an urge to contribute. It must be a disciplined urge that knows how to generate, how to combine. It must stop long enough to record when the combination of components has generated an image, an idea in the kaleidoscope of impressions which stir in our minds.

We might think of a pool table. There are many balls on the pool table. They have position. We have to put them into motion. We have to put them into directed motion to make a point. Ideas come from human internal motion. It is motion of the senses and the mind. They come through the formation of images. They come through the stirring of the pot of our imagination to create a new flavor, a new picture, a new thought, a new combination: "a new idea."

This is the working mood. How do we get there? How can we build up, fan this fire of striving for excellence, this fire for motion towards new combinations, this fire that churns the components in our minds? We all have a tremendous inertia barrier. We could rather sit and relax than wind up the motor of our imagination.

It is not easy to get this imagination rolling at full speed. It is for this that we can apply a first aid to the creative process. There are things we can do, until inspiration comes. We can hunt and explore to get ourselves into the working mood. We can fool around, we can browse. This may seem an aimless and random endeavor. However, it leads us directly to the best possible working mood for idea generation. It gets the creative individual out of his rut. Directed motion is just a special case of random motion. The inertia barrier is down. That is the secret of the "dither". We are on the way to obtain combinations of components in a new image. Any action, any motion, is better than standing still.

In one of my early attempts at painting, I painted the dish of the large radio antenna built by scientists to attempt to communicate with the stars. The painting turned out rather well, except for the sky. I had to make nine attempts at painting the sky to match the idea and the feeling of the painting. On the ninth attempt, while I was fooling around with color combinations and shape, I achieved a proper mood to convey the right feeling.

Persistence is important when generating ideas. There are always more ideas to be found. You may not think so, you have just exhausted your approach. The checklist has just run out. You cannot see over the hill. Keep on climbing, go around that big tree. Do not hit your head against that stone wall, there is a road open to your left. Do not force it, but keep on moving. There are many more ideas. Try a new approach, a new checklist, a new association, a new and different tack. Try a wild and unusual way. What if this problem were not on earth, but on an imaginary planet? What if you were not human, but an insect? What if there were no rules, no past? There are always more ideas to be found.

Idea generation requires overcoming inertia. Strange as it may seem, however, sometimes ideas will come best through relaxation. Sometimes you may want to temper the intentional drive for results. The mind will keep on working if you go for a walk provided it has been given a sufficient push to overcome the inertia. It will keep on working if given a direction towards the ideas you are seeking beforehand. Thus, you can get yourself into the working mood through hunting, browsing, exploring, change of scenery, relaxation, or even through shock techniques.

Inertia is generated by many factors. Possibly the greatest barrier to ideas, is fear of ridicule. Fear of ridicule not only works against idea generation, but it is particularly harmful when you try to devise original ideas. Against this deterrent the creative individual can best apply and strengthen his resolve through discipline. It is the ideas that count, not ego. Many ideas seem wild at first, but turn out to be most valuable after further study.

We must learn that failure is the norm and success the exception. The creative individual learns to live with failure, but without giving in to it. You cannot get ahead every time. Getting angry about a miss will ruin your concentration. Failure to the creative individual must not be a barrier, but an open gate; not discouragement, but motivation for the next try.

The barrier of the first solution, the old one, the obvious one, is equally severe. The first idea, the obvious one is not likely to be the best. In fact, it is most likely to be a result of conformity and prior learning. It is most likely that the first idea that comes to you will be the combination that has been thought of by you or others in the past. Old thoughts and language patterns stifle new ideas. It is important to continue to persevere, not to be too strongly taken in by the first and obvious idea.

We are the slaves of normalcy. A screwdriver is for turning screws; we may not think of it as a lever. But a screwdriver may also serve as a measuring stick, as a weight, or even as a chisel. We think of a brick as part of a wall, not as a hammer. We have blinkers on when it comes to new arrangements, to the formation of new ideas. Idea training removes these barriers, strives to improve our ability to use components in a different way. It helps us to see available elements in a different, a new light removed from old relationships, free of unnecessary restrictions.

The German psychologist Karl Dunker experimentally demonstrated the inhibiting effect of strong associations, such as we will encounter due to the ordinary use of an object. The ordinary, normal associations inhibit the formation of new ideas. In problems where some object had to be employed in an unusual way, those people did very well who had not first been asked to use the object in its normal fashion. In a problem requiring a thumb tack box to be used as a candle holder, nobody had great difficulties if they were given the box empty. However, only half the people got the idea of using the box as a candle holder when it was given to them filled with tacks.

Often we add our own barriers, we close ourselves in voluntarily.

Asked to count the squares in the drawing on the next page most people will reply 16 squares. However, there are really thirty squares. You were not asked to count squares of equal size, but you probably added this additional restriction consciously or unconsciously yourself, voluntarily. We volunteer all too many barriers to ideation. Ideation training removes barriers, frees us of preconceived notions.

We need many ideas to generate good ideas. What method gets the most ideas? Whatever method it has to be, it must be your own method. Ideas are born within

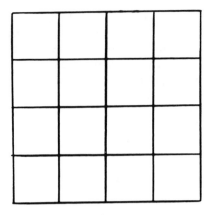

your **mind, within your system**. Ideas are the result of your human creativity. Each profession, but most important, each human being, each professional has his own requirements. **You have to** develop and foster your own best method. You **have to** cultivate **your individual** style of "ideation".

Much **is known to** encourage and develop successful methods for idea generation. But **this should only** assist us, lead us in cultivating, strengthening **our own** unique **style of bringing** forth many, many new and original ideas.

The **first and** foremost principle of any successful method for generating **ideas is** a **willingness, a** trained ability to defer judgment. Ideas are fragile; they **can be** destroyed **quickly** and prematurely. They must not be judged without a grace period. **Idea generation** and judgment must be separated.

WiThhold JudgemenT

A solution, **evaluation**, judgment must not be engaged in until the ideation process has **been given a** chance, until many, many, many ideas have been generated. This means ideation should be a significant, a self-contained, a substantial effort. It also means the professional must learn to separate, to divorce time-wise the ideation process from conclusions, from the evaluation, the selection of a solution.

Many professionals are trained analytically. We are likely to favor analysis over creative synthesis. We have a tendency to immediately judge any idea in our mind. We tend to analyze the ideas of others, either in our minds or out loud. This is fatal to the success of generating many ideas. It has a most detrimental effect on creative problem solving.

Defer judgment! Defer judgment of your own creative ideas. Be willing to express and record ideas even though you might judge them immediately as unsuitable. Defer judgment on the ideas of other. Do not smile, do not laugh, do not contradict, do not say: "this is impossible." Instead, try to reinforce, try to find ways to use the others' ideas, try to strengthen them. Most important, record, record, record.

Ideas must not be judged prematurely. This then means that they also must not encounter prejudice. Bias, prejudice, preconceived notions, these are barriers to idea generation that we must not tolerate. In many professions, law, medicine, chemistry, the professional has developed his analytical capabilities to a high degree. Analysis is a vital tool, but it has to come after the idea generation stage. Ideas must be allowed to spring forth, to grow to a healthy state before they are analyzed, dissected, and possibly chosen or discarded. Prejudice formed by past theories, past dogma, or today's fads, must not be permitted to interfere with the generation of new ideas.

How can we counter the dangers of judgment and prejudice? How can we protect the fragile, newborn ideas? First, they must be recorded, they must be nailed down. An idea is like lassoing four matched horses at one and the same time. They must be corraled and broken to harness to make a matched team. The most beautiful butterflies in the meadow do not contribute to my collection. They need to be caught in the net, mounted and displayed. Human memories are frail. Ideas fleetingly conceived, are readily lost if they are not recorded promptly.

Create your own best system to record ideas. Write it down on cards that you keep in a box. Have a pencil and paper with you at all times. Keep them ready next to your bedside if that is where ideas might occur to you. Use a loaded small tape recorded, if dictating comes easier to you than writing.

Ideas are like beautiful balloons. We must blow them up and they will shine in all their colored splendor. But we must also string them or they will soon collapse or escape into the sky.

If we defer judgment, and record our ideas promptly can we then leave idea generation to chance? Can we increase the opportunities for ideas to be born? Shall we follow a planned approach? Do not sell chance short. But remember lucky accidents do not happen to dead cows. Lightening strikes only the prepared mind. What I am trying to stress is that accidents are where we find them. Accidents are fine, but they need a receptive human mind to kindle an idea. The idea is a human creation. Hooray for the accident which will trigger a worthwhile and original idea. But it will only come to pass if the human mind is ready for it. Let's keep looking for this kind of accident. Let's make it happen. Let's be alert to it, take advantage of it. Accidents are wonderful, but only the ready human can take advantage of them. Let's sharpen our sensitivity, keep our eyes and ears open for that outward happening, that coincidence, that occurrence that can help us generate the new idea.

The princes of Serendip had many lucky adventures in their travels, but they were ready for them. They had the natural human ability to take advantage of the lucky accidents. Serendipity is a talent to look for, profit from. Record and take advantage of accidental, lucky combinations. You can rightfully wonder if they are truly accidental, since it takes a human, a creative mind to recognize them.

Conditioning yourself for the ideation process, is like learning to swim. You have to overcome your fear of drowning, learn the moves and gain the confidence that you can do it. In learning to build your ideation muscles, first you have to overcome your fears of ridicule, of breaking tradition, of acting against your prejudices. You have to learn the freedom of conceiving many new combinations without regard for your innate barriers.

Next you have to learn the moves, but most important you have to have the confidence that you can do it. You are human, you are an idea man. Any healthy human, man or woman can be a genius in his or her own way. A genius is just an individual with an idea at the right time, in the right place.

Like swimming, ideation can be, should be enjoyable; it can be great fun. If you develop your ideation talent, the ideas will come faster, easier. They will be more and more unique, less obvious, original.

How the moves are made is also very important. The champion swimmer has his own well trained individual style, but he learns the optimum way to turn. He studies the moves of the hand, even those of the fingers. The moves are understood and practiced for optimum results. Training aids are used to develop muscles, favor certain motions. Equally in ideation, we can profit greatly from understanding and using the proper aids. Most significantly we can improve our ideation capabilities through practice.

We must learn the moves. We can and must develop a personal style of ideation. Remove all the barriers, mix and stir. Opportunities for ideas can be made, can be improved, can be provided. We can open doors to idea generation. More than just creating opportunities, there can be a planned way, a true method for idea generation. Aimless browsing does not get the same result as directed research. There is a place for aimless browsing. It can relax the mind, create opportunities for new directions. This does not negate, however, the value of a methodical, planned effort at idea generation. There are many aids, many systems to assist you, to help you in a planned, systematic effort at ideation.

We know, that in a way, ideation is a process of fitting bits of information together in a new and unusual way. It stands to reason then, if we start with a bit that is related to the problem, a bit that fits even slightly, we will favor the process. Equally, if we systematically search for bits to incorporate in an idea, we should be doing better, than if we blindly wait for all the pieces to fall in line, without conscious effort. We can increase the odds of achieving effective surprise.

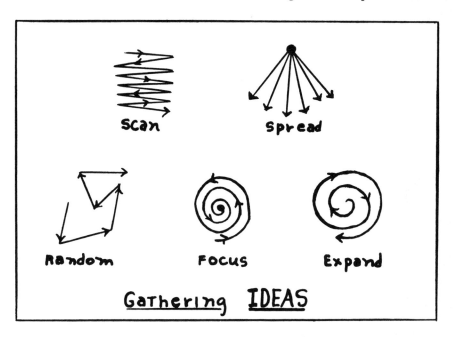

Possibly the simplest way of assembling bits into an idea is a check list, some way to keep your mind moving, to get combinations formed. Alphabet soup. Going down the alphabet starting with "a", thinking of words that relate to, that might generate an idea for the solution of your problem. First a word starting with "a", then a word starting with "b", then a word with "c", and so forth.

Check lists offer a variety of ideation assistance. You may use a dictionary, an encyclopedia or a phone book. The yellow pages offer an excellent list of vocations for example. Check lists stir your conscious mind, and help you in forming new arrangements. They keep you from bogging down and keep you moving forward. Many helpful check lists have been published. Make up your own. I'm sure you can improve on mine.

CHECK LIST FOR IDEATION

Find a   Model
                Contrast
                Opposite

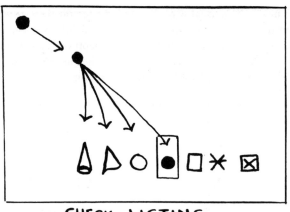

CHECK LISTING

Change	Material
	Color
	Function
Make it	Small or large
	Short or long
	Thin or thick
Just	Add
	Subtract
	Divide or multiply

Another approach to ideation is to analyze and synthesize. You first take it apart, and then use the pieces for a better combination. This is also called "attribute listing". You examine the detail, to recognize components and to encourage reassembly in an improved way. Take a simple object such as a pen and consider its size, shape, color, or material. What could you accomplish by changing each of these? By looking at the attributes of a simple familiar object, and by changing them, you can train yourself to play with, to manipulate, to recombine the elements into a new idea.

Morphological synthesis is similar to attribute listing. It first identifies important characteristics of the problem and lists specific values for each. Then all possible combinations are charted. This invariably produces a very large number of ideas. It also raises the question of inhibiting ideas falling outside the scheme. Like all methods, it helps, if used wisely.

Bionics, the use of analogies drawn from nature or generally role playing and dramatizations can also be very helpful to form your ideation style. Whether you imagine being an animal or a plant, and experiencing the problem, or whether you use even more fantastic ploys, ideas will be flowing freely. In fact this type of game

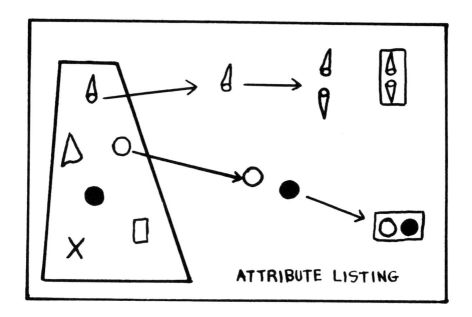

ATTRIBUTE LISTING

is apt to encourage the generation of original ideas. It serves well to break down the barriers of preconception and to free your creative drive.

Examining these various useful aids, these methods to encourage ideation, we find that there are basically three general approaches to the generation of ideas. The first is random stimulation, which may be based on a list of words, a list of questions or similar simple devices.

Next, and always to be kept in mind, is alteration. Alteration makes use of what is already known, what is already available, the ideas that are already at hand. From these we generate additional and new ideas. It is like stepping up various steps. You will go from the known step, to a slightly different or very different step. You can either go very strongly in one direction, looking for likes, or you can go in the opposite direction looking for ideas that are very dissimilar. You might magnify or minify, you might expand, you might contract. In any case you are likely to reinforce the initial idea.

The third method which will be discussed in greater detail when we discuss the group effort at generating ideas is cross-fertilization. You can get ideas, often very original and valuable ideas, by looking at similar problems in other disciplines. You can obtain many different viewpoints and many different attacks on the problems in this fashion.

Remember you are trying to find the right bit from the many millions of possibilities in your brain to fit it into a new idea. While there are countless combinations possible, your mind has a unique ability to combine the bits in such a way that the useful, original ideas come to the forefront.

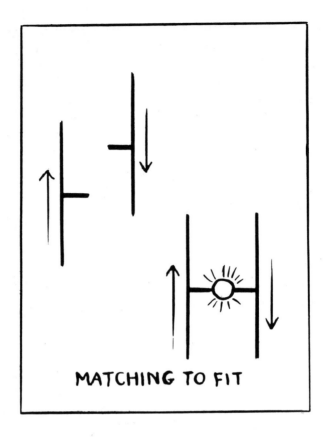

MATCHING TO FIT

The ancient Greeks recognized three doors of association: contiguity, similarity and contrast.

"Contiguous" means something side by side, something near. Similarly, one idea can readily lead to another. A word in the problem definition can be the trigger. Something we have recently run across in our preparation for problem solving can lead to an idea. This first idea then can again lead to something new, close to it, and so on. Similarity and contrast are terms which we readily understand and frequently use. We can get help to form association by looking for contiguity, similarity and contrast.

It is most helpful to ask ourselves questions. A question which is particularly useful to the engineer is: "How can I simplify it?" Other questions frequently beneficial in idea generation are: "How can I use this for other purposes?" "How can I combine various aspects?" "What more can be done?"

We can create our own method for improving our ability to form associations. We can move our mind around, we can stir our imagination to find new combinations, to generate new ideas. We can see to it that our serendipity is active, that we keep traveling until we have the lucky accident.

110

However, associations, and new ideas don't always come the way we want them and when we want them. Associations can also lead us astray. Osborne, in his book on applied imagination, recounts a curious and humorous passage as follows:

"What is a double petunia? A petunia is a flower like a begonia. A begonia is a meat like a sausage. A sausage-and-battery is a crime. Monkeys crime trees. Trees is a crowd. A crow crowed in the morning and made a noise. A noise is on your face between your eyes. Eyes is opposite from nays. A colt nays. You go to bed with a colt and wake up in the morning with a case of double petunia."

When our mind runs in circles it is not always this funny. Many times in our striving, in our desire to solve problems, we may run up against a stone wall. We see only insurmountable barriers. We run dry of ideas. When we are stopped, then it is time to do something different. There is always a way when the road is blocked. Detours are better than collisions. But, it is easy to lose the working mood when we are overtired and over stressed. Then ideas do not want to come.

The working mood can be affected by your physical condition. Where you are, how you feel, can have a bearing on your ability to generate ideas. Emotions can be a barrier to ideation or they can be a motivating force.

Emotions are not always helpful to the creative process. Fear, such as fear of ridicule, keeps us from formulating and expressing wild ideas. However, emotions and feelings move us to act. We will act emotionally even when we have insufficient information to make a rational decision. Thus emotions will help us to overcome our normal, rational barriers. Emotions free us from premature judgment. They increase our willingness to take risks. They can be helpful in generating ideas.

Straight thinking leads us to obvious associations. Ideas, yes, but not necessarily original ideas. Excitement, anger, even fear can bring forth association, ideas of an unusual nature. It can push us towards ideas which we would have trouble finding in the cold light of dawn. Thus, for idea generation, emotional stimulation is apt to be of assistance. It is more likely to favor ideation than to hinder it.

In his excellent article on emotions and creativity, Simonov illustrates this with the fable of the two frogs:

"Two frogs fell into a jar half full of cream. One frog soberly appraised the situation, to struggle was useless and put its paws together and drowned.

The other frog was not the intellectual type and did not stop to analyze the situation. Since he did not have the same information as the other frog, it went on struggling for its life. The rapid strokes of the frog's paws gradually thickened the cream and created a lump of butter. The emotional frog crawled onto the solid lump of butter and jumped out of the jar."

Emotions, however, can also effect our control, they can mislead us. Emotions are not always the best conditioning for idea generation, even though they may contribute to originality.

You may have to experiment and study yourself to find your most effective conditioning, the best time and place and conditions for you. Most people function best with a rested mind. Morning hours, even the routine of cleaning up and getting dressed for the day's work can be favorable to idea generation. But please, do not forget to record. Write down your ideas before you get fully dressed.

Much has been said about sleeping on ideas. No miracles are likely to happen while you sleep. Ideation is a waking hours activity. However, your active, churning mind which has been grappling with the problems may need to rest. It may need some quietude to form those precious associations, to generate and formulate the ideas. The mind can be rested in many ways. You may want to interrupt and go for a walk. You may turn on the record player with a good piece of music, or you may want to sleep on it.

These are some of the ways to favor a rested mind. Determine which is best for you. Most any kind of change of pace is apt to do something useful if idea generation has run at too rapid a pace or a seemingly immovable barrier has been encountered. Some methods may be better for you than others. Find your individual best way.

In any case, even though a driving desire is vital for the working mood, recognize the need for time. Rome was not built in one day. Not all the good ideas will come to you in the first few minutes or even the first half hour or even on the first day. Time may be needed, especially to let you overcome those first obvious ideas. You may need to rest your mind. You may need to free your mind and open it wide to many new, original combinations which do not come necessarily at first encounter with the problem.

Only a healthy mind can bring forth many new and original ideas. Much has been argued concerning the use of drugs and artificial stimulants of the imagination. Idea generation, day in, day out, requires not only a rested mind, but also a clear mind. Drugs can relax or stimulate, but at a terrific cost. The human system is a complex marvel. Over-stimulating it, or relaxing it artificially demands a price in future impairment of capability. Too often the excuse, that relaxation will stimulate the imagination, lower the inertia barrier, leads to continued use of drugs or alcohol. Continued use unavoidedly leads to weakening and destruction of personal capabilities. Alcohol and drugs, upon repeated exposure, will dull your senses, and inhibit ideation rather than favor it.

Idea generation requires a healthy human being, with a healthy human mind. Physical health and a clear mind are closely tied to each other. Fresh air is a better stimulant than drugs. With a little time and help, every healthy human being can relax. You can get the rested mind into the workings mood through your own actions without the penalty of future dullness from artificial stimulants. Ideation is the fun part of creativity. Play it that way, generate many, many ideas. Depart from the unusual and embark on a trip with the Princes of Serendip. Many, many ideas will show you the way to outstanding, to original, to creative ideas.

EXERCISES

List 40 or more ideas for the following:

Conserving energy in your home.
Prolonging your life expectancy.
Getting your job done more effectively.
Finding new friends.
Making a contribution to your community.
Improved driving habits.
A significant learning experience.
An enjoyable vacation.
Increasing your income.
Helping a friend.
Helping a stranger.
Making an invention.

RECOMMENDED READING

Myron S. Allen, "Morphological Creativity", Prentice-Hall, 1962.

Myron S. Allen, "Psychodynamic Synthesis", Parker, 1966.

Edward de Bono, "New Think", Avon, 1971.

Bernard B. Goldner, "The Strategy of Creative Thinking", Prentice-Hall, 1962.

Donald A. Schon, "Invention and the Evolution of Ideas", Tavistock, London, 1969.

Pavel V. Simonov, "Emotions and Creativity", Article from "Psychology Today", August 1970.

John D. Yeck, "How to Get Profitable Ideas", McGraw-Hill, 1965.

Goldner's book is worthy of special attention. It has humor, examples and is easy to read. Many of the books listed in previous chapters also extensively and competently cover "ideation".

CHAPTER 7

INCUBATION: TIME OUT FOR CREATIVE DIGESTION.

Pressure and relaxation   Time out for mental digestion
Daydreaming   Utilize your subconscious
Long walks in the country   The total human being
Training for fantasy   Flash of genius
Hobbies and sports   The surprise solution

At the beginnings of the process there was problem definition and preparation. Then we studied the fun part: idea generation. Ideas can be stimulated. They can be made to flow freely.

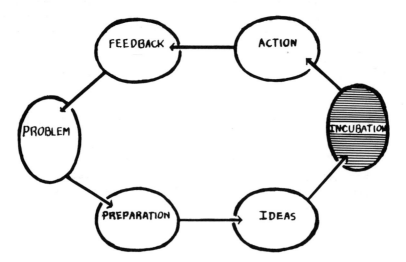

Now we are out of ideas. We have examined the problem from all angles. We have hit a stone wall. New ideas do not come readily anymore. We have been under pressure for weeks. Ideas, facts, prepartion, problem definition, everything seems a confused swirl. We have struggled with the problem for so long we seem stale. We do no longer enjoy pursuing our goal. We do no longer enjoy trying to be creative. We are tired, confused. We still feel the need to solve the problem but we are checkmated.

Or all has gone well, we readily saw and understood the problem. Preparation was fun and interesting and we have generated large number of seemingly attractive ideas for solving the problem.

114

What next?

Stone walls, confusion or profusion of ideas, it is time for a change of pace. It is time for creative digestion, time to let them simmer. Where the previous steps of the creative problem solving process profited from pressure, from diligence, from dispatch, even from competition, now it is time to relax. We must slow down, we must encourage patient delay during the incubation period.

We have striven consciously and deliberately. We have gotten to the point where we are repeating what we have done. We are like a machine going forward but without direction. We have roamed too freely. We have explored so far and wide the many ideas which have been encountered that we have lost our focus. We have gone off the track. Some new factor never encountered before has come into the picture, making it difficult for us to go on, obscuring our vision and blocking our conscious ideation process. We have been slowed down by the strain of our own activity. We have become ineffective in our creative effort.

Ideation can be both conscious and unconscious, or, better, "subconscious". It can be deliberate or it can be the result of daydreaming. It can be the result of playing with the problem just below the surface of our conscious mind. Naturally, this is not a black and white proposition. Like the swimmer, we may want to come up for air during the problem. Any further effort, any new attempt seems like boxing feather pillows, no progress, no light, no way out.

Stop! Hold it! Time out!

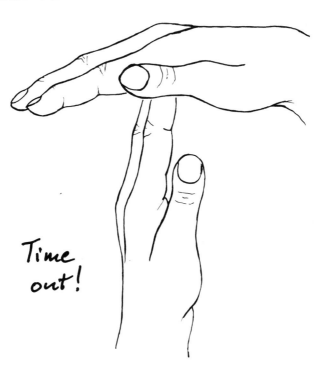

Time out!

It is time for a change of pace. Let your mind relax, allow incubation to take place. Incubation requires a change of attitude, a change in outlook, a willingness to take it easy. Where we were driving, pushing, working hard, where we were firing our own intensive innate drive to create, to solve the problem, incubation requires a willingness to let up. We need a dreamy, a playful attitude. We must change to an attitude that allows conscious activity to give way to subconscious contributions.

This is the time for our sixth sense to go to work. Now as scientists, professionals, members of today's realism-oriented society, we have been trained not to do anything, not to believe anything, without evidence. We are used to realistic, straight-forward, machine-like computer-oriented attitudes. We are only rarely aware of our subconscious mind. Speculations are condemned, realism is the order of the day.

It is not that we do not know that there is more than our alert, systematic, open consciousness. We are aware that there is more to our total consciousness than our deliberate, realistic, direct day-to-day activities. It is not as if we did not recognize that there is such a thing as a subconscious mind. We know that there is more to our total consciousness than our waking, alert, direct activity. It is more, that we do not like to think about it.

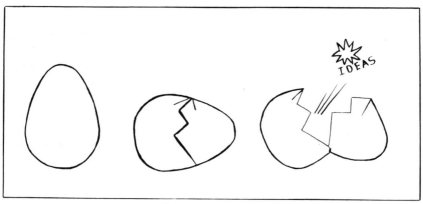

Incubation

It is almost as if we were classifying subconscious activity, the things we have greater difficulty to understand, with magic, with mystical activity. In the words of Dennis Gabor: "Nobody denies that his consciousness exists. Opinions differ only on the point, how important or urgent it is to introduce it into scientific discussions."

Our total consciousness contains all the data, all the knowledge we have accumulated. It is made up of numbers, words, sentences, images, concepts delivered and stored, usually in deliberate fashion. Our intuition, imagination, our feelings, values and drives make up the subconscious part of our total consciousness.

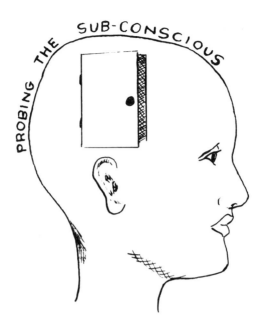

PROBING THE SUB-CONSCIOUS

We must understand that the capabilities of our subconscious mind go beyond and materially add to the potential of our conscious being. Dennis Gabor puts it: "the unconscious mind is a tremendous fact which we cannot dodge. It is like a large office with a great number of clerks in it, each with his 'own time', while the conscious is like the director's office in which only one clerk can report at a time to avoid confusion."

To assure the fullest use of our subconscious mind, our broadest and widest potentialities, we require incubation.

It seems that certainly the simplest way for a change of pace for incubation to take place, should be to sleep on it. Stop the conscious attempts of ideation and wait until the next morning. Go home for supper, play with the children, and sleep on it. It would be nice if we could solve our problems while we were sleeping. Some scientists do believe that winning ideas come to them in a dream, come to them while they are sleeping. R. W. Gerrard reports such an incident as part of Otto Loewi's discovery of the functioning of the nervous system.

Loewi's experiments on the control of a beating frog's heart were giving puzzling results. He worried over these, slept fitfully. Laying awake most of one night, he saw a wild possibility, a way to experiment, which would test it. He scribbled some notes and slept peacefully until morning. The next day was agony. He couldn't read the scrawl, nor recall the solution, though he remembered that he had had it. The next night was even worse, but at three in the morning lightning flashed again. He took no chances this time but went directly to the laboratory and at once started the experiment.

117

Stories such as this have given rise to speculation that ideas may be obtained while asleep. Consider, however, the ideal conditions for incubation. You are trying to sleep. You are physically relaxed. You are focusing on sleep, shutting out all the thousands of influences which are apt to sidetrack your consciousness. What better conditions could you ask for? What an excellent circumstance for your subconscious to advance a winning idea. Even more so in the morning after a good night's sleep, when first awakening, you are in excellent shape to have the good idea. With Dr. Wilder Penfield, the famous neuro surgeon, I believe "it was not that your brain was working on it, but that your brain was not working on it".

It is as if sleep preferentially sweeps away the irrelevant, the unnecessary, the faulty, the extraneous. It helps us to start out fresh with a substantial advantage. We are more likely to remember and associate the relevant, the material, the significant. We see problems more clearly with a rested mind. The ashes of the previous day, the useless images, the discarded associations, do not crowd in. The favored ideas, the potential solutions, the creative images come through more isolated, stronger, more clearly, more dominant, free of the chaff of the discarded, unsuccessful attempts of the previous day.

Most of us should be at our best at problem solving early in the morning after a good night's rest. We must use this to our best advantage. We should have pencil and paper in our bedroom or our bathroom to jot down good ideas. We should deliberately favor our consideration of problems in the morning. We must use this valuable time spot creatively. Please, do not think of the traffic jam you are most likely to face when you get to work. Please, do not turn on the news on the radio or television. Do not listen to all the bad things that have happened during the night. This will kill your creative mood. Rather enjoy the potential peak period of your mind, use it for creative activity.

It pays to be aware of your creative periods. It pays to take advantage of them. You must learn how to relax, how to incubate a problem. how to let a problem simmer, how to bring your subconscious abilities, your whole creative competence to bear on the problems at hand.

Not all of us have our best and most creative periods at the same time, in the same place, or in the same way. Gerrard tells us that Darwin remembered the very spot in the road, while he was traveling in his carriage, where he conceived his hypothesis as to the origin of the species.

A fine scientist whom I greatly admired did not let his vast and responsible duties as a research director keep him from spending much of his time at the glass blowing bench. This was his way of incubation. This was his way of favoring creative subconscious activity. While his hands were handling the glass blowing torch and the hot melting glass, his mind was relaxed and his subconscious at work on weightier problems.

Creative periods, a change of pace, can take many forms. For some of us, it is a time when our mind is fresh or relaxed at play. For others it may not be a question of the time or day. It may be a certain mood, a location favorable to the release of creative potential. We may even have little or no control over these periods of creative outbursts.

Bernice T. Eiduson, in her most interesting book, states that some scientists felt themselves at the mercy of their periods of creativity. A chemist said:

"I can't turn it on and off. I wish I could. The best thing I can do is make use of these periods for whatever they are worth."

A theoretical physicist stated:

"You're working on something. Now when you're working very hard, the ideas are coming good, then you're beginning to solve something. I don't know what happens. You're not daydreaming, but you have moments of absolute blankness because everything is going on inside."

Maslow, in his classical work on motivation and personality, refers to this as "peak experience", as almost a mystic experience. He talks about:

"Feelings of limitless horizons opening up to the vision, the feeling of being simultaneously more powerful and awesome or helpless than one ever was before, the feeling of great ecstasy and wonder and awe."

Maslow's "peak experience" is, however, nothing supernatural. It is the harmonious functioning of our total potentialities. It is the full human in action. It is the in step performance of conscious and subconscious together. It is the fullest combination of understanding, intuition, and imagination. It is creativity at work.

The incubation period, more than any other facet of the problem solving process, requires us to foster our imagination. We must give your intuition free rein, follow paths that might be closed to a hardheaded realistic approach. How then can we woo these subsurface capabilities, these talents which make up, deep down in us, the great strengths of our creative selves?

We must learn to recognize our creative potential when it flourishes. We must learn to make it grow. We must strengthen and train it. Possibly the incubation step requires the greatest effort for many of us in this respect. We are trained in logical thought processes. We have accumulated and stored much realistic knowledge. Whether engineers, lawyers, bankers, scientists, or housewives, we have developed rational, methodical, realistic ways of handling our problems. In our country we have been brought up in the belief that if we spend more money, if we put more people on it, somehow things can always be done. One, two, three, forward march. If Joe cannot do it, let us get Bill. Let's put an experienced engineer on it. Get a good PhD.

Maybe, just possibly, it would pay to have a little patience. We need to be a little less serious. Let up the pressure for a little while and recognize the character of the incubation step. Encourage subconscious activity, find a creative solution, illumination, inspiration, insight is just around the corner. To find them, show the right attitude, show an understanding of yourself and others. Exhibit patience, allowance for the change of pace, time out for mental digestion. Encourage, or at least tolerate, creative daydreaming. Know when to let up on the whip, curb your realism. Favor intuition. Reward imagination.

We must take advantage of our rested mind. This does not just mean alertness to our possibilities for creative undertakings after a good night's sleep. It also means a wooing of our subconscious during the daytime. It means favoring activities which would strengthen our intuition, develop our imagination. This is difficult for many of us. Suddenly we are told "learn to daydream". Where it has been "pay attention, concentrate, work at it, don't dream", now, all of a sudden, we say "play, relax, dream a little".

George Neilson, famous architect and designer, gives us a good picture, when asked what was the relationship between this mood and his ability to create and produce in his chosen field.

> "What comes to mind is like slipping in the clutch, in other words, you disengage the motor and get into a mood of 'no thought' or 'a sort of empty', relaxed and detached mood. What I think I'm really saying is that you turn off your conscious mind with all its buzzing and scurrying and just wait. Then the subconcious does the work."

We can encourage daydreaming. Certainly it will not be stimulated by watching television. In our affluent society, we have fostered the habit that we must always be doing something. We work, we eat, we sleep, we read, we listen to the radio, we watch television, we go to the theater, or a party. We are always doing something Let us daydream, let us do nothing but relax. Do not go to the beach, just to play ball or to swim. Curb your inner restlessness, lay in the sun and daydream. Do not schedule every minute of your day the way you do now, but schedule a half an hour of daydreaming. Make your coffee break a day dream break.

This does not mean you should encourage loafing or passing the time gossiping. The day dream time is not to discuss yesterday's football game. It is a plea for the legitimacy of day dreaming. It should be a relaxed period, a change of pace. Day dreaming is of great value, we do not need to apologize for the time we spend on it. Time spent on incubating the many problems under consideration need not weigh on our conscience. It is a legitimate, necessary and important part of the creative process.

Neilson also describes how he solved the problem of keeping a beach in its natural state while opening it to the enjoyment of the touring public.

> "There was no solution from this point of view and you had to disengage your mind and let the problem simmer. And, as usual, all sorts of seemingly irrelevant images came to mind and this is the most curious part of the thing. It is as if you have a kind of high speed data retriever. The retriever knew what to look for. This is really a miraculous part of the thing. Well, my data retriever gave me a picture of a piece of land with houses on it and boats in the harbor in front of it, which had nothing to

do with this strip of beach. And I thought 'what am I looking at?' And then, if you put buildings on land something happens, quite often for the worst. But if you put boats in front of the land, nothing happens at all. The land remains pure and untouched and the combination of boats and land is ok. Very pleasing! So there was the answer. Put everything on barges or boats and rafts and then not being part of the beautiful stretch of dunes and beach, you do not violate this natural thing."

It seems natural that certain images impress themselves on us more strongly than others. We see the winning combination, we see a special flash. The image leading to the sought for, wished for, hoped for creative solution makes the strongest possible impression on us, both when it first appears and later in retrospect. It came to us in a flash. Suddenly out of nowhere, this image impressed itself on our conscious mind. But our restless creative self, our subconscious mind was at work all the time. It had done the wrestling with the problem. It had produced the insight, the winning combination. Countless combinations had been made and if not filed, were at least examined and screened in a preliminary way. As much as we may try not to cast away any ideas too early, not to judge and prejudge any possible use for the images or combinations, this had been going on. There is a certain way in which we function, a way of individual action or reaction, a certain sorting or specific screening involved in just allowing images and associations to form in our conscious mind. Some are relegated to our subconscious minds, others eliminated, or discarded as not meeting even the broadest requirements of the problem.

The subconscious is usually most tolerant. It has not been imbued to the same degree with the rules of realism, with the rules of effectiveness and efficiency, which we have acquired through education or life experiences. Our subconscious is less regulated, therefore, more open to the unobvious, the wilder image, the im-

DAYDREAM

possible, the unusual, the original idea. It is not surprising then, that in our subconscious we form the winning combination. We seem to have the bright flash of recognition of the most likely solution to our problem. We see the light. We have illumination, The Eureka experience.

Day dreaming, "intentional, purposeful, willing day dreaming", exercises and activates our subconscious. The painter experiments, drawing lines or placing paint hesitantly on the canvas. He gropes, tries for a feeling, not yet formed, but an image coming forward, coming from his subconscious. He works from feelings, from intuition, translating his imagination, the subconscious picture into reality. Almost without his will, without his conscious thought, the images form on the canvas. The more relaxed he is the less he tries to force it, the better. As the great Renoir expressed it: "Like a child, I paint before nature with an artless soul and the instincts of my fingertips".

In the same way, incubation allows our subconscious to push the winning combination to the surface. Intentional day dreaming can bring about "effective surprise." In our subconscious we can strive to imagine the procession of fantasies starting with general, desirable images. We range further and further afield, but always disciplined by our motives, by our desire to solve a well defined problem. Gradually our subconscious targets on the desired goal. Day dreams, fantasies, speculations, they all assist and orient towards the solution of the problem. Speculations and fantasies may be rejected by the conscious mind of the practicing professional, but they will help the subconscious mind to find an original solution.

How can we train ourselves to relax, to allow our subconscious to function more effectively?

Hobbies are invaluable in developing our creative potential. They automatically teach us to change pace, since we will usually pick our hobbies in areas different from our normal problem solving activities. Hobbies foster creativity, whether it is jogging, bottle making, ceramics, whether it is knitting, sewing, or any of the many hundreds of hobbies that are being practiced by people all over the world. In America there are literally millions of interested and active participants. A hobby, an enthusiastically engaged-in activity different from your normal problem solving, is invaluable to the development of your creative skills.

To quote Spinoza: "Teach the body to do many things, this will help you to perfect the mind and to come to the intellectual level of thought."

We have to train our total human faculties. Let us choose a hobby which will consciously and synergistically add to the total of our capabilities. If you are engaged in an occupation which primarily uses the mind on a numerical or verbal level, choose a hobby which involves manual dexterity. If you do not normally use your hands, learn to cook. Practice gourmet cooking, it will bring many of your creative skills into play. If you do not get enough physical exercise and do not want to choose a sport, start jogging. Choose weight lifting or any of the many hobbies which require you to use other than mental skills. Far be it from me to discourage mental activity. If your job is one of a very physical nature, such as work on a production line, then certainly a highly mental hobby such as chess might be best for you.

Generally, in the choice of hobbies the rule should be a change of pace. Thus your hobbies will train and prepare you for the utmost use of your skills during the incubation, the change of pace portion of creative activities.

Artistic activities are an excellent and enjoyable extension of the hobby scene. You may find, you will enjoy creative endeavor if you are just willing to try. Engage in artistic activities such as painting, drawing, sculpture, ceramics, woodcraft. There are many other artistic activities which are taught and practiced in groups within our cities all across the nation. At the artistic level of a hobby you will actually be creatively engaged. There is no better creativity training.

Participation in sports is of substantial value to your creative talents. A good game of tennis, golf, or any of the sports available to us on the participation level, are of great value as a change of pace. While it may be true that even in front of the television, watching a football game, you contort and unconsciously participate in every ball thrown, in every run or every pass intercepted, this is not as good as an hour of tennis. Active participation, active engagements, whether it be in the high jump, in the running, in automotive racing, in tennis, in bowling, any active participation in sports is orders of magnitude more valuable than spectator sports.

Games are valuable tools for teaching creativity, encourage games for young and old. While games can be and are being used for conscious learning, they are also of significant value in the subconscious sphere, in the training of other than verbal skills. We must oppose the idea that play is something sinful, something not to be encouraged. It is not a waste of time, it can be a positive activity.

In our society we have formed the habit of encouraging work and learning and discouraging the play of children. We stress that school is positive and play is negative. Somehow we have gotten the idea that play detracts and is nonconstructive. This is not at all the case. Games and play are particularly useful in encouraging creativity and in fostering the total mind body. Play has a significant and important role in the development of our creative talents. It is at play that the young child first learns some of the major lessons needed for his or her future life.

The mood of play, the playful attitude, the willingness to play around encourages creative performance especially during the incubation period. Play can be used in many ways to further our creativeness. DeMille's imagination games have already been mentioned, they serve to establish the rightful place of imagination in the early years. They also serve to convince the parent, the adult, of the legitimacy of playing with imaginary situations.

Much has been done to use games for educational purposes. Play and games are not reserved to the young. The adult profits as much from playing with children as does the youngster.

Games are of value in training our subconscious. We play, we let our barriers down, we relax, we accept, we enjoy. At the same time the game has a purpose, a goal, we compete. A game is a playful copy of the problem solving process, thus an excellent training device. Learning with games, benefits of play, are part and parcel of creativity training. They are of special value to incubation, the change of pace.

Incubation serves not only to let your subconscious focus on the winning ideas, it also paves the way to the next and final step of problem solving, that is, selection, action, implementation of a solution to the problem. By letting it simmer, by taking time out for mental digestion, our original preferences for one solution or another, our commitment to a favorable idea weakens. We are gaining distance, we are gaining judgment. Judgment, selection automatically brings in the dangers of prejudice. The break, the incubation period, clears a way to make the honest, the true, the proper, the successful selection step easier. We take time to step back, to look at the big picture, we back off and see the entire system. We avoid premature conclusions, we loosen up. We make inspiration more likely, you might almost say we prepare for inspiration. We put ourselves into a state of mind where it is easier, it is most likely for the flash of genius to hit us. We generate a mood, an attitude, we are relaxed, turned inward, ready for insights, for effective surprise. We are in the best frame of mind for inhibitions to disappear, for our intuition to show us a successful way out. We are willing to see the wildest and most unusual pictures our imaginations may paint for us. We are poised for the surprise. Oops! Originality! The solution! Effective surprise, not just an ordinary solution, but an original, a creative solution. Imagination is here. We are ready to face the problem. We are ready to implement, to act!

ACTION PAGE

INCUBATION

Incubation:	Sleep Dreams Awakening
Incubation:	Day dreaming Day dreaming Day dreaming
Incubation:	Hobbies Sports Participation
Incubation:	Games Play
Incubation:	Instinct Imagination Change of pace

Incubation

EXERCISES

If you have not already done so, put that paper and felt pen in your bedroom for easy access. Use it.

Each morning for the next five days, select one problem you have been wrestling with the day before. Mull it over in a relaxed way. Contemplate it in the shower, or while you are shaving. Write down anything positive, anything constructive that comes to your mind.

Pick the busiest part of your day. Whenever things are most hectic and you are absolutely rushed, stop. Put your work on the table before you, close the door if necessary. Close your eyes and relax, try to keep it up for five minutes.

Practice daydreaming for one half-hour each day for one week. Try to clear your mind, get completely relaxed, allow your self-conscious to function.

Take up a new sport: indoor tennis, horseback riding, skiing, anything that you have not done before.

Organize a group of friends or family to play games with. Purchase and select one new game each for the next six months.

RECOMMENDED READING

Clark C. Abt, "Serious Games", Viking, 1971.
Elliot Carlson, "Learning Through Games", Public Affairs Press, 1969.
Bernice T. Eiduson, "Scientists: Their Psychological World", Basic Books, New York.

G. M. Ferber, "Control of the Mind", McGraw-Hill, 1961.

Ralph W. Gerrard, "The Source Book for Creative Thinking".

Irving John Good, "The Scientist Speculates", Heineman, London.

Robert G. Graham and Clifford F. Gray, "Business Games Hand Book", American Management Association, 1969.

A. H. Maslow, "Motivation and Personality", Harper and Row, New York.

Jasie Reichardt, "Cybernetics, Art, and Ideas" New York Graphic Society, 1971.

Carlson's book is of great help as an introduction to the use of games for creative problem solving. "Cybernetics, Art and Ideas" is a stimulating picture book and conversation piece. Dennis Gabor's chapter in the "The Scientist Speculates" make for fascinating reading.

CHAPTER 8
SOLUTIONS, SURPRISES, ACTION.

Only action counts   Discovery, invention, innovation
Implementation is the thing   Pick the unusual
Always many solutions   Delegation and motivation
More than one right answer   The unfair advantage
Any action, better than none   That first step

Action, action, action! There is no creativity without action. Ideas, incubation, inspiration may be the wings of the creative process, they may be air currents carrying the jet of creative force, the flight of originality and surprise, but there can be no creativity without action. Action, implementation, reduction to practice brings the creative process back into the realm of reality. It locks the creative process firmly into the real world and enables its contribution to progress. Action thus completes the creative process, contributing value and the creative product.

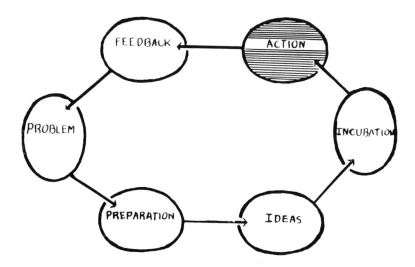

Action generates the permanent mark, the new, the original work of art, the poem, the novel, the sculpture or the invention, the new machine of the engineers, the technologist. Let us not confuse the creation, the product, with the creative process itself. The painting is the result of creativity, not creativity itself. It is the finished, permanent embodiment of the creative process. Without action, without implementation, without solution of the problem first posed, the creative process is not complete. Creativity is not fulfilled without action.

127

The creative process started with preparation and problem definition, both determined activities, steeped in reality. Preparation, the hard drudgery, the intense concentration of learning, collecting the many pieces of potential future usefulness, selecting what might contribute to the creative process, this was an activity in the reality sphere. So was the problem definition when, with both feet on the ground, we explored the real world to find, delineate, describe, and focus on the real problem, to distinguish the real problem from the surrounding distraction, to isolate it so it could be tackled by the creative process. Preparation, problem definition took place in reality.

When we got to the idea stage, we put our wings on. We started to look up, to rely on our imagination. We suspended judgment and encouraged flights of fancy, we took off for the land of dreams. We went on random excursions, we consciously and intentionally broke the bounds of convention, used tricks and games to encourage many, many, many, many wilder and wilder, more original ideas.

Then in the incubation period, we soared ever higher, leaving the world of realism, forsaking conscious activity for the stimulation of the unconscious. From the realities of logical thinking, of deliberate, awake idea finding, we progressed to the use of our total potential, intuition, imagination, fantasy, all put together to arrive at the optimum inspiration, we nourished ideas better and more original, more valuable than any we could have generated by earthbound conscious efforts alone. But like the bird sailing happily in the ocean breeze, like the glider riding the upwards drafts of warm air currents, we have to land eventually. We have to return to reality to complete the creative process. We must not and cannot remain in the realm of incubation forever.

Action must be a deliberate choice, a solution of the problem, a decision. From the many ideas, we must choose among the alternate solutions. There may emerge one or more combinations. It may be a variant or a reinforcement of an idea first seemingly useless that offers the best way towards implementation. Maybe you have a difficult time choosing. Likely even, there are a number of solutions since, as we have always stressed, most problems have more than one solution. Survey all the new ideas, organize them, shuffle them like cards, mix them up and review them, recheck some of the ideas against your definition of the problem. What is the relationship of time, people, resources to the ideas under consideration? Consider, if you select certain ideas, how you can implement them. Is there a unique and original solution or are there several desirable alternatives.

Thus, action first means a choice, a decision. You have to conceive a solution. If you are fortunate, lucky or have developed your creative powers to a high degree, conception may be a strong, a forceful, an almost explosive illumination, a happening. You may have a "eureka" experience, a flash of genius, an almost automatic recognition of the right thing to do. "Oops! Never thought of that." You suddenly experience "effective surprise". You see the light; the solution becomes obvious. All other ideas fade beyond the conceptual vision, the inspirational image of "how to do it". You do not need to choose. Your total being, your subconscious has

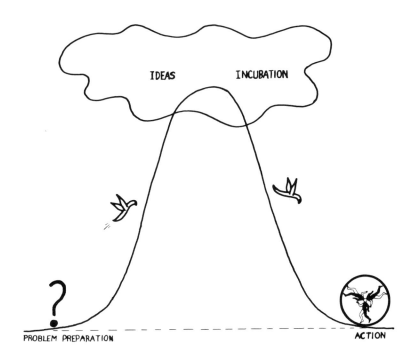

IDEAS   INCUBATION

?

PROBLEM PREPARATION   ACTION

already made the choice for you. Surprise, originality, the choice seems obvious, right now, no other way seems possible. You are most fortunate—the first step towards action—the choice—the conception has almost been made for you. You have a strong forceful image, an idea of what to do. You have found the solution, you have had a vision of the way to overcome, to solve the problem. You are now ready to reduce it to practice, you are ready to put it into action, to translate it to reality.

But this is only the first step. The conception, the vision, the idea is not enough. Now you must implement, you must fulfill your dream, you have to act. Conception is likely to still be in the imaginative world. Action only—doing something about it, setting in motion occurrences in the real world, will lock your conception into the flow of progress. Implementation, real doing, is required to bring the creativity process down to earth. For most of us it is easier to think, to dream, to play with ideas, even to have unique original ideas, even to experience "effective surprise", than to do something about it.

All of us, especially as we grow older, as we acquire more and more knowledge, as we experience the real world, have built up an inertia barrier. Inertia is doing nothing, protecting the status quo, standing still or moving forward only in the same old routine ways; in this world of change, we hide defensively behind the wall of inertia. We are used to doing things a certain way or not at all. "That is not my job, the government should do it." "Why doesn't the mayor, why doesn't the Congress, why doesn't the President do this?" Everything is somebody else's responsibility. We like to blame everyone but ourselves for what goes on or doesn't go on. We do not like to act. We do not like to be involved.

But, only when we move, only when we make something happen can we complete the creative process. Whether it is an experiment, starting to build a model of a new machine, the stroke of a paint brush on canvas or meeting the stranger whose help you need, action means overcoming our natural tendencies towards inaction, overcoming the inertia barrier.

"Action is the thing." Now first of all, to overcome the inertia barrier, we must be willing to do something wrong. When we look at our sports heroes we do not expect perfection. Any action is better than no action. You cannot get a hit unless you go to bat. No one has a thousand batting average in baseball; .330, one hit in three, is considered excellent. Why not so in life, nobody in school, industry, or college should be expected to bat one thousand. Are your tests and expectations out of tune with real life? Are you afraid to act because you might fail? Only through action, through frequent continuous action, can you expect to improve your batting average. We must be willing, not only to excel but also to fail. This will help you break through the inertia barrier.

Practiced action, repeated action, continued frequent action can put you on the road to excellence. We rightly admire perfection, the artist is often judged on perfection standards. One slip of the memory, one false piano passage, one failure of the opera star's voice and a critical audience gasps. Perfection standards are the ultimate goal of the creative individual, the final seldom achieved result of the striving for excellence. They cannot be reached without practice, life-long continued practice, a willingness to act, to try and try again. It can only be attained if there is a willingness to fail as well. We cannot give in to the fear of failure.

Try and try again, inspiration or judgment may be followed by experimentation. This may lead to verification or failure. If the desired result is not achieved we need feedback to repeat the process in a better way. Feedback may be "fine, the solution works", or "improvements are needed", or "no, we must start over". Feedback is necessary to revise the judgment, choose an alternate idea, a different solution and act on it.

What is failure and what are its consequences? Many times failure is not of the real world but solely a product of our imagination. Action is in the real world. Imaginary failure should never keep us from it.

The real risk of action may be very small compared with the ceratin failure of inaction. We may well want to be wise, however, in the employment of our resources. We may want to minimize the risk of failure. It is a foolish gambler who risks all his winnings on one throw of the dice. If your resources are irreplaceable and the potential risk is large, it may well be wise to move toward the desired goal stepwise.

For the creative individual, it is important to understand the value of stepwise commitment. Where action is concerned we most often deal not only with our own hesitation, but with the caution, the inertia of others.

130

It is nice to get there all at once, to reach the goal on the first try, to take a shortcut, to hit a home run, to win the sweepstake, to become a success overnight. However, most of us are not likely to be that good or that lucky all the time. It may be better to hit a single and to get around the bases one at a time. The first action may be easier than going all the way. It commits less and it accomplishes less. This is quite true, but the second step may come much more easily, if the first one is successful.

I've been told that the introduction of the zipper to men's clothing was delayed two years because management's lifelong traditional habit of thinking in terms of buttons could not be shaken. It would have been easy to equip just a number of pants with zippers. This limited test might well have led to an earlier full acceptance of the total change.

When you act you are changing something. Change is inherent in the definition of action and so is resistance to change. The bigger the change, the more original, the more radical the concept you are trying to implement, the greater the resistance. How much wiser, how much more in keeping with the teachings of creativity to try it the easy way. Make a feasibility study first. Build a model, a prototype, make a sketch, a beginning. If this first step towards your concept is successful, it will prove that your idea is a winning one. If you can demonstrate the first step, how much easier to implement it further, to convince others now of its value. A working model can be highly convincing. The first step is a tough one. Like moving a vehicle from a standing start, it takes the most energy. It is much easier to keep the ball rolling once it is in motion.

If your concept is valid, your idea a winning one, even if it is the true pot of gold, and thus to you it seems that it should sell itself, the implementation will not come automatically. It requires action, it requires selling on your part. Thus if you have a major concept to implement, if it requires large resources of people and money, break it down. The first successful step is likely to make the entire project much easier. Do not commit all your resources at once. A creative start towards full implementation requires ingenuity. You must find the easiest way to get moving, the creative choice of the right starting point.

Similarly if there is a risk of failure you can minimize that risk by choosing that first step that is most likely to succeed. Partial success is likely to convince other to take the total risk. It will help to overcome their fear of failure and yours.

The creative individual must never underestimate the power of even the smallest acts. Small acts may have large consequences. The banana peel inadvertently dropped on the floor may lead to somebody else's downfall and a broken leg. Both positive acts, and, deeds left undone can be significant. The creative individual must cultivate a spirit of action, an inclination towards movement, towards doing rather than not doing. It is important to condition ourselves. We should practice our willingness to act, a constant alertness, an attitude, a vibrant readiness to move. Certainly it is easier to start if you are ready mentally and emotionally. Willingness to act in small matters generates greater ease of action when it really counts.

However, hardly any action is small, even though the consequences may not be readily detectable. Positive action, seemingly minor, may have major consequences, major effects in the long run. The kind act you perform for another may cause a kind act of his towards others. The chain may continue and even come back to yield benefits to you. The good example you set by a positive minor act such as removing a tripping hazard may lead to safer living for many. The loose screw you tightened on a piece of machinery, the worn tire you replace on time, the helpful suggestion to a son, to the neighbor, the tactful criticism voiced to a co-worker, all these seemingly small actions may have major consequences.

We can train ourselves for the actions required of us by fostering a lifestyle of willingness. We can cultivate a style of voluntary action, a habit, a practice of keeping the inertia barrier low. Volunteering makes action come easier. We can develop a habit of action or of inaction. The creative individual must choose the lifestyle of action. It is a vital part of his makeup.

In implementing the concept, in reducing an idea to practice, not all actions are alike or equally effective. We have already discussed the advisability of limited action, the importance of the first step. It is especially important that the action attacks the target, that it be chosen to have leverage.

To accomplish the goal, to reach the target, to achieve the concept, it is not always best or most effective to attack directly. A sledgehammer approach may be too risky. It is often best to attack the weak spots, to find a way of action that will get the most efficient, the most productive results. While we must focus our action on the concept we are implementing, the result we are desirous of obtaining, the change we want to effect, the most direct route may not always be the most productive.

We may want to attack a weak spot to gain leverage, to achieve the total change. Just as we have used the creative process in finding the new idea, the concept, so we want to use the creative process in deciding the best way of implementation, the course of action most likely to succeed. We want to act in a unique and original manner. We may need first to gain attention, to be recognized by others, to secure their assistance. Our credibility, the image that others have of us as a result of past associations, may first have to be changed to gain the desired success. We may have to gain the confidence and approval of others before they are willing to commit their resources to our common goal.

Another consideration is the timeliness of actions we take. Our ideas, our concepts, the ingenious original solution, the value of which we are convinced of, may be out of phase with reality. We cannot force yesterday's or tomorrow's ideas onto today's reality.

My friend, Gordon Buehrig, automotive designer of classical car fame, was unable to sell his patented design for a convertible with removable solid panels in the 50's. However, it was quite in style seventeen years later in the late 60's when General Motors brought out its elegant Corvette sportscar. Nothing is harder to implement than the brilliant idea out of step with its time.

132

It is the nature of most creative individuals not to be patient. Creativeness is often coupled with a sense of urgency. Ideas, more ideas! Evolution of concept, the continued exercise of the imagination and as we have stressed the need for active implementation, all of this is likely to generate a sense of urgency impatient of obstacles and the slow reaction of others. Time means conflict in terms of the inherent untimeliness of any original concept. Any new and original idea in itself means change, often drastic change. Most important is the need for the time that it takes others to catch up to the creative individual, others who may be vitally needed for successful implementation. There is a natural tendency for the creative individual to consider his conception, his effective surprise as obvious, as easy. He may have taken years to get there. It has required his highly specialized training and preparation to get there, but now: "Oops, I should have thought of that" and also: "Oops, everybody should see that".

The creative individual transfers his impatience, his urgency to the rest of the world. This impatience manifests itself as an unwillingness to wait for others to understand, to catch up, to build agreement and enthusiasm. This urgency leads also to complete frustration with the inertia of others, their opposition and their difficulty of reaching the same conclusions.

A truly creative individual must expect these difficulties. It is practically part of the creative process, the worthwhile successful implementation, to see, that such opposition is quite normal. It is to be expected that there be resistance to change— to new ideas. The more original, the more significant the concept the more a break with tradition, the likelier that prejudice, fear of change will generate resistance. A related obstacle frequently encountered by creative individuals bent on change is the NIH factor. NIH "Not Invented Here" is a normal reaction of many of us. It cannot be worthwhile or we would have thought of it ourselves. It is difficult for all of us to accept creative competition, to adopt and promote the work of others.

It is helpful to distinguish between three types of creative processes which can be practiced by one or by separate individual human beings as the case may be. These three processes are discovery, invention and innovation. While all three of these processes require creativity and can best be carried out utilizing the mechanism of the creative processes, they are distinct and different.

Discovery is finding something new and different. Columbus discovered America. He was looking for India but he discovered, he found America. You can discover treasure in the ground by digging for it. This may be very routine and not at all a creative activity. On the other hand you may be highly creative in discovering a law of nature. In discovery you find something that was already there, a location, a pot of gold, a scientific clue.

Invention by contrast requires creativity. It is the essence of the creative process. Invention involves action, originality and value, generating some original new and useful object or process. The process of invention is a creative process.

Innovation is the essence of implementation. It is the process of instituting significant useful change. It is the activity of promoting and effecting useful progress. Innovation may be based on an invention. However, innovation does not necessarily require an invention. The change may be based on old, known principles. The innovator promotes significant change. Establishing a national chain of quick service food establishments may be an innovation, without requiring invention. The innovator may need all his creativity to succeed, but he may need even more patience and persistence.

It is important to consider that these are distinct and different processes and that as such, they may be practiced by one and the same individual or by totally different actors on the stage of reality.

Discovery often leads to invention and invention can lead to innovation. The discoverer and the inventor may also be innovators, but often they are not temperamentally suited for this role. The innovator, the entrepeneur requires a persistence, a patience, a driving continuity that few inventors display.

Creative process solving techniques may be of great help in all three of the distinct and separate processes, of discovery, invention and innovation. However, it is of the essence only for the process of invention. When the main process, the overall objective will not yield to the creative process, the individual steps, the subgoals, the many individual problems which are part and parcel of discovery and innovation will lend themselves equally to creative problem solving techniques, as the overall process of inventing.

Regardless of the process, however, whenever we want to get results for creative action we must try and try again. Seldom does a real obstacle yield to the first onslaught. No creative individual is likely to give up at the first try, the unsuccessful attempt at implementation of his burning idea, his urgent conception. Perseverance, repeated attack is vital. It gets attention and sparks results. However, repetition must not be boring. Repetition with a new twist is recommended. You can be creative even original in the way you again and again attack and try to conquer the same obstacle. Repeated similar requests for action by others are likely to bring only limited or unsuccessful results. However, repeated attacks on the same goal from different angles, with a variety of clever arguments, with a variety of new tricks, may well succeed. Do not be discouraged. The first try may be more successful than you think. It may lay the ground work for future attempts and ultimate success. Different approaches, changes in the tactics of implementation, may find the way. After many tries, there may be a means of finding the weakness, the hole in the fence, the door in the wall of resistance, the stairway, to overcome the obstacle to successful implementation.

Action, implementation of the creative concept, may also be favored or hindered by the surroundings, the external circumstances under which the creative individual functions. Just as the surroundings significantly affect the ease of idea generation and the ability to use your subconscious mind, so the right surroundings can play a major role in the implementation, the reduction to practice. It can facilitate it or hold it back.

Overorganization holds back action. To act is vital and therefore it is important to have the courage of your convictions, to act when you believe in your concept. This means action without asking too many people too many questions. This means setting up each organization in such a way, that action can be taken at each level without excessive checks and consultations. Act out your convictions. If you succeed, you are a hero, and if you do not, you may still be respected for trying to act. Consider how much or what you have to lose if you fail. Often there is no real loss to you if you fail, possibly some head shaking or loss of your image, pride or credibility. But this may well be outweighed by the recognition that you showed worthwhile initiative. Often it takes a significant amount of time to get permission. It takes somebody else's time and effort to make a decision, a judgment, whether and how to act. You could have and should have acted on your own. Would it really be so bad if your initial step, your first and significant act did not succeed? At least you have tried, you have shown your initiative to move towards the desired goal. The creative individual should be willing to try, willing to fail. He must cultivate the experimental mood. The approach of high initiative is likely to lead to frequent success. Let us all be willing to at least experiment, to move, to act towards the implementation of our original ideas.

There are many conditions favorable, many environments which can be set up, to help the creative human to act readily and promptly. Living amongst the tools of the trade can be very helpful. Many creative individuals do not function well in cold, sterile surroundings. The artist in the studio may be more ready for active painting, among the many brushes, among the half finished canvases, than he would be in a well ordered clean and excessively neat workroom. A laboratory to be a favorable surrounding requires a certain warmth, a climate of "men work here" rather than super orderliness. Informality breeds motion, activity. Action, performance comes more readily without excessive rules and restrictions, in surroundings that naturally lend themselves to creative output. It is easier to overcome the barrier of the empty canvas in a friendly workroom. Paint just flows better with that old brush which has been a companion of many prior successful creative performances. That cold well-ordered stainless steel laboratory, that sterile orderly room just does not produce the required "dither". Its coldness serves as a break to creative action. It favors immobility over mobility. It is in itself a barrier to creative implementation.

Action is multiplied through the help of others. Your own limited ability for action can be vastly expended if you can get others to assist you, to act with you towards implementation of your winning ideas. Delegation multiplies your assets, especially your most precious and irreplaceable asset—fleeting time. While you do your part, delegation allows others to do their part in the same time span. How can you best multiply your ability to act with the help of others?

Action is favored, is made easier if responsibility is well defined, clearly spelled out. This doesn't necessarily mean detailed instructions, guidelines covering all minute specifics. On the contrary, good delegation makes use of the ability, the capability, the assets of your fellow human beings, giving him or her as much freedom to act as possible. You want to spell out only the main guidelines, the major directions required. However, the target and the role of the individual, the extent of responsibility needs careful defining.

When implementing with the help of others, when the ultimate goal depends not only on you, but on the performance, of others, a steady line, a continuity of responsibility is important. Once you have delegated, once you have asked somebody for his assistance, once you have assigned a specific responsibility, do not interfere. Show confidence, expect successful performance. Be patient and use your own time and energy for action elsewhere. Do not change responsibilities too often. Continuity of action and assignment has great value in building experience, skill, excellent even in this world of rapid changes.

Avoid unnecessary formalizations, strict and bureaucratic delineations and multi-levels of responsibility. Your friends, co-workers, helpers, even strangers, whose cooperation you need, are motivated by trust, by your expectation of success, by their own inner drive to contribute not, by stale rulebooks or formalized organization charts. Informality favors the motivating factors that are so vital to success. It discourages attitudes such as: "this is not my job", "let Joe do it" and "it is somebody else's baby". Informality is more likely to generate the volunteer spirit such as: "let me help you", "can I do this for you", "how can I best contribute to the common goal".

Finally, acting with and through the help of others requires creative communication skills. How much input does he need to be able to help? How much teaching does a new member of the team require before he can materially and successfully contribute. Does he or she really understand what is expected of them? Do you understand how to communicate with them? Are you sending one way signals that can be misinterpreted? Is there room for feedback? Good communications are a necessity of successful delegation.

Motivation also plays a significant role as to the proper choice of assignments. How should we assign the tasks that require action? How can we get best results, most effective action when distributing the many subtasks that lead to the ultimate goal? We may have to choose between two systems both of which are widely practiced in many industries and professions.

The initial development may have been carried out by a single individual or a small team. For example, a laboratory worker discovers a new process for the manufacture of a chemical. In the formalized and specialized organization this phase often ends with a report. Then the project is turned over to the larger specialized scale up and development group. This may be an engineering department or an other highly specialized organization. From there the project may go to construction and finally to a start-up and production team. In each case, a project has been carried through various stages of action by new people, new teams, new organizations. In fact, the only thing that really moves is reports, drawings, paper.

The creatively more favorable alternative is that people, the inventor, the innovator move with the project through the various stages of activity required. This less formal approach favors motivation. It is the innovator, the entrepreneur, the inventor's project that moves. He moves with it and pushes it, leads it, removes the obstacles in its path. He has a more personal stake. He is the champion, the driver, the spark plug — he assures continuity of action, for it is "his" project and he moves with it.

Action, driving for the success of an idea, the success of a project does not necessarily make friends. Results count, where action is concerned. The method required may not always find favor in the eyes of others. This is a competitive world and the success of one, may be the downfall of another. Innovation may bring changes, which will affect the well-established routines and privilege of others. This has always been the peril of the innovator. Even in the days of Machiavelli, he stated:

"There is nothing more difficult to take in hand, more perilous to conduct or more uncertain in success than to take the lead, the introduction of a new order of things because the innovator has for enemies all those, who have done well under the old conditions and lukewarm defenders in those who may do well under the new."

Motivation for major action may require a certain edge, a certain unfair advantage, a head start, protection from others who might want to jump on the bandwagon. This is what the patent law is all about. Its aim is not just to reward an inventor, but it is primarily to stimulate an innovator. The patent motivates him to put into action that beneficial change to society, that advantage to all of us, that can accrue from the invention. That is what patent protection is for—a motivating force driving the inventor and innovator towards commercialization, giving him an edge. He needs an advantage to apply all his energy and resources, so that the invention can be made available for the benefit of all.

Many actions require large committments of assets in people, money, and other resources—some unfair advantage, some additional weight on the scales, some protection through patents or other means is required, to supply the motivation for the committment of these assets. Besides patents, it can be an ability to be there—fastest with the mostest—especially when unique skills are involved which cannot be readily duplicated or imitated. Thus action may require some degree of protection to assure motivation. In this competitive world of change we must run faster than the hounds. We have to jump some difficult hurdles to stay ahead of the pack. We have to be tough to succeed. Nice guys don't always win.

Action then is the driving thrust from the world of imagination into the world of reality. Even brilliant ideas are worthless in themselves, they must be selected and implemented for successful solutions. Only action, reduction to practice counts. Ideas do not solve problems, action does. Dare to act on an original idea, dare to take the unusual action. Do not stand still, motion puts you on the road to overcome the inertia barrier.

The first step is the most important one, action may become easier as you move along. A partial solution gets you further than no attack. Be willing to fail. Action is its own reward. If at first you cannot budge a target, try again, try a variety of different modes of attack.

If your own assets are limited by time and the extent of your personal capabilities, multiply your actions through the help of others. Committment of assets, people, money requires an advantage, some probability of return, some motivating factor toward success. Whether it be a patent, a head start or another "unfair advantage," these motivate the innovator, the entrepreneur, his team or his organization. They are driving forces essential for successful action.

EXERCISES

Make a list of twelve significant action items that you have put off doing in the last six months. Do at least one in the twelve months to come.

Analyze three recent failures, your own or others. Are they really serious? Are there any long range consequences? Examine whether the risk would have not been worth the possible benefit.

Consider three tasks you thought too big, too difficult for yourself. Determine the first step. Do something that would make just a dent in the big goal.

Consider these same three tasks, analyze them, to find the weak spot, the place to exert leverage. Do it.

You're frustrated by others. They do not see the value of your original idea. List the barriers that you would expect them to have, barring acceptance. Try again and again, tackling each recognized barrier separately.

Next time you want to ask your boss, stop, check, is it really required. Should you go ahead? Next time you do something important, stop, check, should you inform your boss?

You have an important job to do. Stop, consider, should you ask somebody elses help. Would it be safer that way? Would the result be better, more original? Would they be happy to help? Go and ask them.

RECOMMENDED READING

Ernest Dichter, "Motivating Human Behavior" McGraw-Hill, 1971.
Buckminster Fuller, "Ideas and Integrities", MacMillan, 1972.
Joel Hildebrand, "Science in the Making", Columbia University Press, 1961.
Garvin McCain and Erwin M. Segal, "The Game of Science", Wadsworth, 1969.
A. D. Moore, "Invention, Discovery and Creativity", Doubleday, 1969.

Buckminster Fuller's book is particularly stimulating and thought provoking. It illustrates the creative process and practical implementation in many fields where he has supplied unusual original solutions.

CHAPTER 9
THE CREATIVE GROUP: MULTIPLICATION OR DIVISION?

Essential cooperation.
Synergism and multiplication.
Complimentary talents.
Brainstorming, no cure-all.
Freewheeling and reinforcement.

Problem definition.
Choice of group.
No negatives please.
The multi-person organism.
Synectics — operational creativity.

Can the creative process be practiced by more than one individual? Are there advantages? Can there be synergism through participation of more than one human being in problem solving? When human beings attempt to work together creatively, will there be multiplication or division?

Some say that since creativity is a unique human talent, and since ideas are formed in the conscious or subconscious mind of an individual being, creativity is a one man or one woman activity. This thesis states: only the individual, only each one of us, one at a time can be creative. This thesis negates the possibility of a group performing a creative act. It maintains that the creative act is only the output of individuals, members of the group and therefore a blossoming of the individuals, single, unique creativity. However, the question we must ask is really not, how to trace the creative performance back to the individual, rather can there be synergism in a group. Can group interplay multiply the talents of its individual members? Is there potentially greater creative power in a group than the sum of the individuals creative capabilities of its members?

The unequivocal answer must be: "yes." The creative potential, the creative capability, the creative power of a group is not only desirable but often essential to success. Man is a social animal. Many of his problems can best be solved by group action, rather than by total reliance on the outstanding individual.

In the arts we are quite accustomed to the necessity of group interaction to achieve a creative result. We do not expect the composer of the new musical to go it alone. We expect the final polished performance to be the result of the creative harmony of the choreographer, director, conductor, and performing artists. Procedures for their successful creative cooperation have been well developed. Rehearsals, road shows all lead up to the premier performance.

Outside the performing arts, however, creative group activity has been developed to a much more limited extent. In fact, the possibilities of creative group action are often not recognized. Whether out of pride, habit or lack of recognition of the possiblities, creative group action is not sufficiently practiced in many fields of human activity. Professionals especially are proud of their ability to go it alone.

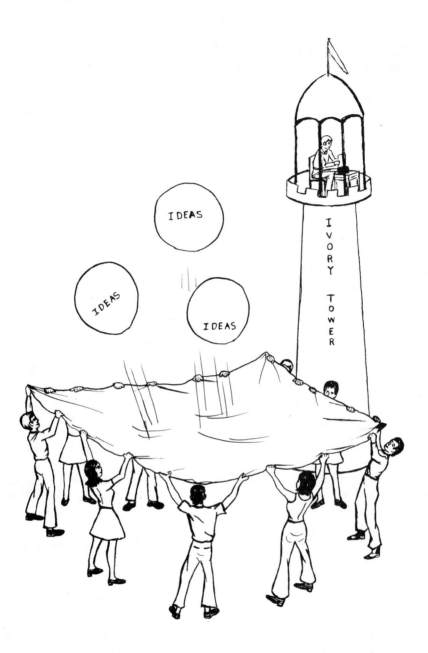

They shun the significant synergistic advantages that can flow from creative group interaction. They had better examine why and how to take advantage of the help of others in the practice of the creative process.

First, there is preparation. When we prepare ourselves for the solution of a problem, sooner or later we encounter the limitations of our background. There may be mathematics we cannot master without very expensive and time consuming efforts. The preparation may take us into fields in which we lack the necessary understanding, the ability to quickly and readily separate the essential from the vast amount of detail which surrounds it. The lawyer may have a case involving the detailed knowledge of complex chemical processes. The chemist may require the understanding of difficult biological phenomena for his fullest preparation.

You might say that we can consult the specialist, the man who has the tools, and the background. We may hire a consultant to assist us in our preparations. True, but in the preparation phase we often do not know enough to utilize his help effectively. Does this not guide us properly and correctly to the conclusion that this specialist, this expert consultant has a contribution to make throughout the entire creative process.

In our complex world even the greatest genius, the most creative individual will be limited by a narrow background, a slim base of preparation. A group is likely to be better equipped as far as their general preparation is concerned. The group will bring a broader band of knowledge, a larger array of tools to bear on the problems than each of its members.

To get optimum results, the group should be carefully chosen to provide a variety of talents. This is the secret of success of the research teams, that have moved science and technology forward at such a fast clip in in this century. Whether at a university, in industry or at a non-profit research institute, the working together of interdisciplinary groups, and the mutual reinforcement of their creative powers has and is playing a magic role in the march of progress.

Needless to say that the creative ability of the individual members is vital but the ability to compliment each other is very significant. Successful group action is not reserved to the technological arena. It is equally important in social affairs, politics, business and finance.

In a well chosen creative group not only can general preparation and background be synergistically applied to the creative process, but also specific preparation can be divided, assigned, delegated in an efficient and effective manner. Thus a group can be of major advantage in the preparation phase of creative problem solving.

What of problem definition, recognizing the real problems, focusing on the needs, the change required for positive action? Here too, the different and varied talents of the participants are apt to make a contribution. In a given industrial problem, it is often not known and recognized initially whether the real problem is one of technology, economics, marketing, advertising or maybe even law. How much easier for a well chosen creative group to define, to nail down the real problem than if the task is left to one of the specialists or even to a generalist who might not have the special insight required.

For creative group action, the choice of the group becomes by necessity a part of preparation. It has to be made carefully in the early phases of the problem solving process. How should the group be constituted? There are some natural groups. They are formed not deliberately to engage in solving a specific problem but they have been formed without taking this activity, this capability into consideration.

The first group that comes to mind is the family. We are born into it, we marry into a family. We do not choose it for its creative problem solving competence. We may have a limited choice, we have to accept the members of this group and like it. Certainly few of us think about creative problem solving when we get married. However, the family group more than any other is faced day by day, with the need to solve problems in a creative manner. In fact, part of the success of the family depends on group participation in solving their problems as against individual solutions which may not harmonize with the total needs.

At work, in the laboratory, the factory, the office, groups are often formed without due consideration of their suitability to solve problems together. Each manager, each department head may be the best man to fulfill his assignment, his specific responsibility. However, has it been considered whether the resulting staff group has all the necessary talents to solve the company's problems? Too often we try to solve problems in groups that are determined by organization charts rather than considering the requirements of the problem solving process. If legal background is required, a lawyer must be a member of the group, regardless of his role in the organization, if costs are to be considered, the accountant is needed. We should not rely on the scientist to supply this type of information second hand.

Besides the regular groups which meet to solve problems, there must be mechanism to form groups as the need arises. These groups needed for the task of resolving a given situation or determining the source of specific problems must be carefully chosen. Proper choice of the individual members can contribute greatly to success.

From the beginning the group should be dedicated to creative cooperation. It should focus on the problems. The group must realize that its success depends on the rules which govern successful creative problem solving. If they want to achieve their goal, this is a consideration not to be taken lightly, especially in groups of outstanding individuals. Cooperative creative problem solving is a difficult undertaking.

When the individual undertakes to solve a problem, he has only himself to cope with, only himself to watch. If we apply the rules of problem solving such as "no judgment during ideation", the individual can exert control. In a group, it may be much more difficult to adhere to this all important direction. In a group staffed with several strong powerful, creative, vocal individuals, adherance to the all-so-vital rule "no judgment during ideation" may take some real doing, some training, some practice before it can be accomplished. The most common danger in a group is that of deferring to authority. If a group is constituted of people with varying degrees of responsibility in the organization, there is a tendency by the manager to assume leadership, and to exert authority. Even if he tries to avoid it, there is an inclination by his co-workers to defer to his implied or assumed authority. This must be guarded against. It pays to constitute the group with regard to equal rank in the organization. Insist on leaving rank outside the door before the group starts to work.

Another danger especially for groups that meet regularly or are a constant part of the organization, is that they lose themselves in routine acts or information exchange without concentration on the task of solving specific well defined and delineated problems. Efficiency is easily affected by discussions of the golf game or the party of night before last. Even worse, there is often a tendency on part of the members of the group to interrupt, to sidetrack creative problem solving by unrelated information or routine matters.

Most to be guarded against is interruption through the introduction of different and unrelated problems. We can only tackle one problem at a time. For a group to be successful, it has to work together, applying the same lessons which we have stressed and learned in the context of individual problem solving. Each problem constitutes its own specific creative challenge.

Group action is particularly effective in the generation of a large number, a great quantity of ideas. It is in the ideation step of the creative process that very material advantages can be gained. Here we truly encounter multiplication and not division.

Brainstorming is a well known technique which has been widely and successfully used. It is somewhat unfortunate that the word "brainstorming" visualizes for us a wild, undisciplined stormy undertaking. As is the case with so many human endeavors when we apply labels or such a key word as "brainstorming" then the word, the slogan leads to misunderstandings and worse, expectation are raised that cannot be fulfilled.

"Brainstorming" is a method for creative group action, for generating ideas, many ideas in areas in which a problem can be well defined. It should be narrowly focused and should require only limited preparation. "Brainstorming" is not an all encompassing way of carrying out the creative process. It is no cure-all. However, it is an excellent way for the generation of ideas. It may also serve to foster the creative behavior, to bring the creative talents of the participants to a higher level.

"Brainstorming" is group action for ideation. Preparation and problem definition must be completed before the "brainstorming" session begins. Usually the problem is in a well-focused form. It has been transmitted to the members of the group several days prior to the actual meeting. Preparation may be broad but it is usually not lengthy, indepth preparation. However, as in all creative processes, preparation is important. Especially the leader of the "brainstorming" session should do everything in his power to prepare himself adequately. You should not call people together on a moments notice without letting them know the target and say "Now, let us have a brainstorming session". Even with participants of broad general background and with excellent overall preparation, this is not likely to lead to success.

For every "brainstorming" session: *Define the problem; Choose the group; Give them time to prepare before the meeting.*

Possibly a few words should be said concerning the size of the group for "brainstorming". This depends largely on the type of problems that are being tackled. New product "brainstorming" groups are normally made up of five to ten persons. For a highly specific task such as naming a new bridge, a much larger group may be acceptable. However, too large a group may be hard to handle. It may slow down the tempo and, therefore, limit the success of the activity.

A variant of "brainstorming" is the "buzz group" in which the larger assemblies are broken down into groups of about six people each in order to tackle the problem. One word of caution: exclude the boss or any dominant personality whose presence would have a dampening effect on the free and uninhibited participation of the other members of the group.

Let us repeat: define the problem as one problem; choose the group and alert them, to give them time to come to the "brainstorming" session well prepared, mentally ready.

The basic rules of the "brainstorming" session are identical to those which we have studied for ideation by the individual. They may be somewhat harder to adhere to, but they are vital to successful performance.

First, all judgment must be deferred.

There is to be no evaluation, no criticism in a "brainstorming" session. Ideas are to be advanced, not judged. The spirit of a successful "brainstorming" session must be that of a game, of fun, of play, of a hunting party looking for shiny bright Easter eggs of ideas. This is not the time to look for the *worm in the apple.* This session is for roaming far and wide, trying wild ideas on for size, looking for and advancing the unusual, the unobvious. A rapid pace is encouraged.

Research has shown that even the mildest forms of antagonism have a dampening effect on the advancing of ideas by the participants. Using tools similar to the lie detector, it was found that fault finding, even statements such as "I hate to be negative, but . . . . ." had a similar effect on the subject as a gentle slap upon the arm.

The real strength of "brainstorming", the advantage of group ideation, lies in *the possibility of reinforcement.* Not only should there be no evaluation, no judgment of ideas during the "brainstorming" session, but there must be a deliberate policy of *building* onto the ideas advanced.

There must be a specific effort to make them stronger, to reinforce them. "Free wheeling" speculation can be solidified through "hitch-hiking", building upon the idea, the speculation of others. Thus, "half-baked" ideas, ideas that are just in their formative stage, can be solidified and strengthened. What first was a nebulous, groping attempt, can be brought to full flower through the help of other members of the group.

The reinforcement policy can be formalized in what is called the 6-3-5 variant of "brainstorming". In a group of six participants each writes three ideas on a card. These cards are then passed five times to the others who are requested to reinforce the ideas and to build on them. Thus each participant is given the specific task to strengthen all the other ideas put forward.

This, however, may interfere with the free wheeling, with the gamelike motivating atmosphere of excitement and competition desirable in a good "brainstorming" session. Competition should be in terms of wanting to contribute as many ideas as possible, not in wanting to push an individual idea, or setting one idea against another, or even trying to show how smart a given participant is.

Equally important is *the rule of recording*. Write it down! This is part and parcel of all successful ideation. For successful group sessions, we need visualization. It is desirable that the ideas be fully visible during the entire performance. This encourages further reinforcement. One excellent device is for the secretary of the session to write in heavy felt pen on large poster-size sheets which are mounted with tape around the walls of the room as they are filled.

We thus have three cardinal rules of "brainstorming": No judgements; reinforcement desired; record visibly.

There are some procedural points which can greatly assist in making a "brainstorming" session a success. They serve to assure the necessary discipline. There should be a leader whose role it is to assure orderly progress and a tempo of action that maintains a spirit of excitement, a gamelike atmosphere. Participants should raise their hand to advance an idea, snap their fingers to indicate "hitchhiking reinforcement." The leader is responsible for the spirit of the entire group. A warm-up session is suggested to get into the swing of it. Maybe the group should start by trying its hand at a humorous problem for a few minutes before getting down to the prepared serious task.

For example, you might ask for ideas to rename the town you are working in, or how to get along without the automobile. Another good warm-up exercise is to pick an object such as an ashtray on the table and ask for alternate uses for it.

During the "brainstorming" sessions, the leader must keep things moving. He may want to keep some of his own ideas in reserve so that he can inject them whenever the tempo lags. His job is to maintain, support, and keep up the enthusiasm vital to success. However, this is a true group effort not an authoritarian leadership affair. It is team play at its best. Under no circumstances should the leader identify ideas with individuals, they are the group's ideas, the team's output.

"Brainstorming" is an excellent tool for the generation of ideas in quantity. Often they are also of high quality. It is time and quality effective. Much is accomplished in terms of generating and gathering ideas in a short time span. The talents of a number of people with different specializations, different viewpoints, differences in experiences, can be focused entirely on a single problem. The enthusiasm of the game, the cooperative tackling of the single task, going at it from every angle, in many different ways, is apt to stimulate each participant's creative potential, and to motivate him or her to come up with original solutions.

However "brainstorming" groups are not well suited to the completion of the creative process. Yes, the group may be reconvened after a lapse of time and after they have been given the written list of ideas generated, but incubation is a very personal activity. The plumbing of the subconscious in an individual experience not that of a group. You cannot generate the same enthusiasm in an evaluation session, that existed in the original "brainstorming" game. Thus, in the evaluation and the action steps brainstorming groups are of limited help.

To go beyond group ideation, to achieve fuller group participation on more than one or all levels of the creative process requires a much closer and most unique relationship between several creative individuals. It requires devotion, understanding, unselfishness and friendship.

Abelson in his thoughtful study of group interaction between collaborating scientists stresses the motivating influence arising from this interaction. He cites the mutual stimulation and contributions to each others' work of the three Hungarians: John von Neuman, Eugene Wigner, and Leo Szilard, stressing that friendship can greatly contribute to mutual creative interplay. Abelson makes an interesting distinction between scientists organized as a team to accomplish a specific task, and a group engaged in less well-defined, more creative problem solving. His example is the famous group at the Radiation Laboratory at Berkeley from 1935 to 1939 under Professor Ernest Lawrence. The brilliant young men of the team had two goals, the first was to develop and build the cyclotron, a giant machine, the second much more creative task, was to exploit its potential. Construction of the cyclotron offered little opportunity to be creative, indeed, there was no place here for innovation once the design was set. The life of the young scientists might have been sheer drudgery if it had not been for the encouragement by Lawrence of the highest degree of creativity in the realm of research using the new tool, exploiting its potential for new knowledge.

In the field of science, through friendship, common drives and mutual interests, group interaction can extend itself to practically all phases of the creative process. Abelson calls it: "a banding together of individuals to create a microenvironment which offers intellectual satisfaction to those within the group and which also meets the needs for human fellowship".

Such groups can extend their creative cooperation even into the phases of judgments and creative action. They can, by overcoming tensions and personal egotism, by harnessing their individual personalities engage in research almost as one multiplied human being.

However, such humans are rare. Usually our individual interests, our drives and emotions, our selfishness do not allow such intimate creative group action to succeed or to continue for long. It takes wisdom and creative insight to realize that such groups are possible, not only among brilliant scientists but among all of us, and that much can be accomplished by this type of multiplication of human effort.

Jerome Bruner described such a group of six people. They were active for a consulting firm on projects both inside the United States and abroad, such as dam construction, power plants and similar major undertakings. The group consisted of Bruner, himself, a Harvard professor, a young Navy flier studying linguistics and accoustics, a young furniture designer, a middle aged architect, a highly skilled shop technician, and the leader who was very religiously oriented but whose field of specialization was paleantology. Made up of such diverse talents they had succeeded in establishing a relationship which resulted in true group creative effort. Among the factors responsible for their success was not only the multidisciplinary composition of the team but, to a larger degree their "detachment and commitment". They were organized as a group of their own, set apart from any other organization or unit of the firm. Their detachment was planned. Commitment resulted in that they had developed a pride of creative accomplishment, a commitment to creativity, an attitude of creative performance. Equally noteworthy was their "passion and decorum". Passion, they had a wild almost inefficient latitude for the expression of impulses in connection with the work. Almost anything was allowed, provided it could be transformed into the grammar of the problem. The principal source of decorum lay in their adoration of elegance and generality. They allowed any proposal, any idea, any hypothesis to be wild but the solution had to be elegant and as generalizable as possible.

Whenever and wherever we have a chance in our lives to join a group for creative action, to expand, to multiply our personal efforts through joining with others in a bond of friendship for greater creativity, we should not fail to take advantage of this golden opportunity.

Such groups can only function successfully if each member displays a high degree of unselfishness. The group becomes overriding, the group becomes the creative organism, the group's success is the motivating factor.

Groups of highly creative men and women develop their own special and effective group style. However, William J. J. Gordon, over more than two decades has developed a method of "operational creativity" to train specially selected groups to operate, to function as one creative body, one creative organism.

Where "brainstorming" is fun and games, Synectics is a well-defined scenario, a drama or comedy, role playing and theater. The members of a group play parts together according to well-worked out, practiced rules. The entire process is put together like a play with a first act, a second act and even a fourth act finale. It follows definite scripts, which while they encourage ad-libbing, move the players from one scene to the next in a predetermined fashion.

As a result of extensive research and experimental work into the nature of creativity and the behavior of creative human beings, Gordon and Prince have authored an operational method, welding a number of creative individuals into a highly capable group for tackling and solving problems of all kinds. Their emphasis is on problems encountered in the modern technological business and industrial organization. The method plays particular attention to problem definition, to the analysis and understanding of the problem.

Great emphasis is placed at bringing into play the total human being, at stimulating subconscious activity. While the Synectic's group may not be intimately engaged in the ultimate implementation, the Synectics process encompasses a well-developed and worked-out mechanism aimed at effective inspiration, illumination and evaluation. Feedback is stressed, if the first attempt at solutions should prove unsatisfactory.

Synectics stresses an understanding of the psychological foundation of creativity, an emphasis of emotion over intellect and the creational as against the rational. It attempts through a multitude of clever, unique devices not only to take advantage of the variety of experiences and capabilities offered by well-chosen participants but also to force the participants to act in unusually productive ways. The method creates situations within the groups activity that favor the appearance of "effective surprise". Synectics groups not only generate ideas and solutions, they generate more ideas leading to an original solution.

To the serious student of creativity, training in this method is highly recommended. It involves the use of a detailed and unique sequence of steps, a flow chart leading from the *problem as given* through an "analysis" and "purge" to the *problem as understood.* One problem at a time is chosen for further processing. The actual treatment of the problem may take several routes depending on which of the many provocative devices is employed by the leader. Discussion ranges often intentionally far afield and is brought back to the problem through a forcefit and a viewpoint which serves to assure feedback and recycling of the problem if necessary.

Among the many intricate devices employed, most noteworthy is stress on making the strange familiar and making the familiar strange. This serves to stimulate our creative potential in that it makes us look at situations and problems from unusual angles. Recognizing the inhibitions to our creativity, our innate resistance to change, our recoiling from anything new and different, the mechanism of making the strange intentionally familiar serves to break down these barriers. On the other hand, the mechanism of making the familiar strange, distorting what seems usual, transposing it into unusual realms such as fantasy or the world of nature, bionics, stirs our subconscious. It fertilizes our imagination, thus stimulating creative productivity.

Other elegant ways of stimulating the Synectics group are deliberate methods of engaging them in a scenario. What is meant is that the problem is literally discussed and treated in an alternate world. This may be the world of personal analogy where the participating humans identify with the elements of the problem. In the discussions, the individual group member becomes a part of the machine that will not work or becomes a component of the instrument that is to be designed. The participants, so to speak, crawl into the problem in a highly personal direct way. Alternatively there is added to the more commonly employed direct analogy, another scenario of symbolic and fantasy analogy in which the problem solution is searched for among the world of abstract symbols or in the realm of fantasy.

In all these cases, the goal is illumination, the *original* solution. The devices employed are only part and parcel of the group methods style itself. It is a device to train effective groups as well as to develop creative functioning of the individuals.

Synectics study is unusually creative in itself, constructive and helpful, a significant contribution to the science and the art of creativity stimulation and development. It is highly recommended.

In this complex world, group activity, multiplication of our powers and capabilities is a must, a basic foundation for progress. The individual genius, the lone inventor will always tower above the rest of his fellowman. We must take advantage of the multiplication factor inherent in creative group action. A group of human beings working together in a creative way can accomplish more than the sum of the individual efforts. Groups can be trained, they can be helped, taught not to engage in devisive efforts where everybody is striving to dominate or enforce his will on others. Division can truly be replaced by multiplication in the creative group.

The trend to group efforts in our society is bound to continue not only due to the complexity of the problems requiring the application of many disciplines to their solution but also due to the high cost of modern tools, such as computers, laboratories, accelerators, satellites, and so forth which are required for their solution. Let us summarize some of the advantages which can be ours by suitable creative effort recognizing that with any advantages there are also likely to be drawbacks.

Group spirit provides cross fertilization of ideas and inspires contagious attitudes of creativity. Groups are less prone to fear of criticism. Errors may be avoided through cross checking, if they do occur, responsibility is shared by the group. Most importantly, interdisciplinary teams can cover broader ranges of problem solving activity. The participants can synergistically contribute the missing link to an original solution. Motivation in a good group is apt to be high, one inspires the other to outdo himself. The interplay of competent individuals can generate results not otherwise obtainable.

Finally, the group offers some assurance, some possibility of continued and sustained effort. Continuity of programs may be assured even against the loss of an individual brilliant contributor. In contrast the loss of the lonely genius may destroy the project. Last, but not least, participation in a creative group may serve as a mighty stimulus to the training, to the development of the individual participants creativity. There is no greater stimulation than by example, no greater development than by practicing, by performing. Performance in a group gets results and develops the individual.

EXERCISES

List meetings you participate in regularly, each day, week or month.

What special meetings, do you call, attend? List and review for creative problem solving activity.

Select two or three social, community, church or business problems. Invite 3–6 friends to your home for a "brainstorming" session. Be sure to follow the rules of preparation, freewheeling, reinforcement and visible recording.

Pick a number of outlandish topics and play a "brainstorming" game with friends or family.

> Example: How would you communicate with a Venusian?
> How to paint without a brush?
> How to teach an old dog new tricks.

In the next three meetings you attend count the number of times, somebody is interrupted or put down. Try to keep yourself from doing it.

In the next three meetings in which you are the normal leader, make a special effort to reinforce everybody's ideas, rather than your own.

When organizing or leading a meeting try to be the catalyst, not the dictator. Put others before yourself. Time the periods you listen, in comparison with the periods you speak.

List 40 ways you can keep a meeting moving, ways you can inject interest and strength into the proceedings.

Develop several means or tools to make the record more visible during your meetings.

Search out and participate in group training for better meetings, such as Synectics.

RECOMMENDED READING

Phillip H. Abelson, "Relations of Group Activity to Creativity in Science," Daedalus Summer, 1965.

Jerome Bruner, "The Conditions of Creativity", Atherton Press, 1967.

J. J. Gordon, "Synectics", Harper & Row, 1961.

Howard K. Hughes, "Individual and Group Activity in Science, Essays on Creativity and Science", New York University Press, 1963.

George M. Prince, "The Operational Mechanism of Synectics", Journal of Creativity, Winter 1967.

George M. Prince, "The Practice of Creativity", Harper & Row, 1970.

CHAPTER 10

COMMUNICATIONS: DO YOU HEAR WHAT HE IS SAYING?

People problems.	Master or slave?
Contact and interaction.	Words and deeds.
Feedback required.	Map and territory.
Language, creative tool.	Language and behavior.
Body language secrets.	Creative communication.

You're working hard. You're concentrating. Your concentration is focused on the papers before you. The balance will not quite come out right. You're absorbed. You're puzzled. Suddenly you are aware of a slight hissing sound. A whistling, short, modulated, intense, patterned. You look up and stare at the strangest apparition. You look at a ghostlike, a transparent exclamation point about two-thirds the size of a human being. You see a shining metal ball slightly larger than your head floating at its top. It moves. It vibrates. It seems to beckon to you and it whistles at you almost frantically. You almost faint. Then you exclaim, "what is this? Who are you? Where are you from? Is this a joke? Is this a projection? What am I seeing? What am I hearing?" All the while, the being from outer space is addressing you with its hissing, its whistles. You're talking at it. You're both sending messages madly, but no communication takes place.

How *would* you creatively communicate with a man from Mars? Did you know that we sent a message beyond our galaxy? Very sophisticated! It was addressed to a civilization that would be highly intelligent. How would you have done it? What is creative communication?

There was a time in April 1960 when a group of men thought they had made contact with beings from another world. They were radio astronomers at the Green Banks Observatory in the Appalachian Mountains. They were part of Project Ozma, an attempt to discover whether intelligent radio signals were emanating from the galaxies. This was not idle speculation or mere fantasy. This was real. This was living science fiction.

On the afternoon of the second day with their telescope aimed at Epsilon Eridani, a far distant star, they picked up pulses, regular spacings suggesting some sort of intelligence. Then the signals stopped. Great excitement. But confirmation was still lacking. Disappointingly, continued research showed the signals had originated on earth. Had they originated in space, could they have been decoded? Could we have established understanding?

Communicating with space may be a difficult problem—yes. The Mars man is unlikely to speak our language, unlikely to even communicate by sounds. Human communication is something we usually take for granted. We underestimate its sophistication, its complexity, its difficulty. Sometimes, however, it almost seems as if we were trying to communicate with people from outer space. Many times we believe we are communicating when we are just making noises. Communication is a "must" to solve people problems.

How did we learn to speak? How did we develop that all-powerful tool, "language"? Do we communicate by words alone. Even on our own planet, sound is only one of many means of communication, but speech, language stands out as a unique human attribute, the strength of man.

Some animals can communicate by sounds although we have been unable, to date, to break their language code. Whales sing strange, melodious songs. Dolphins emit intriguing sequences of sound. Dogs bark and cats purr. However, we notice also that dogs sniff each other's trails and leave odorous signatures at signposts for their friends. Bees have been observed to perform strange dances when they have located the nectar. Many other strange ways of signaling have been observed in our animal world.

Communications are particularly vital to us humans. Communication skills are essential to a creative life. While we are all strong individuals seemingly self-sufficient in our shell of human competence, each one of us is also a social animal. To exist, to succeed, to enjoy our short visit on planet Earth, we have to be with others, live as others, contribute to others and allow others to contribute to us. Man is part of the group, a member of the herd, a number in the social flock. We live in a permanent duality, our shining individual self, the bubble among bubbles, the bright, high-flying balloon and on the other side, just one of the multitude, just a cog in the machinery. We are part of the family, the local community, the village, county, town or country. We are part of the work force. We are an employee, an engineer, a lawyer, a banker, an executive, a machinist. We are members of the distinguished and necessary profession of garbage collectors. We are social animals. We are people. We cannot function creatively without others. We cannot solve people problems without the creative mastery of communication skills. Communication is a social affair. It is the cement that holds human groups together. Without good communications, we do not just drift apart, we fall down, we explode, we fight each other.

The very word "communicate" means "share", come together, cooperate. When we truly communicate, we are one, not so much a union but a unity. Communication is establishing a real bond, a tie between two or more human beings. It requires a common understanding—a common meaning. Communication involves the conveying and sharing of a message.

There is some communication between man and animal. Certainly your dog understands you when you tell him you are going to take him out for a walk. But for creative living, for people problem solving, we are primarily concerned with the difficult, the complex art of communication among humans.

Most of us take communication for granted. We speak incessantly, we shout, we rave, but seldom do we make a real effort at communication. We speak to hear ourselves—talk to pass the time—to give vent to our emotions—to keep somebody else from talking, but seldom are we communicating.

Communication is to make creative contact with another human being. It is sharing, communing, establishing within two individuals the same message. Communication is the attempt to get the same or similar impressions, conveying similar thoughts, making both minds see the same image.

To live a creative life, to solve the large number of people problems that we face daily, we must not only understand communication, not only grasp its function, but we must also be fully aware of its importance. Is it speaking? Is it writing? Is it reading? Listening? — It is all of these and more? Communication is a state of mind as well as a process. It is a willingness, an awareness of the need and the difficulty of reaching another human being.

Approximately three fourths (72.8% according to a recent study) of our waking time is taken up by communication activities. There is hardly any occupation which does not require us to spend more than half of our time communicating. In fact, two-thirds of the time, when we are not sleeping — we are either speaking or listening.

Considering the role this activity plays in our lives, do you feel you've had sufficient training? Are you good enough at it? Have you learned not only to read and write, to speak, but also to listen? Are you giving proper attention to the perfection of the skills in this important area of your life which consumes so much of your time and energy?

To try to understand communication, we have to realize how it functions. We have to know when we are trying to communicate. If we shake our heads, stick out our tongue or shrug our shoulder, we are signaling but we are not communicating.

I operate the keyboard of a computer, punch in a program or insert information, is that communication? A TV set playing in an empty room, a newspaper unread in the gutter, is that communication? You send a gift to a sick friend in a hospital, are you saying something and is this communication?

First and foremost for communication, sharing to be established, there has to be more than one-way action. Sharing means participation by two or more. Communication means involvement of two or more human beings. If I shout for help in the wilderness and nobody comes to my rescue, there is no communication. Whether this is because I am in the desert where nobody can physically hear me or whether I am on a crowded street where nobody wants to become involved, there is no communication in either case.

If you wire your aunt in Australia for money, all the complex facets of the communication process may become involved. You form a message in your head, you break out of your shell, code the message in words, transmit it to the telegraph office where it is coded in electronic signals, send it out over the cable or wireless channels to far-away Australia where it is decoded and finally delivered to your aunt. It may even be received by her, your needs penetrating and being recognized in her mind, inside her personal shell. Truly all this accomplishes nothing. There is no communicatiion between you and her, no sharing, no real bond has been established until she wires the money or sends a telegram saying that she is unable to help you.

In contrast to our normal oversimplified image of communication as an action from a sender to a receiver, communication is a cyclic process. Human communication requires action, back and forth between human beings until an effect, a goal has been accomplished. There has to be creative contact between the meanings of the sender and the understanding of the receiver. We may fail to make contact, or our message may be incomplete or unintelligible. To achieve communication, the receiver must become the sender. There has to be feedback to complete the sharing, to establish full cyclic communication. In most cases, to truly achieve communication, to make a full understanding possible, the sender and receiver will alternate their roles and the communication process will go round and round until full understanding has been accomplished. If we have not fully understood, as it is often likely to happen the first time around, we must ask questions and keep the cyclic process going until a truly creative and full, clear contact has been established.

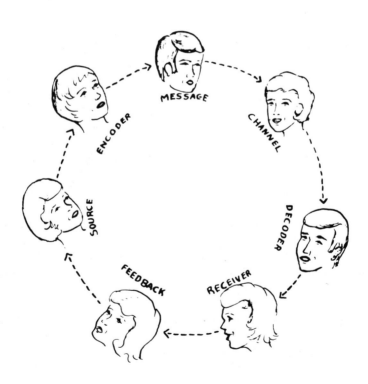

Consider a typical exchange between a boss and his secretary. In a hurry, he walks by her desk and tells her, "I would like to talk to Mr. Cooney". His mind is clearly well past the message. He is occupied with the next thought process. He really meant in his shell: "I want to phone Mr. Cooney of Abraham Construction Company in Springfield, Massachusetts". Now he has a good friend named Tooney, so the secretary asks: "You want Mr. Tooney?" "No" he replies, "Mr. Cooney in Springfield." Again sadly enough, very incomplete and ineffective, since he has business dealings in at least three of the many cities named Springfield, the one in Ohio and Illinois, as well as Mr. Cooney in Massachusetts. But most important, without the firm's name the secretary cannot get the message, since this is a piece of information not previously at her disposal.

Messages all too frequently are complete and clear only in our minds. We presume that even the slightest clue will result in the same complete picture in the recipient's mind. The opposite is nearly always the case. Fragmentary transmission cannot establish successful communication. A significant, careful effort must be made to transmit the message in all its important details.

Communication is a cyclic process, one that cannot readily be accomplished until the proper message has been established inside the shell of all the participants. Understanding this basic truth, successful communications means several things.

There is no sender or receiver, we are all participants in the ring of communication.

A clear and complete message is vital to establish the full communication desired.

We must not stop until we are sure that creative contact has truly been made.

Communication joins two human beings in a single shell. It is a cyclic process. Communication is not established, not complete until creative contact has been established between two or more human beings.

Communication is the basis for our social existence. Our society, our fate here on earth depends on the quality of our communication efforts. To achieve results, take your masks off and join the human race. The creative individual is a universe unto himself. To communicate he has to break out, he has to share his bubble, he has to realize that to live on this earth, it is necessary to cooperate, to make a creative contact with others.

In solving people problems, in dealing with other human beings, it is wise to realize that it is difficult to change, to manipulate, to influence others. If we want to improve communication, if we want to be successful at this difficult art, we must work primarily with ourselves. By example, this may help to improve others. We can work effectively really only with ourselves. What then can we do, fully realizing that communication depends as much on us as on the other party or parties?

Personal effort, your personal attitude is the key to effective communications. For good communication, there must be integrity of purpose, full respect for others, some healthy self-understanding, a sense of humor, belief in the message to be imparted, and willingness in fact, eagerness to receive the messages of others. To get your message across, to eliminate the many shells, the barriers which may affect your communication and that of the other human beings you are trying to reach, requires attention, understanding, acceptance and action. It is truly a creative process.

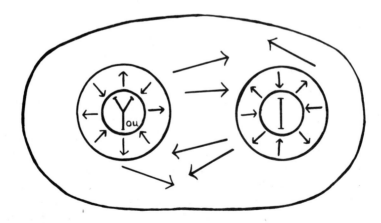

First, there is the question of attention. Do you succeed in reading people correctly? Can you tell whether they are attentive, whether your message is getting

156

through? How do you affect their facial expressions, posture, gestures, hesitation and response, lifted eyebrows, the tone of voice in their questions and comments. Are you listening?

While you are speaking, have you created a shell keeping you from paying attention? Are you open to your audience's feedback? Are they hanging on your every word or are they gradually falling asleep? Are you open to their questions, their reactions? Are you attentive to their behavior? Are "you" paying attention? Are you aware that you are not alone, that to establish communication, he, she, they, you, all must participate.

Next to attention, then we must make a successful effort to be on the same wavelengths. Are you able to establish a bridge from mind to mind? Let's see you talk to younger people. Are you sincere, and interested in communication with them as equals, or are you a little afraid of the modern generation? Are you showing a superior attitude? Can you let down the shell of apprehension and truly tune in on them? Are you preventing communication by being apologetic, defensive or are you over-confident and patronizing? It is vitally important to be on the proper wavelength to achieve effective communication.

A friend of mine and I recently discussed ecological problems with a fellow executive for whom we have the greatest respect, a lawyer highly trained in engineering and with excellent technical understanding. We had great difficulty establishing proper communication and found a complete lack of understanding of the ideas which we tried to explain to him. We finally discovered several basic factors contributing to the shells around each of us. We were unable to get in tune, to get on the same wavelengths because a recent experience had put our lawyer friend on the defensive. We had not, on the other hand, bothered to inform him of our degree of experience and knowledge in the ecological field. He thought of us as ivory tower scientists while we thought of ourselves as practical engineers. No wonder with this total inability to fully tune in and to consider the others difficulties, meaningful communication did not result.

To be successful, we must get on common ground. We must share our shells. We must make true and objective contact, with one another. This means not only words but also gestures. Sincerity shows not only in what we speak. You can easily give yourself away through the blinking of an eye or the shrug of the shoulder. It is important to practice your empathy.

To establish full and successful communication, we not only require attention and empathy, there also must be patience. There must be no haste. There must be a willingness to succeed, to try and try again to make contact. There must be no shell holding back a possible communicator. There must be no interference, no unnecessary intermediaries. Communication is a personal and a human undertaking. You must be open and available, spend time and give encouragement. Ask questions, be willing to explore the seemingly irrelevant. Curiosity is an excellent door, a wedge to improved communications. Encourage discussions, do not close off prematurely. Do not cut off before all attempts at making creative contact have been truly exhausted.

Thus for personal creative communication, work to improve your capabilities at paying attention, your potential to establish empathy with others and above all, give the complete task of communication all the time and effort it needs.

Communication starts with the inner self of the human being. Here deep inside lies the source of the message, here is the origin of the signal. Now the message also has to take form. It has to be encoded, put into suitable shape for transmission. We think naturally, first of all, of coding in words, using the effective human development of language. But messages can take other forms than words. Communications can be acts, gestures, smiles, kisses or a fist raised in anger. We use tokens of communication, whether they be road signs, money, stocks and bonds, table manners or even an old-fashioned courtesy. In fact, a silent language, a language of behavior is part of our culture. What people do, often speaks louder than words.

The silent language, the action code gives us a chance at truly creative communications. If you want to get through creative communications. If you want to get through that impassive shell of others get attention, use a creative approach. Think of a most unusual act, of an original way to stir your audience. This will open the doors, it will act as a key to effective communication. A message sent with a dozen red roses is apt to make contact with a lady even in the less romantic period of the 70's. A call early in the morning or late at night is apt to be taken more seriously than during regular business hours.

It is important to consider customs and their differences in different countries and cultures. In the Middle East, it is pointless to make appointments too far in advance because their system places everything beyond the week into a single category of "future" in which they do not like to plan. On the other hand, on United States business and professional calendars, advance planning even for a whole year is not uncommon. In South America, a wait of forty-five minutes or longer may be very acceptable, while it will communicate an insult or at least a lack of courtesy in our country. Especially when we try to communicate with foreign nationals, with people who do not share our background or our culture, we must be aware of the pitfalls of the silent language. To effectively communicate, we must not only learn the language but also the customs, the culture of the people with whom we deal.

Just as time, so space talks. If we want to make a point which is important to us, we are apt to move closer. We move in on the individual we are trying to convince. Normally as Americans, we do not touch, we keep our distance, not so in southern climates. Communication is apt to be practiced with much greater closeness. The distance between individuals is apt to be less. Hugging and embracing are a common sign of friendship between men in countries such as France. Space and time play a significant role in your communication pattern, in the form of encoding.

It pays to have an original way of going at it—a creative approach—a creative personal style, a code that is "creatively" you. Churchhill's voice was his trademark; so were his unique features and his cigar. Hitler's mustache was the unique attraction that immediately identified him. Do you have a unique way, an original way to signal your communications? Try using a special color ink in your work, one that quickly identifies your signature, quickly denotes your contact with a given report, a document, an idea. For many years, I have used green ink in this manner. How about an original stamp, a unique symbol as your mark on your stationery. The form of your communication, its originality, can help significantly to get attention. A scientist of my aquaintance used to clap his hands merrily greeting the various co-workers as he entered a room, thus establishing a friendly, slightly humorous contact every time he came in. A custom of wishing a co-worker a happy birthday shows a style of communication going well beyond the immediate happy birthday message. Encoding the message does not just mean words. It means a creative original approach, an attitude of "let's make contact".

We have the sender who originates the message, and the channel carrying the coded message. We have the need for decoding, receiving the message. We have a need for feedback. The cycle must get back to the sender through an act or a new message whether it be questions to clarify the message or answers. There must be a means of making sure that the communication ring has been closed, common ground has been established.

Needless to say, in this day and age of mass and electronic communication, the system may be much more complex, with devices of all kinds in the total cycle. We have the telephone, telegraph, television, radio and printing, to mention only a few. The more complex the system the more chance for interference or noise, the more chance also for garbling the message. The more people involved in the cycle, the more things can go wrong.

Surely you have played the game where a group of people start with a relatively simple message which is passed from one to the other around the room. When it finally reaches the last person, it is usually unintelligible or at least entirely different from the original message. The more complex the system the more we require a clear signal, well differentiated from noise and clearly linked to the communicator's purpose.

The most common code, the great, the magnificent tool that distinguishes man from the animals is the word—the realm of language. It establishes a common ground, helps us to bridge the gap between us, provided we have a "common" language. Now if we both speak English, we have a common language. Right?! No, not necessarily. Even when the words we use are the same we may be far apart. Due to our upbringing or past experience, words may have different meanings to us, evoke different images in our different minds.

Most of my life, I have been fortunate enough to work for helpful, understanding men who assisted me, were generally kind to me, and whom I greatly respected. So the word "boss" means to me a man for and with whom working is a pleasure. "Boss" for me is very much a "white hat" word — an accolation — a good word — a favorable word. Imagine my surprise in one of my creativity classes when I encountered an almost violent reaction by one of my students to this word. To her it meant "oppressor, dictator, exploiter". She saw red, she got emotionally angry when somebody mentioned the word "boss". A good English word but totally different meanings in two individuals.

SLAVE OR········

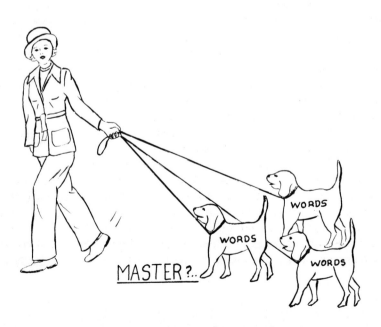

MASTER?...

Is language for you a mirage or a creative tool? Are you its master or its slave? Do you control words or do they control you? Who is in charge? Words should have value only as tools of the communication process. They facilitate the sharing, and the cooperation, the relationship between humans. That is what we are striving for. Words enable social contacts; they make work possible; they are the foundation of the culture of our times. Equally important, the written word, the printed word, video tape and the many forms of embodying communication in a permanent fashion, enables language to carry wisdom from one generation to the next. Knowledge, experience of the past is carried forward not only to the present but also into the future. Without language we are lost. It is said that the great Inca culture crumbled for lack of the written word.

Language can be of great value. It can be the mainstay of human understanding but also it can be a source of trouble. It can be the origin of strife and discord. Language is a symbolic process, we must recognize, understand and use it as such. To succeed we must be its master not its victims, its rulers, not its slaves.

Recently, there were long and hefty debates in Congress concerning the word cigar and cigarette. Federal laws bar ads for cigarettes on television and radio but permit commercials for cigars. Moreover, cigarettes are taxed much more heavily than cigars and other tobacco products. But what is the distinction? The word cigarette really means little cigar. According to law the difference is defined primarily at present as to whether the tobacco is wrapped in tobacco, or wrapped in paper. On the other hand, what we are really concerned about is the health hazard of smoking, and this is closely related to inhaling. Usually cigar smoke is so strong that people do not readily inhale it. On the other hand, little cigars are, according to witnesses, inhalable.

So, what do we do? Do we do what is best for human beings or are we getting ourselves into a long discussion as to the right word. Do we want to protect people from health hazards? Do we want to exempt certain tobacco products from tax or are we caught by the words cigar and cigarettes? What is the meaning of this "word"?

We must remember that symbols acquire meaning by agreement. We can make any word stand for anything. Just think of the confusion that Marshall McLuhan introduced to the generation of the last decade with the reverse use of such words as "hot" and "cool". We learn words in school, use them at home, and live with them as we grow up. Thus it is easy to forget that *we* make the words, *we* assign the meaning to them.

We must forever keep before us the truth that there is no necessary connection between the symbol, the "word" and what it stands for in "reality". Words and facts, words and objects, words and abstract notions, words and images—they are independent of each other.

If somebody calls you a "pig", that does not make you a "pig". You may have dirty habits, but you do not get them by being called a pig. If you are competent, have done a good job, that is not at all changed by some one calling you a "failure".

The word cannot make you a failure. Equally if you have struck out and cannot succeed, to make up for it with words is impossible.

THE WORD IS NOT THE THING

WORLD OF NOT-WORDS

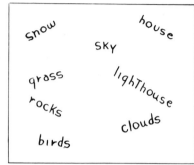

Language, words, symbols are not reality.

We owe a great deal to Alfred Korzybski, who in his book, Science and Sanity, first published in 1933, shed a great light on the effect of language on human behavior. He investigated in depth the relationship of reality to symbolism, real life to talk. His studies pointed out how often in human endeavor and especially in the humanities, in daily living, man's words did not fit the facts.

To be effective in creative communication, we must be masters of the language. We must lead the words not let them lead us. To quote from Hayakawa's outstanding book, Language in Thought and Action, we must be aware at all times that

"The symbol is not the thing symbolized."

"The map is not the territory."

"The word is not the thing."

In the realm of communications there is a world of words, a world of language which, whether we like it or not, takes on a character of its own. Each word we use has associations in our memories. It awakens feelings. It is tied to our own individual personality. It is part and parcel of our mind, our memory, our makeup. Single humans, are unique beings—therefore, words cannot truly be alike for any of us. The verbal world we live it is inevitably tied to our past, our lifelong experience. Since we are unique, it can never be entirely the same for any two human beings. Just as perception is tinged, colored, ruled by our personalities, our creative human fountain of competency, so our language—our verbal world—is equally characterized and styled by our creative self.

For successful creative communications we must remember that each one of us has a verbal world different from that of any other even the closest human being. Your verbal world is slightly different from that of your teacher, your father, your mother. This is inevitable. Realizing this truth, we will avoid many communication difficulties.

162

Besides our verbal world, the world we are experiencing through language, there is a real world out there, a world we are capable of experiencing directly. I can burn myself on a hot iron even though I am told— it is cold. For good communications, it is very desirable that our verbal world not differ too much from the real outside world.

Korzybski introduced the helpful parallel of the map and the territory. For a healthy life, good and sane human behavior, the relationship between our verbal world and the real world is like a good map to the territory it depicts. We will not get lost if we have a good map, if we read the right map. However, picture yourself trying to find your way in Los Angeles with a New York City plan! People problems can be solved with the right language but often human relations break down because we have the wrong map.

It is not as difficult or unusual as it may seem to acquire the wrong map, to live in a verbal world vastly different from the real world. In fact, all of us experience this shortcoming in varying degrees. While we may have a good map in some areas of our experience, there is a likelihood, that due to areas of prejudice, areas of upbringing, areas of exposure to strong influences, we have in our past life acquired some wrong maps.

It is difficult to avoid teachings of superstition and prejudice. How many of us have been taught that all Scotsmen are stingy or that it is bad luck to walk under a ladder. How easy is it to talk about somebody, to spread false rumors. This can hurt him with other people, but it does not change the reality, that he is not guilty of any of the verbal falsehoods. The verbal word can have powerful effects, and wrong maps can be extremely dangerous.

We draw the wrong conclusions and express our thoughts in words. We see smoke and shout "fire". Maybe it was only steam. We can get false maps not only from others, we can easily create false maps for ourselves. When you communicate, does your map correspond to the territory? Is your message factual, truthful? What are you communicating?

Just as in perception we cannot take in all the sights, so in expression we cannot use all the signals. In language, we must choose, we must develop a simplified scheme to describe, to verbalize the real world. The territory comes first. It is real, it is the starting point. It must be where we develop the map. We must simplify—we must select—we must choose to arrive at the useful map. Just as no map can fully represent all the features of the terrain, so the language cannot give us all the details of the world it is trying to represent.

We abstract, we choose, we select from the real world. There is a strawberry on the kitchen table. It has size, shape, taste, color, many detailed distinguishing characteristics, but I abstract, lump it all together with a label. All these characteristics, even the taste I know the strawberry possesses, is contained in the word "strawberry". We must realize our limitations. Whenever we describe, we cannot get the true detailed picture. We can only attempt to choose to abstract effectively from reality. Speech is not reality. The word is not the thing.

163

Many a lawsuit could be avoided, many a fight prevented if we just in all our communications remembered "reality comes first". Facts first, that is where the verbal world originates. The verbal world should not dominate. The real world must precede. We are masters of the words and they are our tools. It is *our* language if we start with the real world. We are slaves of the language, the word if we start with the verbal world rather than with the true, the factual world. Words must not lead us. We must lead with words.

This is not to neglect an understanding of the power of the word. Since words are associated with feelings and other words in the memory of human beings just the sound of a word can have power over us.

If you crossed a tomato and a carrot successfully and wanted to name this magnificent new food, you surely could sell a "carrato", a "tomrot" would never do. Our mind forms both obvious and inadvertent associations. Even totally new words must be accomodated within the framework of our specific individual receptive memories and makeup. The advertisers are masters at exploiting our weakness for words. They know and use the right words, they build up the Tradename to key our buying impulse.

We all respond favorably to words familiar to us, to language we are used to. On the other hand, we react radically to certain signals or to languages foreign to us. Thus, communicating wtih a disadvantaged person or persons from a totally different background than your own may take a special language. It may require that you make a special effort to ascertain that the words mean the same to both of you, that they raise the same feelings, get the same reaction. Only if you use the right words can you be sure that communication, the cycle of coding, decoding, understanding, participating in a common message, can be accomplished. It is not enough that the message reaches the intended receiver. It must be possible for him to get the meaning of the message. Understanding is never easy and often does not happen.

An interpreter for the early missionaries in British Guiana found some of the Christian words difficult to translate. Untranslated such words as "temptation, wicked, conversion, Christmas, salvation", would appear in his sentences. These words can to be recognized amongst the Patuma tribe as "powerful words". Powerful words in their primitive religion served to curse your enemy. Now, one Patuma explained, "a person can go to the prayer meeting, kneel behind the one he wished to curse and while everyone is praying out loud, he can mutter words like 'Christmas, salvation'".

We will not always find such huge differences in the meaning and understanding of the words on the communication cycle, on the ring of understanding we are trying to establish. However, often differences do exist. We must overcome these differences through extensive, effective participation of all human beings involved in the communication attempt.

It is vital for all of us to do the best possible job of coding our messages in such a way that they can readily be encoded and fully understood. You address fellow workers, you talk about the difficult business climate of the coming year. You try to convince them of the need for utmost effort in cost reduction. Let us look at the signals starting in their head. What does it mean to them. "Difficult business climate". What is the message? Are you succeeding in having them see what is in your mind?

There is a shell around you. You have difficulty getting the message crystallized—getting out of the shell. Now, with whom and where do you want to place the message. You are addressing fellow workers. Who are they? What do you know about your audience—the other party—the various humans you are trying to motivate? They are also mature individuals. They are surrounded by their own shell of prejudice — by their intellect — by their obstinacy — by their inability to hear you — by their inability to see your images and realize the meanings that you are trying to communicate. How well do you know them? What do you really know about their background? What do you know about their feelings, the sensitivities that they have acquired in former years? As difficult as it is for you to get the message from your heart and mind through the shell of your own inhibitions, your own insecurity onto the communication channel, so it is equally difficult for you to penetrate the shell of your partner, to reach his heart and mind, to get reception, to get participation, to get effect, to get understanding and to motivate him by your message.

Difficult! Yes, by all means. Not at all easy. Difficult: That is the world of communication. Realize how difficult it is and employ the patience, the care, the effort necessary to truly establish creative communications. Associations to words can be strong enough to cause violent emotional reactions. I remember the father of one of my best friends who would get red in the face and very angry any time the word "Roosevelt" was even mentioned.

It pays to be aware of the power of words, of good words, not so good words, and bad words. Even in jest, it does not pay to call a friend a "crook". Some words just do things to people. Some words just sing and bring back pleasant memories. "Roses", "beautiful", "sweetheart", these words are likely to arouse similar feelings in others as they do in you. Be aware of the effect that words can have on those that you are trying to get on the same wavelength with you.

Avoid words that are difficult to understand. One of the great failings of the professions and especially of science is the ever increasing tendency to coin words for specific situations. Words, whose meaning are not agreed upon, cannot really serve as a communication link. Meanings must be established in all the minds participating in the communication circle. Some of my fellow professionals need even be on guard against coining words which in their own minds have no fully established meaning.

Are you using words out of habit, words you do not fully understand? How do you expect to successfully communicate meanings with words that are not clear to you in your own mind? How do you expect to establish creative contact with others if you have not truly crystallized the meaning of the message within your own self? Talking over somebody's head, using big, unintelligible words, is a selfish game, it is not creative communication. It does not pay to use babytalk with mature individuals, but neither is it right to use intellectual gobbledegook when good-down-to-earth English is in order. Do not use complicated language to hide your ignorance, communication cannot be achieved that way.

Professionals are particularly guilty of using highly specialized language with people who cannot be expected to have the ability to connect the words they receive with meanings similar to those acquired by the specialist.

Much of the dissatisfaction with the delivery of medical care can be explained by communication failures between doctors and patients. A recent study of medical communications showed that nearly one fifth of the mothers felt that they had not received a clear statement of what was wrong with their baby from the attending physician. Almost half of the entire group was still wondering when they left the physician, what had caused their child's illness. This communication failure had a substantial effect on the number of mothers who carefully carried out the doctor's medical advice.

The medical profession is only one of many that deals almost entirely in people's problems. Communication, a true establishment of a common ground of understanding requires special attention and training. It demands a willingness to use language that can be understood by all participants.

A particular pitfall obstructing effective communication is the use of "in-language". There are certain words that suddenly become fashionable. They may originate on TV or in the literature of a specialized field. It is easy to succumb and use these words without really understanding what we are talking about. With the great influence of the media in our times, "buzz words" are often quickly adopted by large numbers of people. Only if all these people truly understand what the word stands for and use them in similar fashion, only then can they truly serve as tools. In a way, "communication" is a buzz word. So is "creativity". Beware of buzz words. Use them wisely and only if you are sure that you yourself understand their meaning.

Sometimes the buzz words have Greek roots like "heuristic, charisma". Watch out for glib phrases! The more syllables, the more you need to watch out. How do you like "market segmentation"? Or "marketing concept" or how about "linear programming".

Communication is a participatory activity. Communication is an ongoing effort in which the meanings of the sender make creative contact with the understanding of the receiver. It is a mutual activity, it is a participating circle, a closed ring.

You talk to your boss. You talk to your fellow workers. You talk to your family. Do you tell them? Are you with them or alone? Are you sending, without their sending back? You are swinging, is anybody swinging back?

Creative contact does not occur between an active sender and a passive receiver. You know how passive we all are—whether it is because we had a drink for lunch or because we are worried about something at home or because we just listened to an adverse newscast. Maybe it's too hot and too stuffy in the room! Every one of these factors contributes to our passivity. Only if you are active, if you do not have something else going through your mind, only then can you participate in the communication circle. To establish communications, a creative contact, we must assure that there is an active receiver. We must motivate him to participate. Communication is a mutual activity, a full wheel, a linking chain, a circle. Meanings on both sides must reach out for each other. Unless the receiver is an active participant, there cannot be real communication. Thus listening is as important as speaking, viewing as projecting, reading as writing, feedback as the message.

Let't remember that we are in the people business. Creative problem solving means, more often than not, the solving of people problems. If we want results, contributions, performance, than we must realize that we are not in the message sending business. Communication is a tool, a means to an end. Successful communication must build bridges. Discussing the weather may serve to politely open a conversation with a stranger, however, talk by itself, talk without saying anything worthwhile, speech without a meaningful message, this is not creative communication. Communication must elicit not only a response but a resulting creative effect. We are solving a people problem. We are motivating. We are out to accomplish a goal. The effect is the last step in communication. It must indicate itself in some way or fashion. It will show whether the communication has been successful.

Successful communication is vital to a successful life. To assure successful communication, we must understand its nature as a participating effort, a symphony in which all players contribute to the ultimate effect or at least a chamber music concert or a duet. Communication is a circle not a one-way street. It isn't just sender and receiver, it is feedback, understanding, sharing, participating and contributing to a common cause.

Communication is not exclusively practiced with the tools of language. However, it requires, in most cases, a full understanding and the proper use of language. We must realize that the verbal world, the world of language, is not the real world. To use words successfully, we must be their masters, not their slaves. We must understand the difference between the map of words and the true territory of reality. Finally, we must not coin a special map that might be difficult to understand for others not as knowledgable as we are in a given field. We must, if such maps are necessary for communication among specialists, to be sure to interpret the map in understandable fashion to people out side the field. Communication is an effort at solving people problems. Only when the result is successful, proper action is obtained, can communication be considered complete and effective.

EXERCISES

In the next six meetings you attend watch for the silent language. What can you observe about body movement, hands, what about time and distance? Are there significant giveaways of meanings in the silent languages of the participants of the meetings? Analyze your own non-verbal signals. Are you communicating when you do not intend to do so?

Who are the ten people with whom you most often establish communication in your daily life? How well do you and they succed at at achieving effective closure of the communication circle? Do you close the ring or do you take the participation for granted? Prepare a written analysis of your communication effectiveness with each of these individuals.

How creative are you at getting attention? List twenty ways to improve your ability to have people notice your desire to communicate.

Choose ten words at random, examine their meanings in a large dictionary. Did you realize that there were so many different meanings even for seemingly simple words.

Take twelve professional communications, whether they be business letters, reports, testimony, or similar documents. Analyze the sentences for communication content. What words, what portions of the sentence are meaningful? What conveys specifics to you, and what is just verbage, just words without meaning, just fill-in material? Tabulate and compare the two types.

Collect some professional articles, medical, legal or scientific. Evaluate their meaning. Count the number of words intelligible only to the specialist. How well did the writer succeed in conveying meanings to you?

Choose three pictures from a magazine. Take each picture and carefully write a detailed description. Be conscious and consistent to start each sentence, each word with the picture, the reality. Review your writing to check whether the words or your habit of using them have led you astray. Can you go back and relate the picture to your verbal description?

Take a passage from a novel, a paragraph, a page, or similar excerpt from a short story. Can you draw a picture? Can you visualize or represent reality? Try to sketch, try to document what you are reading. Analyze the words, the sentences. Are you able to fathom the meaning of the writer? Write down and try to see whether more than one meaning is possible. Analyze and attempt to document at least three different meanings.

RECOMMENDED READING

David K. Berlo, "The Process of Communication", Holt, Reinhardt, 1960.
Edward T. Hall, "The Silent Language", Doubleday, New York.
William V. Haney, "Communications and Organizational Behavior", Richard D. Irwin, 1967.
S. I. Hayakawa, "Language in Thought and Action", Harcourt-Brace, 1972.
Irving J. Lee, "Language Habits in Human Affairs", Harper and Row, 1941.

H. Norman Wright, "Communication: Key to your Marriage", Regal G-L Publications, 1974.

Hayakawa is"must" reading for you and anybody you know who can read. It is fascinating and reading it will help you lead a better life. Hall's book relates language and culture in excellent fashion. For the serious student I would recomment Haney's excellent work on communication and organizational behavior.

CHAPTER 11

CREATIVE MEDIA – WRITING, SPEAKING, LISTENING

The importance of listening.
Outrunning the speaker.
Contact with strangers.
First the message.
Know your audience.
Total performance.

Single minded visuals.
Your personal style,
Organize your writing.
Reading for a purpose.
Modern tools, use them.
Media and reality.

"Creative contacts" with others, communication is the key to success in the professions and in our daily lives. We make speeches, we watch television, we write reports, letters, and short notes. We read newspapers, journals, magazines and books, and we listen. Oh, do we listen! Contrary to our normal reaction, that speaking and writing are our most important communication skills, it is listening which takes up most of our time, and requires our best efforts.

How do we communicate? How do writing, reading, speaking, and listening compete with each other? How much time do we spend on each of these important activities? Needless to say, this will differ from person to person and from time period to time period. But on the average, it breaks down as follows:

Listening	45%
Speaking	30%
Reading	15%
Writing	10%

Listening, then, is the most important of our communication activities. Have you learned to listen? Have you sharpened your listening skills? Do you listen creatively? What do we mean by listening? Do you think only of hearing, or are you aware that good listening involves your total human being, all your senses.

Listening is more than hearing. The good listener uses his eyes, his ears, his nose, even the sense of touch. He uses all his senses to participate in the communication exercise to establish the common ground of understanding. If you watch a football game on television and get half out of your seat with a long pass, that may be funny to your wife, however, it is but a sign that you are really listening. Good listening involves your total creative self, and participation in what goes on. You must want to listen, to be willing to totally involve yourself in the process of listening, of wanting to establish full and successful communication. Are you as good a listener Sunday mornings in church as you are at the Saturday afternoon football game? Are you as good a listener when somebody walks in your office complaining, or alerting you to a special situation, as you are when you go to your evening class at night school?

We usually take our listening skills for granted. Listening is not easy, especially if

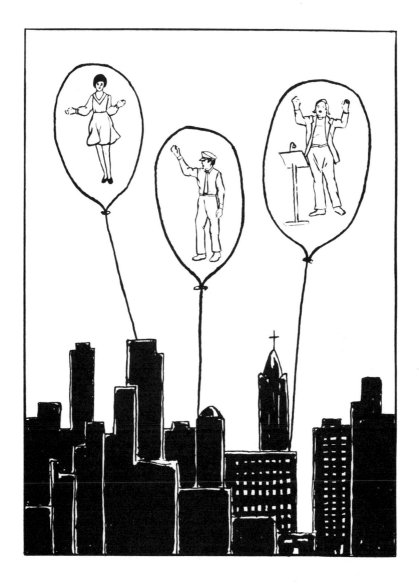

you have developed your creative potential to a high degree. The creative urge, the natural impatience, the inclination for our mind to wander, are likely to make our listening more difficult. We have an urge to speak. We succumb to our ego, speak, not listen. We compete, interfere, make communications difficult if not impossible. Listening requires patience and control. To begin with, the rate of talking does not coincide with our rate of listening. We can hear and understand at a much faster rate than anyone can speak. A normal speaking rate may be on the order of about 100 words per minute, while a good listener can easily hear 500, maybe even 1000 words per minute. Add to that the normal urge to speak as soon as something occurs to us, the urge to interrupt, to correct, and you can readily see the difficulty of putting speaking and listening onto the same beat, the same time frame.

Since we can listen at such a fast clip, at such great speed, there arises the danger of distraction. What do we do with the extra time? Do we use it to listen more fully? To listen successfully, we must not stray or be diverted. We must find a creative way to use the extra time to reinforce, to strengthen our listening. This can be done most creatively by exercising total perception. We can be looking for clues to the meaning, concentrate on the contents of the message. We can analyze it, examine it, weigh it, focus on the significance of the message. Instead of straying, moving outward in the extra time, we must concentrate, move inward, find creative ways to more fully participate, to be one with the speaker.

Truman Capote trained himself to remember *verbatim* his conversations with the criminals he wrote about in his book, "In Cold Blood". He had only the usual listening ability before. He did not use a recorder.

Memory, as we discussed elsewhere, is a function of repetition and association. To improve our listening, we must not only use our fullest potential to establish the full circle of communication, but we must also endeavor to memorize the essentials of the message.

This means, first, as in all forms of perception, a selection process. We listen to thousands of words, see many images, whether they be multimedia, or the motions and gestures of a live speaker. The process of listening to be successful must select and identify the essentials of the message. What was meant? What can I learn? What should I do? How do I react? How do I participate, learn, gain something from what I hear and see? Once we perceive, select the message, then the process of problem solving, the creative act, comes into play. How can I take advantage of the message, retain it, record it, associate it with something so that I will not forget it? Also, to close the communication ring, how can I accomplish feed-back to assure that communication is successful; that I got the right message. How can I improve or complete the message to ascertain its correct meaning. How can I make sure that I have succeeded in establishing common ground.

To be a good listener, we must concentrate, avoid all diversions, focus, become totally absorbed in the process of communication. We cannot allow ourselves to roam. We can overcome the time gap. We can use the time differential for improved perception, repetition of vital portions of the message, and for creative associations, to reinforce our memory.

Good listening means that we must not use the extra time to get ahead of the speaker. We must control, we cannot draw inferences too early. We cannot jump to conclusions, which may be unjustified based on what is going to be said next. As in creative ideation, good listening means withholding judgement. Listening to it all before you become too selective or critical, is vital. Good listening looks for reports, verifiable facts; it distinguishes, and analyzes between the speaker's facts, his

172

WAIT AND LISTEN

inferences, and his judgements. The good listener himself defers judgement until all the speaker's ideas have been advanced, until all his arguments have been presented. Listening is a creative act.

We require preparation for good listening. Who is the speaker? What is his background, his purpose, his associations? Is he likely to be well-informed on the subject? What do I know about the subject? Good listening requires preparation. How can I avoid distraction? Can I see the speaker well? Can I hear him well? I should be comfortable, so that I can concentrate. How do I avoid being diverted by the pretty girl in the front row?

Good listening requires problem difinition. What is this all about? How can I participate? What can I do to assure that I will benefit from listening? Do I want to listen? Do I have prejudices as to the speaker or the subject that create a special problem?

Creative listening means an open mind, a willingness to establish the full communication circle. It means a willingness to openly receive all ideas, defer judgement, as in the ideation stage of the creative process. It requires not primarily idea generation, but understanding of ideas. They need non-critical reception, reception without prejudice or preconceived notions. We must hear the message as it is meant to be heard. We must not, as we often do, look for what we *want* to hear, but really for what is *there* to be heard. We must listen to, hear, understand the ideas that are advanced, in the context of the speaker, the sender, not in the context of our own possibly wishful thoughts. The most important part of good listening is deferred judgement, is patience. Listen, do not talk. Yes, we may want to talk eventually, sparingly, to assure feedback, but we must exert a willingness to delay our input, our comments, our criticisms, to allow the speaker the fullest degree of his input.

We must also be on the lookout for difficulties of language. Do the speaker's words mean to him what they mean to us? How close to reality is his language?

173

Does his map fit the territory, and does the map we get from listening to him, fit the territory? Are we listening to meaningful words, or to words that do not relate to any reality? We must take some of the extra time we have, due to our high listening speed, to evaluate, to consider what the words the speaker uses really mean. What does he understand them to mean? Are we decoding the words the way he encodes them? Are we relating the words he uses to reality in the same way he does? Are we only hearing the words, or are we relating them to the same images, the same objects, the same reality he sees?

We must not only watch for his words, but for all other signals, because often the real meaning, the true message, may not be expressed in words. Words may hide the real message. We must learn to listen for hidden messages, for feelings as well as facts. We must be able to listen beyond words.

The passenger who sits next to you on the airplane and makes a polite comment on the weather does not really send a message which reads, "Beautiful weather today". His message is most likely to mean, "I am willing to talk to you." Human traditions and conventions often do not allow the direct, honest message. It would be unlikely to succeed in establishing a conversation. So we must read beyond the words.

We must listen carefully for the non-verbal comments as well as the language. When the boss calls you into his office for a directive, he may mean to communicate the importance of that directive. Listen not only to the words, but also to what may be behind the words. Pay attention to the context, the timing, the surroundings. They may convey as much or more than the message itself. Pay attention, listen to the total verbal and non-verbal communication. Establish a full and functioning circle, so that the meanings of the speaker can make creative contact with you. For good and effective listening, then, we must listen totally, not just hear, but see, feel, taste, and devote our entire attention, our full potential to the listening process. It is the most important of our communication activities.

The good listener is a powerful solver of people's problems. Many human problems can be solved creatively just by good listening. Creative listening can add a new dimension to the solution of human problems. It is listening which gives full scope to the communication process, establishes a bond, an empathy, a commonality between people that by itself can solve many of the seeming problems of the day.

Many of the problems among human beings are the result of communication failures. Often, merely establishing understanding, succeeding at communications, allowing meaning to flow from one human being to another will be of great benefit. Good creative listening can solve many problems.

Through feedback we can add our own creativity to the listening process. We may add to the meaning, establishing common ground with the speaker. We will see his problem, and possibly he will see his problems, in an expanded view, a widened horizon.

Through good listening, we will contribute to broader, more meaningful understanding. This is the basis of the need for better listening, and better listeners.

Listening done in a creative way goes into the depth of other people's problems, and through perception and feed back, contributes significantly to their solution. Listening can and must be a creative activity, just as speaking, writing, painting, which we readily recognize as such. We need specialized instruction, help and training, exercises in creative listening, just as we do in creative writing or other facets of human creative expression.

Speaking and writing are more readily recognized as requiring creativity. In a recent poll of 1500 scientists and engineers 95% stressed the importance of written and verbal communications in their work. More than 60% believed that technical people do have a unique communication problem. The group was almost unanimous (93%) that training in communication especially in speaking and writing, should be part of their college curriculum. It was interesting that they emphasized oral communications, since they felt that most of their contacts with supervisors and co-workers were face-to-face. This underlines the importance, not just of speaking to and before groups, not so much public speaking, but direct one-on-one verbal contacts.

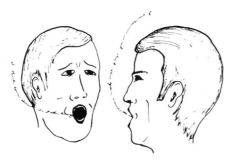

In the technical professions, we are apt to get involved in the material parts of our problems, and forget that people problems may be of equal importance. The technical solution is of no value if you cannot get the engineer to see it, to understand it. He has to translate it into action, and carry out the next step. Technical solutions without successful communications can be worthless. In fact, upon closer examination of our troubles, we will find that insufficient, incomplete, improper communications are most frequently at the root of our problems. We lack communication skills. We do not get our message across.

Much of this situation is caused by our inability to express ourselves, to talk in such a way that we build the communication circle, that we complete the ring, that we reach common ground. To succeed in making a speech before a small or large group, or to convince a single individual face-to-face we must consider three simple, and at the same time, often complex questions:

What is my message?
Who is my audience?
How do I communicate?

Each of these questions, each part of the speech, is a problem in itself.

To speak successfully, I must have something to say. I must know what I am after. I must establish the goal of the communication. I must have defined the message. In your daily activities, the messages may flow out of the requirement of your technical or business endeavor. You need to know something; you want something done; you want others to understand, to know, to act. Arriving at the message defining, formulating what you are going to say, what you will say next, is a creative activity. Thus, if you want your boss to approve a project, if you want to convince the interviewee to accept employment, if you want to formulate the scope of a research project, or if you want your teenager to be sure to come home by midnight, you must creatively solve the first problem: "What is my message?"

If you are willing to give public speeches, address your local luncheon club, selection of a topic will be the first step. What are you going to say that will be of interest to them? What do you want them to carry away from the meeting? What do you want to accomplish? Selection of the topic lends itself readily to the application of the creative problem solving process. After some preparation, you may brain-storm the problem with the man who asked you. You may generate a large number of ideas for possible speech topics. Give yourself some incubation time before making your own choice. Keep in mind that you are after an original presentation. Even if you want to talk to them on safer driving, or energy conservation, you want to define a speech topic with an original angle.

Titles, abstracts and outlines can be important, because they serve as a bridge between you and your audience. They lie somewhere between our first questions, "What to talk about" and the second question, "Who is our audience?" In reality, it may often be difficult to clearly separate these two aspects of your speech; thus, a bridge will be helpful.

Title, abstract and outlines may decide whether you will have an audience, since it is often the only motivation for many to attend the meeting. Here particularly we are dealing with a problem which requires our utmost exercise in creativity. A catchy original title, a brief interesting novel outline, will serve as bait for the audience. It raises their expectations, catches their attention, and sets the stage for your delivery. Be original. Take the trouble of applying the creative process, of developing many ideas, of allowing inspiration to come before you settle on that catchy, effective title, the "come-on" to your speech.

Who is your audience? Whom are you trying to reach? Who will join you on common ground as a result of your speech?

Analyze your audience. You must reach that other human being, you must touch him, make him understand, motivate him to listen, to participate, to communicate, to act with you, to reach common ground.

To reach that audience we must know it. To decide how much detail the execution of a communication requires, we must know the receiver, his background, his reactions, his prejudices, possible barriers to communication which require a special approach. The good speaker analyzes his audience consciously, be it one individual, a group or a large crowd. Each audience has special requirements. Whether to speak formally or informally; highly technically or as simply as possible; whether certain words can be used without defining them; these are just some of the questions answered by audience analysis.

Even if we are dealing only with a single individual, the more we know about him, the better. What is his training? What is his preparation in the subject you want to talk about? Very important, if you can determine it: What is his attitude towards you, the speaker? Will he be on the defensive? Will he be influenced by differences in responsibility or position? Is he likely to be receptive or hostile?

Know your audience. If you deal with a group of people in a discussion or meeting, make an effort to find out the strengths and weaknesses, the preferences and prejudices of each member of your audience.

It is important to highlight the positive aspects in audience analysis. Do not underestimate the people you are dealing with. Talking down to people makes successful communication almost impossible. Better to somewhat overestimate the group you are dealing with, than to fall short of their expectations. To be able to fulfill the needs of your audience, to live up to their expectations, to make them listen, understand, to motivate them you must make an effort to know them. The success of a speech is based on your recognition, your understanding, your feeling for your audience. This is the starting point, the basis for success.

Needless to say, you can be creative in many ways to find out more about your audience. Ask the people who are your contacts to open up and transmit to you specific and unusual information concerning this audience. Look up the individuals in reference books, such as "Who's Who". Open the session with provocative questions, the answers to which will shed light on your audience's reactions and attitudes. Surprise your audience with an original and unexpected opening statement, and analyze their response.

How do you successfully communicate, how do you face them? You note I do not ask how to successfully "speak", since all communication involves more than only speaking. Success requires fullest use of your total creative potential. It requires a total performance, not just speaking. Speaking may not be enough for successful face-to-face communication.

Success requires attention to detail, from your appearance to the seating arrangement, from the room temperature, the lighting, to the noise level. There are many factors to consider: "how to deliver a speech". Remember, you want your audience to join you in the ring, to participate; this means a creative approach to the problem of distance. If you have to be in front, don't let your audience be in the far distant back. If you want to establish a common bond, do not leave a heavy desk between you and them as a bulky barrier of separation. Get close; sit around a common table; get into the crowd; make them identify with you; identify with them. Bring somebody up to take part in the demonstration, and the crowd will identify; you have brought them closer to you. Avoid spatial barriers, such as empty rows, speaker stands, tables, and similar devices that separate you from your audience.

Most important, avoid the barrier of a script to read from. You are not the President or Head of the State Department, who has to make sure that every word they say is evaluated as to its possible consequences. Reading a speech raises a suspicion that you are not master of your subject, that you do not fully understand or believe in your message. You cannot communicate with others, if you yourself are tied to that manuscript. You must know your subject, your speech, your message. A good performance is not possible without learning the script.

This does not mean that complete memorization is a necessity. There are many tricks that you can use: Outlines, key words. Possibly the most creative and effective approach is to prepare visuals and demonstrations which reinforce and complete the presentation of key ideas. At the same time they can serve as a guide, a road map, a memory aid to assure the order, the sequence, and the completeness of your presentation.

Good communication means involving as many of your senses and those of other participants as possible. This means demonstrations, gestures, visuals — anything that will help to put your message across.

Regrettably, it is in the area of visuals, of using the eyes to supplement the ears, that many of our highly knowledgeable speakers fail to keep up with the times. First, all visuals must be considered through the eyes of the audience, not the mind of the presenter. This requires adherence to some obvious rules. Obvious? Yes, but more violated than followed.

> Visuals must be: Simple
> Interesting
> Visible
> Single minded

One idea at a time. Do not crowd your visuals. Use no more than seven words per line, no more than seven lines at a time.

This is where a creative approach is most desirable. When your words are long forgotten, a good visual that is original, stimulating, maybe humorous, and presents the idea well, may long be remembered. Many people have a strongly visual memory. Visuals can help the listener focus, help him fill the extra time he has. Be sure that the visual is in tune with your talk, in harmony, and properly timed with your text. You want it to be a help, be a reinforcement, not a distraction.

Blackboard presentations belong in the past with rare exceptions. A sinner against all principles of good communications is the scientist who writes equations on the blackboard at such a speed that the students have to make a choice between copying at the fastest speed possible, or concentrating on trying to understand what is being presented. Even worse is the one who erases with his left hand while he writes with his right hand. Good communications would take advantage of previously prepared overhead slides, or posters, to allow maximum time for explanations and feed-back. Blackboards and their erasure make it difficult to refer back.

178

Something that has been presented previously cannot be reconsidered to accomplish fuller understanding.

An excellent aid for small and medium size groups is to draw or write in heavy felt pen on large newsprint tablets. Rather than turning over the sheet after it has been filled, have one of the participants mount it with masking tape around the walls of the room.

A variant of this device is a "poster talk". This is a good way to overcome the handicaps facing the speaker at lunches and after dinners. Instead of being barricaded at the head table behind the podium, the speaker can roam about freely. Previously prepared visuals on poster size sheets are taped on the walls of the room in strategic locations. The speaker can point to these, or even better, walk from one to the other, while he delivers his talk. The food stuffed audience will have to move to see and follow. This will overcome their natural tendency to relax and not pay attention after a good meal.

Involvement of the audience is the creative approach to good communication with them. One creative avenue is to single out someone in the audience, address that person directly, have that person get up and perform. Do something, refer to his hobby, to an unusual interest, to somebody in his family, this makes the audience wonder how you know so much. (You've asked the host before the speech began, of course!)

Visuals, tricks, humor, participation will make your talk successful. Be sure, however, when you use a picture, a model a joke, that it rings true. It must be relevant, it must fit, it must be part not only of your talk but also of your style.

Our personal style, our own creative specific way of presenting ideas, of attempting to convince, to influence others is vitally important. We must develop our own personal way of successfully facing and convincing an audience. It means first of all self-confidence. Even if you are somewhat shy by nature, you can face groups. If you are prepared, you can contribute. You have something to offer, so do not play yourself down. Do not apologize, be sure and confident of your own strengths.

Your style should be in keeping with your personality, but you are here as a performer — as a performer who has a goal, who has a message. Remember, the listener has all that extra time and your job is to keep those listeners on the subject, to keep them from being distracted.

In developing your style be aware that you are trying to fulfill the other participant's expectations. You want to make an impression in keeping with the goal you are trying to reach. Informality may be in order for monthly staff meetings, but not for a presentation of a major project to the President or the Board of Directors.

Cultivate a behavior, a performance, that is sincere and in keeping with your individuality. At the same time it should aid in the establishment of mutual understanding. This may mean avoiding some habits of speech, or gestures, that might be distracting. One of the worst gestures, usually due to shyness, is to keep your hands in your pockets. This gesture will be read by your audience as a lack of self-confidence. On the positive side, you may have your own distinctive attention-getting characteristic, whether it be face adornment, hair style, bow tie, or pearl studded jacket. You want to give your audience something to look at, something that expresses you, that is in harmony with your personality. Just as the listener is an individual with the right to be accepted into the common ring with his entire creative personality, so you participate with your own personal style, as a speaker. The more creative you are in bringing your personality to the surface, whether it be in the use of certain words, gestures, or actions, the more it will contribute to your successful performance.

Knowing what you want to accomplish, what your message is, knowing your audience, you cannot help but establish a successful bond, if your format appeals not only to the ears, but to the full potential of their senses, and you have taken the trouble to develop an effective personal style of presentation.

Always keep in mind, however, that you are not just speaking; the secret is to close the ring, to get on the merry-go-round, in the circle with your audience, whether it be one or thousands.

To the professional, and especially the technical man, speaking holds a spot of great importance. Much that has been said about communication in general and face-to-face presentation also holds true for reading and writing. However, as in painting, the artist has to reduce the multidimensional landscape, the tastes, the feeling of nature onto a flat, two-dimensional canvas, so in writing we are restricted to words on the printed page.

It is to the credit of humanity that so much has been accomplished, so much can be conveyed through our language, through the written word. Some artists are truly able to paint, to reproduce not only the image but also the feeling, the essence of an image, through the written word.

In the context of this book, however, we are concerned with the creative approach to the more mundane writings of the professional. As with his face-to-face presentations there are difficulties. Many of our professionals write a lot without necessarily succeeding in communicating. The rules we laid down for speaking apply equally to writing. Thus, we must define the goal of our writing, we must know our audience, and we must reach our audience through an effective style and format.

Define carefully what your message is. Use the creative problem-solving process to arrive at the formulation of your message. There is a way to make sure that this is done readily and easily, especially in technical reports. There is a foolproof general rule, especially for written communication:

First:	"Tell them what you are going to tell them."
Second:	"Tell them."
Last:	"Tell them what you told them."

In conveying subject matter of all kinds, whether it be technical proposals, plans for a new housing project, a new budget, or an idea for a new product, we are somewhat slow in catching on. Various individuals have different speeds of mental digestion. Also, it helps to get your audience oriented. So in your writing, first:

"Tell them what you going to tell them."

A well-written introduction and summary may be hard to compose, but it will be worth its weight in gold if you succeed in catching your reader's attention and interest. In this busy decade, people like to know whether it is worth their while; should they read the entire writing. A well-written introduction and summary serves this purpose. It is the bait, the eye-catching "come-on". It is vitally important.

"Tell them."

After the introduction comes the main body, the essence, the detail of your presentation. This is the full writing. It may be of many different kinds, depending on the goal you are trying to reach. Here is the vital essence, the detail, the complete presentation.

"Tell them what you told them."

This again must be followed by a summary, a drawing together. Any good report, any good writing should end with summary and conclusions. You owe the audience an indication what now, what to believe, what to do. The reader must be told how to continue, how to benefit. What are the lessons he should have learned, that is what he wants to know.

Again, it is vital to know your audience. Who are you writing this for? Are you writing for the boss, or his bosses? For the Engineering Department, for the judge, the customers? What do you want him or her to do, who will read this? Can the individual who reads this understand? Will he provide feed-back? How can you both get into the communication ring? Writing is more difficult in this respect than face-to-face communication, when back-and-forth chit-chat can be possible, where gestures may serve as feed-back? How do you make sure that you and your reader reach common ground? Did you give him references, exercises? Did you give him the insight on how you reached your conclusions? Can he know you for your writing? Can he know what to do next, how to profit, how to continue? Your writing must establish a bridge from your mind to that of the reader. Do you see the reader? Who is he? Are you writing for him, the real reader?

Across the bridge of your letter, your report, your manual, your article, you are sending words. Only if these words can be understood, if they can be visualized, digested, by the reader is your bridge-building successful. You are trying to convey information, ideas; you are trying to have him see the images you have seen; you are trying to influence him, to make him act, to make him profit, to make him participate. Keep in mind that for your writings to be useful, your words must have meaning. There must be meanings similar in your mind to meanings in the reader's mind. The words serve not just to carry dictionary definitions, they carry associations from your mind to his. They are likely to be found associated with other things in "his" memory then when "you" formulated them into sentences and paragraphs.

Keep your communications clear and free-flowing. Avoid special language, long words, and long sentences. Keep in mind that language, the words you use, are the tools, the means to present the real world. It is the ideas, the facts that count, not the words. The words are a means to an end, not an end in themselves.

Write your sentences, use your words for a purpose. Visualize what you are trying to convey, and thus describe it. Do not use words or sentences for their own sake. They are nothing in themselves. They are your way of conveying reality, of transmitting abstract ideas, they are your messengers. As in all presentations, style, a clear personal way of presenting the truth, is important. In your writing, you express your full creative self, your personality in condensed form, compressed into words.

It is well worth the effort to develop your own clear personal style, a style easy to read, but which conveys your ideas eloquently. This means mixing short and long sentences; it means cultivating the effort of translating your images into words, putting your feeling on paper. Be original with words, your choices and how best to use them.

A last word about your creative writing. Just as in other creative problem solving processes, the best ideas do not always come first. Let your writing simmer, take time out for the incubation of your writing. Then read it again, and let inspiration guide you. Re-write and improve, and finally, edit your own writing. Polish it; get it in best possible shape for the reader. Never forget, the purpose of your writing is to achieve full communication. Concentrate on what to communicate and with whom to establish the circle of communication.

We may not always think of it in this fashion, but the professional's reading also requires creative approaches. We live in an age of media saturation. There is more to hear and see than even the busiest, most effective professional can handle. So, reading means selection, it means creative choice of the valuable, the significant, the relevant. How can we select the right material at the time it is available to us? Modern duplicating devices offer an answer. You can duplicate anything that seems of interest. Then later you can organize it, before reading it. This also allows you to read it at your leisure. Duplication also has the advantage that you can readily use reading aids such as underlining significant passages, without worrying about damaging the journal or book in which the material first appeared. Determine the purpose of your reading. Are you reading for pleasure, for learning? Do you want to pass the time in an entertaining fashion? Are you looking for just one specific piece of information or do you have to memorize, to retain, what you are reading?

Depending on what you want to accomplish there are different ways to read. You may scan rapidly until you find the passage, the item you need. You may speed read, retaining the overall story, the grand design in your mind, getting the feel of what you read without dwelling on detail. For the detective story the description of the flowers in the garden may be immaterial. Or you may savour in detail the word imagery offered to you, the description of an olive grove by the great novelist may be an enjoyable work of art.

Select your reading matter creatively. Organize it well, and read it with concentration and focus. Associate what you want to retain in your memory with sign posts as a memory aid. Remember, that your memory has a limited capability. It needs help in stressing the significance of material that you want to recall at a later date. Know where to find things again; collect and organize your clues to what you have read.

We have discussed creative approaches to listening, speaking, writing, and reading. We live in the closing decades of the twentieth century, a time of change. We can write and compose pictures on the computer. We have video films and multimedia presentations. How do you apply the modern means of conveying ideas? What about using film, multi-screen slide projections, computer graphics, and most important, videotape?

These modern tools can be highly effective if properly used by creative individuals. However, they can be expensive. They require special skills and substantial effort if you want to use them effectively. Just as a picture, a visual has to be relevant to the message, so in multi-media presentation the various media employed have to be used creatively and in concert. The basic concepts of communications apply whether we deal with Egyptian hieroglyphics, or with a video-taped experiment. Communication is a process between humans. The medium can be modern and effective; certainly, video-tape can catch many of the details of an experiment that a written report might miss. But video-tape can be worse than a written report unless the camera operator is a skilled and creative individual. Certainly, a speech using two or more screens to get visual effects can be highly effective. Not only can you leave each visual on for some time while you change the other, you can also artistically combine and play "games" with the images, setting them off one against the other. But you still must weld the speech and the images into a creative whole. You must supply more creative ideas, work harder and be more skillful than when you prepare a single visual presentation. Thus, the cost, the effort, the work required, as well as the creative demands, are multiplied in comparison to the simpler and more direct means of delivery. This does not excuse, but explains the continued love-affair with the blackboard.

The camera and video open the door to events and new ways of conveying insights, not otherwise readily conveyed from human to human. In the age of television, our new generation has grown up with the "tube", the directness of the transmitted event. We must learn, we must make the effort to apply modern technology to our communication efforts. Yes it is difficult. It requires new skills, greater efforts, but it is well worth it. The video screen can be for the professional of the future what the black-board was for him in the past. Video can take over just as the electronic calculator has replaced the slide rule. We live in a decade in which the media have reached a high degree of influence. To compete with the success of the public media, our successful communication must take advantage of the opportunities offered by their tools.

We are exposed to public media every waking moment of our lives. To live creatively we must make a choice. Just as in perception we learn to select, so we must take from the media what is good for us, what aids us to develop creatively, what helps our communication needs. However, we must exert self-control. The temptation is great to listen to the same news over and over again, to fritter our time away.

Just as verbal language captivates us, can become a world unto itself, different from the real world, so the media have a captivating effect. There is a media world of TV, radio and printed matter that is not necessarily the real world. Just as the language map does not always correspond to the territory, so the media map, the world of images, and press stories, is not the real world. The creative individual knows how to relate this media world to the real world. He lives in the real world, in this wonderful nature and culture of our times, and he uses the worlds of language and the media world for what they are: Tools, mirrors, images — not reality. He grows creatively with the real world's territory, not the maps which attempt and sometimes succeed to represent it.

EXERCISES

To improve your listening, write down key words during the next five lectures you attend.

After the next three meetings you attend, prepare minutes for yourself of the significant items you heard.

On your next airplane trip get to know at least one fellow passenger. Put him or her at ease, then listen.

Volunteer to speak, you have something interesting to say. Use the creative problem solving process to arrive at a topic, an outline, a title. Define your message, the purpose of your talk.

Analyze your audience. Number, age, background, attitude. Get specific information.

Be aware, endeavor, during your next ten face-to-face communications, to assure ring closure for success. Make the other persons participate. Ask at least three questions to determine whether you have been understood.

Brainstorm titles for a luncheon talk. Decide on the topic, then write down 20 original titles. Alternately leave the topic open. Write down 30 original titles and topics.

Collect 100 jokes suitable for livening up your oral presentation. Collect 30 short episodes, illustrating some thought or other that appeals to you.

You have some convincing to do, be it your boss, your husband, or your son. Prepare 3 simple visuals to make your points.

Select 6 examples of your recent writings. Check for content. Did you tell them what you were going to tell them, then did you tell it to them, and did you tell them again what you told them?

Think of an extra, some way to be different, when you appear in public. An elegant, beautifully tailored or colored jacket? What is "your" style. Practice it.

RECOMMENDED READING

Merrill R. Abbey, "Man, Media and the Message", Friendship Press, New York, 1960.
Mortimer J. Adler and Charles Van Doren, "How to Read a Book", Simon and Schuster, New York, 1972.
Fred M. Amram and Frank T. Benson, "Creating a Speech", Charles Scribner and Sons, New York, 1968.

Thomas E. Anastasi, "Face-To-Face Communication: How to Manage Your Speaking", Management Center of Cambridge.

Taylor Caldwell, "The Listener", Doubleday, 1960.

John Halverson and Mason Cooley, "Principles of Writing", MacMillan, New York, 1965.

W. F. Keefe, "Creative Listening for Better Management", McGraw-Hill, New York.

Norman Lewis, "How to Read Better and Faster", Thomas Y. Crowell, New York.

W. A. Mambert, "Presenting Technical Ideas: A Guide to Audience Communication", John Wiley & Sons, Inc. New York, 1968.

Jud Morris, "The Art of Listening", Doubleday, 1960.

Sidney Passman, "Scientific and Technological Communication", Pergamon Press, New York, 1969.

Robert R. Rathbone, "Communicating Technical Information", New York, 1972.

Taylor Caldwell's book is enjoyable and makes thoughtful reading. The student workbook "Creating a Speech" applies the lessons of creative problem solving to speaking, it is well worth your while.

CHAPTER 12

OCTUPUS WORLD: ORGANIZING FOR PROGRESS

The need for organization.
Meetings and frustration.
The leadership complex.
Image and "brownie points".
Suggestions please.
People working together.

Participation for results.
Project organization.
Freedom and restraint.
Management by exception.
Make your boss look good.
The human chemist.

The creative loner can still accomplish great deeds in our day and age. There will always be a place for the isolated genius, however, we live in a crowded world. Change alone, the ever-new surroundings, the changes in values, needs, expectations, demands, introduce pressures, make creative problem solving, creative living, an ever more difficult task. Problem complexity requires a pooling of talents; creative humans working together to solve problems which individuals cannot readily cope with by themselves. This calls for organization.

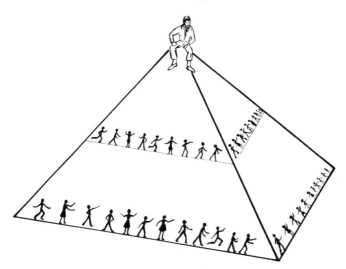

Organization is a combination of creative human talents, for a special one-time or for a continuing purpose. We think in terms of governmental organization, the state, the town, the county. We work or deal with business and educational organizations, the partnership, the corporation, the school district, the university, to mention only a few. Organizing for creative action can solve the most complex human problems. It has put men on the moon, almost eradicated polio and smallpox. Organizing for the wrong goals also has brought us a Hitler and two World Wars.

Organizing, combining several human beings into a constructive whole, means rules, means regulations, certain restrictions, for the individual human being. It is important that the act of organizing be carried out in such a way that creativity is not hindered but encouraged. Successful organization means fostering originality, encouraging creativity, rather than submerging it and blocking it.

Men cannot be ordered to invent, to be creative. However, men and women can be put together, allowing each of them to give the fullest scope to his or her creative possibilities. The group, the team, the organization can perform and function creatively.

Organization in itself is a constructive activity, even though organizations can be formed for harmful as well as beneficial effects. We can organize to feed the multitude or to rob them blind. The organization is not a goal in itself, organizing is a human tool to accomplish a purpose.

The creative organization is a function of:

Its goals and objectives,
The quality of its human talents,
The effectiveness of the combination,
The creative problem solving process.

Goals and objectives come first. Whenever an organization becomes a means unto itself, rather than a means to an end, it ossifies. Creative functioning is made difficult, if not impossible, when an organization considers itself more important than its goals.

Creative performance, functioning of any creative organization, demands direction, goals and objectives. The only reason for an organization's existence, whether it be a two-man partnership or the largest corporation in the country, is to achieve goals, solve problems, reach objectives, which cannot be accomplished by individuals.

Whether it be to supply us with food, energy, or leisure time entertainment, whether to keep our streets clean, or to protect us from thieves, our organizations, business, industrial, or governmental, are created, organized by individual creative human beings, for specific one-time or continuing purposes. There is no justification for the existence of an organization unless the purpose is recognized as real, and is being accomplished.

The perpetuation of purposeless organization is an ever present danger. Just think how hard it is to close down a governmental agency, once formed, even though the purpose for organizing it has long disappeared.

There is a tendency for organizational bodies to want to perpetuate themselves. This we must guard against. Good creative organization is a road to a goal, a vehicle to get there, not a goal in itself. An organization without a valid purpose is an empty shell.

The problem which requires the most exercise of our creativity, is the actual organizing process. How do we combine human talents in an optimum way to solve complex problems?

188

We want to combine these talents to:

Solve complex problems.
Exercise individual creativity.
Exercise group creativity.

In essence, we want to choose people and combine their talents, foster an environment which encourages the exercise of their creative talents, organize them to achieve a common goal.

Much has been done in the past which renders this problem more difficult today than ever before. We remember the dictators, and the villains of yesteryear, the robber-barons and the exploiters. We are also apt to think in terms of individuals, when we look into the past, for heroic deeds. We know little about the creative helpers, the members of their organization. One man stands out and contributors are soon forgotten.

We are apt to think in terms of a pyramid when we visualize organization. We think of the boss who runs things, the strong man who pulls all the strings.

Going back to the German military influence, we might also think in terms of line organization. The staff, when added to the pyramid of functional responsibility, gives expert advice. Staff organizations are teams of highly competent men and women who can study any subject in an expert fashion. They can explore in depth. The best talents are available for each complex segment of special problems.

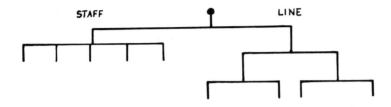

How do we organize for problem solving not only in space, but also in time? How do we combine human talents for the long pull, and on the other hand, for the specific demands of the day? Project "X", must be completed in three weeks, how do I organize for this specific need? We can see needs of project organization, different than the needs of longer range, more administrative organization. To the question of line and staff, we add the question of specific project as against more general administrative organization.

Finally, with larger organizations, we have to concern ourselves with the question as to how many people can constructively function with each other on a day-to-day basis. We have the question of large centrally organized bodies, as against the specific, the individual cell, which is of a certain size critical for accomplishment of the task, and not so large that creative cooperation is made difficult. Modern organizational ideas and theories favor project, cell-type, specific organization for well-defined tasks, fitted into the larger, longer range organization. They need to be arranged and organized in a compatible way.

To achieve results, to safeguard creativity, it must be realized that organizing itself is an exercise in creative problem solving. We want to use a number of people, select and combine them in an original fashion, and motivate them to creatively perform a complex task. Likely, we are going to organize not just for the moment, not for a frozen static picture, but for a constantly changing need, a dynamic objective.

Imagine casting a play for which the script has not yet been written. You need the best actors, you must select them well, and assign them their roles in the most creative fashion possible. You must spell out to them a creative purpose, lay down the rules.

In the modern organization, in the society of change, we cannot write the script. It is up to the players. That is why the choice of the performers is so vitally important. The success of an organization is a synergistic function of the combined talents of its members. It is a creative result, based on the selection of the human individuals and their creative capabilities. It is a composition, an artwork. Once assigned a role, the creative individual makes his own job. Do not ask, "What am I supposed to do", but ask yourself "What can I do to contribute in the most effective way". A great actor transforms his part to achieve his individual creative impact. There is the widest lattitude in any good organization for the contributor to make his mark, to go beyond the usual, the expected, to participate in a creative original fashion.

Just as the organization rightly considers its contributors, its professionals, as assets, so the individual creative professional must consider his organization as a major asset for the exercise of his creative potential. Like a doctor makes use of a hospital to exercise his profession of medicine, so we use our organizations, be it a chemical laboratory, the teaching department of a university, or the local bank.

We are part of the total scene, part of a system. We rely on the other participants, the members of the team, the fellow workers in our organization, who enable us to make our creative contribution. It is project performance more than performance on demand. A creative organization works best by cooperation, rather than by the pressures of power or authority. Even if the structure of the organization might grant you the power, it is better to rely on cooperation.

When my oldest son returned from Viet Nam, we discussed how difficult it was to get things done under conditions existing during the reduction of American forces there. I asked how he, as an Army officer, was able to get such a high degree of cooperation from many people in different units. "That was easy", he replied, "Everybody had a jeep, and our unit could get them fixed."

Cooperation is the key to good organization. It makes the other fellow look good, makes him feel wanted. Help him, and he will cooperate, together you will be able to achieve creative results.

Creative people perform best in an environment which requires much of them, they seek a challenge. The orgainization is set up to work on established goals. The individuals are assigned specific roles. As a result there must be some rules. Rules must be strict enough to prevent abuses, to maintain control, but flexible enough to allow free and creative input of personal contributions. Rules can strangle an organization, if they do not keep up with change. They can stifle individual performance. Rules, by nature, are past-oriented. Creative, original performance, on the other hand, is future-oriented. Rules must be subject to change, with changing conditions.

The creative organization is "change-rule" oriented. It is created to achieve a dynamic objective. It serves to cope with complexity beyond the individual's capability. The result, the goal, the objective is dominating, it is the sole reason for an organization's existence.

Choice of creative participants and the assignment of their roles within the organization determines the success of the total. While synergy, accomplishing more than just adding talents, can readily result from organizing, each individual contributor and the extent of his creative talents is of vital importance. Organizational mechanism, line, staff, project organization, are tools that may be manipulated to achieve optimum cooperation. However, it is the people, not their combination, that counts most. Success will be determined by the individual talents of the people available.

Rules are necessary to maintain control and prevent abuses in any organization. However, rules should be drawn and administered in a fashion that provides for adaptation to changing conditions and allows greatest possible freedom. We need an environment favorable to the free exercise of individual and group creativity.

The organization uses many communication tools, many methods to foster co-operation, to stimulate constructive working relationships for the common goal. Most widely used, probably most widely misused, is the "meeting". We do not use meetings, business meetings, political meetings, governmental meetings, as an effective means of creative endeavor. How good are *you* in meetings? Do you participate constructively? Are you able to get others to contribute? Are you able to keep a meeting from going astray?

Sadly enough, in our culture, we are meeting-prone. We appoint a committee, call a meeting at the drop of a hat. We call meetings to prevent action, to escape responsibility, to hear ourselves talk, to impress others. We call seemingly legitimate meetings for truly illegitimate purposes. We call and attend meetings, where nothing gets accomplished, and leave them frustrated and disappointed. We seem to have a knack at defeating synergy in meetings. We function at an ever-lower level of our capabilities, much more so than when we act alone. Sit back sometime at one of the meetings you attend regularly and listen. Does anybody talk to the purpose of the meeting? Are their or your comments contributing to solve the problems at hand?

We shy away, we avoid, we hesitate to attend the traditional business, government, even church meeting. Why? First of all, it is likely to be uninteresting. The good people do not speak up. When an idea is advanced, somebody is likely to ridicule it right away. You can hardly open your mouth before somebody interrupts you. Meetings are likely to stray and ramble. It is hard to determine the purpose for which you have come together.

These are only some of the feelings we are likely to share about going to meetings. Now, you would think that creative people, trained in the functioning of the creative process, could hold a successful meeting. After all, they are experienced in analyzing problems, they are taught to define a specific problem, then prepare properly to equip themselves with ammunition to solve the problem. They have even learned that after preparation, comes ideation, and from a wealth of ideas inspiration will select the best. Last, but most important, they have learned that action follows, that implementation is vital for the performance of the creative process. Why not apply these lessons to our meetings?

Sadly enough, human behavior is seriously affected by group influence. As soon as several of us get together, we act differently. Just as perfectly rational human beings turn into a lynch mob, so human behavior in meetings seems to undergo a not-so-subtle change. The individual is apt to forget the common goal, even though it has just been recited, even though it may be in front of him on the blackboard. Instead, he attempts to assume leadership, or he sits in his corner and sulks because

192

somebody else assumed leadership. All too often, the task of reaching a common understanding is submerged by ego-seeking, lack of individual control, and other detrimental attitudes. If I cannot have my way, I will not play.

We must get used to the idea, we must indoctrinate ourselves, we must realize as creative individuals that to hold a constructive meeting it is necessary to submerge our individuality. We must control ourselves, we must want to be part of the group. We must realize that a constructive meeting is a team effort, a common undertaking. Together we want to accomplish a, b, and c. To accomplish as much as possible, we require a common understanding, a consensus as the basis for action. There is no room for individual feelings, for self-seeking, for hostilities, even for friendships in a good meeting. We are trying to establish common ground, share information, establish a well-reinforced ring of communication. Together we are engaged in creatively solving problems, assure action. The good meeting must stress the positive, it must create the proper environment for the fullest contribution by any participant. It must creatively build contributions, one on another, and oppose all negative influences.

The good meeting is not only an exercise in good communications, it is even more so an exercise in good behavior. The success of any meeting is based on our ability to control ourselves, to assure an unselfish constructive input to the common undertaking.

Some suggestion might be in order to make your meetings more creative. First of all, avoid meeting unless there is a real need to meet. The monthly staff meeting must have a purpose. It must be worth the time, it must be interesting, it must be significant. Do not call a meeting unless there is a need.

Meetings get more difficult as far as constructive results are concerned, in direct relationship to their size. Therefore, keep your groups small, select the attendees, the contributors, according to their ability to contribute to the purpose of the meeting. Unless absolutely necessary sending representatives of two organizational levels to the same meeting should be avoided. You *or* your boss should go, but seldom both of you. Do not go to a meeting just because you feel every level of the organization must always be represented. You have more important things to do.

Do not double up, and do not fill your meetings with representatives of organizational segments just for organization's sake. If somebody is needed, he can be called to the meeting. Do not tie up people's time, when they are not needed.

Observe the rules of creative problem solving. Define the problem, prepare before the meeting. Agree on the leader, so that leadership fights can be avoided. It is important to solve the problem together, not who is the leader. A meeting must be a group effort; it does not matter who contributes, not how much you contribute. Establish common ground, communicate, solve the problem. Keep supervision out of a problem solving session. Use specific, creative problem solving techniques for those meetings where they are applicable. Synectics can help to select new products, establish new services, and similar problems of the future. They lend themselves specifically to the creative problem solving technique. However, in the day-to-day activities of your organization, even the seemingly most routine meetings can be conducted in a creative manner, then can be a success.

You may be in the position of leadership, either through choice, by reason of organization, or by agreement of the participants. If this is the case, remember that this is an exercise in creative communications. You must establish common ground, close and reinforce the ring of understanding. You are the catalyst. It is your task to keep the wheel spinning. Encourage questions, ideas, comments, but *never, never* cut short or *ridicule* anybody's contribution. No contribution is too small, no contribution too negligible. It may carry the seed for the ultimate breakthrough.

As during ideation, a meeting calls for reinforcement, cutting off or premature criticizing, can be fatal. A critique, even when called for during the selection part of the meeting should never be personal. Ideas, comments, all contributions to the meeting should be kept as impersonal as possible. Avoid falling into the trap of defending your idea at the expense of others. Avoid identifying with an idea, a solution, a criticism. There is no room for partisans, for advocates in a well-conducted meeting.

Keep in mind that all participants at the meetings are different. Each one is a unique human being. Some are slow thinkers, others react quickly. Some talk readily and freely, some are reticent, and do not speak up without encouragement. Your job as a leader is to bring their talents into play, to facilitate their contributions to the common goal. Do not just call on the favorite few. A good device that overcomes shyness and lacks any flavor of favoritism, is to ask for comments going around the room. Thus, each of the participants can have the chance to speak up, to contribute. The success of the meeting depends on making everyone, each individual contribute. Only if the individual has contributed, feels part of the meeting, can he be expected to support the conclusions and actions.

The leader must clearly state, and possibly re-state, the purpose of the meeting. If a meeting starts with a problem analysis, the problem definition arrived at should be spelled out clearly. The use of visuals is recommended. Keep the goal before everyone on a poster, a chart, or the blackboard. As you arrive at partial answers, at conclusions, or as you gain a multitude of ideas, post them, put them before the meeting. Display them in a visual way.

Keep the meeting going. Ask questions. Assure that communication has been established, that common meanings have been reached. Keep pointing the meeting towards its action goal; what next? What is going to be done as a result of this meeting?

If you have not appointed a secretary to take minutes, at least record the action items. Get agreement, and spell the agreement out clearly in writing. Be sure that each participant and anybody else who needs to, is properly informed as to the consensus, the action items.

Meetings can be conducted constructively. They must be oriented towards a common goal. Their purpose and intent must be clarified and properly stated as early as possible. The individual must participate as a team player, interested in common success, not to favor his own individual image or recognition of accomplishment. Original approaches, interesting topics, special visuals, are needed to make the meetings interesting. An outside viewpoint, a guest may add much to the flavor. Nail down the action items, as consensus becomes established. The meeting has a purpose; see that it is accomplished. Even a small step forward is better than standing still, or moving backwards. Meetings can be fun. It is possible to introduce an element of play, possibly some competition or humor, some lighthearted spirit for common motivation. Generate a common sense of accomplishment, so that each one may leave the meeting feeling that his time was well spent.

Not only at meetings is the creative individual apt to be affected by being a member of an organization, affected strongly the larger, the more complex the organization of which he is a part. How can we handle creative people in a creative way? How can creative people perform creatively as members of a large organization?

Management, administration, supervision, guidance, leadership: these are the people problems in the modern organization. The more complex your organization, the more difficult the task it must accomplish, the more the exercise of creative skills is required. People problems will affect significantly the performance of the overall task. Creating an environment, in which creative individual effort and creative group effort can fully contribute to the common goal, is a "must" for human progress.

Creative solution of these problems requires starting at your own personal end. You may not be able to move the mountain towards you, but you can move yourself to the mountain. When I was a student in Paris, I had a summer job with a chain of stores selling hats and caps. My first experience was being assigned to a workshop in which old hats were cleaned and re-blocked. I was sent to a converted apartment in the tenement district, and was received with displeasure by a huge, formidable old Frenchman with a large white beard. He was the proper embodiment of the old style autocratic, dictatorial boss of yesterday. The few employees in the shop were in almost mortal fear of the old tyrant, who had complete power over their livelihoods. It wasn't much of a livelihood. No chance of changing him. The only thing to do was pitch in, work hard, and act as if I didn't know that the last thing he wanted, was having a foreign student in his shop. When I left, many weeks later, he even granted me a few friendly words.

Much has been changed since the thirties. In the intervening years, the work-or-starve philosophy of that decade has been replaced by a philosophy recognizing the society's, the state's responsibility to each of its members. Many a newly-appointed supervisor still has, however, visions of having people to order around. He might like to handle people like that old tyrant did. This is not for today. Today creative style supervision is not to command, but to want to work with your people, to encourage them, to help them, to advise and direct them, not to order them around.

Work at any level is a contribution, whether it be better garbage collection, which means cleaner and healthier places for people to work and live in, or whether it be the design of a space laboratory. Any job is a good job, and can be creatively fulfilled.

Getting results not only directly but indirectly through others, is an extension of your creative self. In some way or other, most of us are responsible for not only our own actions, but in a limited fashion, for the actions, the success, the performance of others. Whether we are supervisor or group leader, team captain, teacher, marketing director, research manager, clerk of court, judge, or just a member of a family, we have authority over and responsibility for others. We can be creative in our relationships with these creative beings.

First and foremost, we must act in an open-minded fashion. We must show a willingness to say "yes" rather than "no". We must be constructive rather than critical or analytical. We must encourage rather than discourage. To assist the individual in developing and utilizing his full creative potential, we must be positive not negative. Maybe you are concerned about the consequences, but unless you are sure of a debacle, it might be better to let the co-worker gain the experience. He needs to learn for himself. He should experience the pleasure of success, even though there is a risk of failure.

Exercise that balance between encouragement and wisdom, which allows the necessary control and discipline without foreclosing original ways of solving the problem. Creative supervision is the ability to establish an atmosphere in which originality is encouraged. Creativity must be allowed free rein even at the expense of a few failures. New ways of doing the routine, of solving old problems are all around us. Encourage those who are willing to try an original attack. Business and governments are serious activities, not happenings, but this should not foreclose novel ways of solving problems, of making progress. The television camera can improve and assist courtroom procedure, the computer can facilitate police work. The electronic calculator not only can, but has displaced the slide rule.

Keep in mind the very important balance between substance and style. Each job, each problem, has a facet of substance, a facet of style. To borrow a phrase from the modern artist, most jobs have form and content. If you are an engineer, the way you propose a plan for a project is form, is style, the technical detail, the soundness of the project is content, is substance. You hold weekly group meetings; that is your style, your form. The technical substance and success of these meetings is content. Some assignments, problems, jobs, are truly machine problems. You can not readily apply your creative talents, to the substance of these problems. However, almost always there remains room for originality to be applied to the form, the style.

Substance comes first; first: focus and substance; then: flair and style. First: "knowing what to do"; then: "trying how to do". The goal, the purpose, is foremost. While an effective style is to be encouraged, people should not become prisoners of either procedure or form.

Value a demanding environment! Creative people, with few exceptions, work better under pressure, often self-generated pressure. The dedicated, able, creative individual wants and demands pressure of the right kind and at the right time. He likes challenges, he wants to be called upon for more. He wants to contribute in ever-increasing amounts. It is especially important to issue challenges which will allow the creative individual to grow in experience. Experience comes from experience. It is through doing and learning by doing, that you and those for whom you are responsible can do more.

Delegation is the key to organizational success. Assign responsibility and give a clear understanding of your expectations. The creative leader will multiply his own effort through delegation to others. He will extend himself way beyond what a single individual can do.

In a very nice and interesting letter, published in the September 1968 issue of Science and Technology, the author addresses a friend who has just assumed technical managerial responsibility. He states.

"You will now have 50 pairs of hands, rather than just one, with which to carry out your experiments. You can be in on the analytical and decision-making phase of many projects, rather than just a few. You will be interacting with good technical minds, with your men at the moment of their peak involvement, with their own problems."

Creative management of creative individuals means catalysis. Creative supervision is not looking down from the top of a pyramid. It is not the quarterback of a football team, looking at his line, he only sees their behinds. For a truly creative view of supervision, you turn the problem upside-down. Think of yourself carrying your organization on your shoulders. If you look at supervision upside-down, if you look up at your co-workers, at those to whom you have delegated responsibility you will be a successful manager, a motivating leader of men.

Consider the lines of an organization chart not only as lines of authority but also as lines of responsibility, lines of helpfulness, lines requiring creative catalytic input. It is for this reason that management training today requires an understanding of human behavior, an understanding of the ways to motivate human beings to use their fullest creative potential.

Good management is not only concerned with the people we are responsible for, it must also be concerned with the people we are responsible to. Most of us, in the large organizations that are the hallmark of modern society, are both boss and employee, both supervisor and supervised, both foreman and worker.

Just as we examined a creative relationship with our co-workers who are our responsibility, so we must consider our responsibility towards our supervisor, our boss. Remember, creative people-problem-solving, involves primarily ourselves.

It is our job to make the boss look good. In any organization, this must be a basic concept. A successful job makes the boss look good. Keep in mind: "He is the boss". He is extending his creative capabilities through you and you are there to cooperate to perform in a way that will make him successful. This seemingly obvious truth is often neglected. Feelings, vanity, ego . . . we forget that we are there to "Make the Boss look good".

Actually, in most organizations, the better you do the job, the less you are apt to see the boss, or experience his direct action, as far as your job is concerned. In the complexity of the large modern organization, the most frequently practiced management style is that of "Management by Exception". This means your boss delegates the job to you; you do it creatively in your own way. He will enter the picture only if major or unusual decisions are necessary, or if you are in trouble. Management by exception means, no interference if the job runs well, management enters only in the exceptional case, when it is needed. This allows you the greatest creative latitude in the performance of your tasks. This also means that you keep your boss well-informed, but request his decisions, his assistance, his time, only when it is truly required. Equally, you will not provoke a crisis unless it is necessary.

Respect and appreciate your manager, the width of his knowledge, the breadth of his responsibilities, the pressures he works under. Assist him; help him. Do not add to his burden unless it is necessary and important. Never, never fight with your boss, unless you are ready to take the consequences. Make sure the goal, the objective, is worth the depth and seriousness of the disagreement you may have with him.

Many years ago, working for a very outstanding and distinguished man, I was engaged in the start-up of a new plant. He had the overall responsibility, but was geographically located many hundreds of miles away. A serious disagreement arose between engineering and the start-up team over a pump packing. All attempts at getting the boss to resolve the agreement in the required fashion were fruitless. I ended up shouting at him over the telephone in order to get a proper solution. I am convinced today, that this was necessary to get him to act, to get him to recognize the seriousness of the disagreement. However, I believe he never quite forgave me, even though the decision saved much time and several hundreds of thousands of dollars. Support your boss whenever you can. Weigh the importance of any disagreement.

Supervising creative people, then, means participation and acting as a catalyst. Decisions must not be arbitrary or unilateral. The supervisor is often the intermediary, the communicator, rather than the agent or representative of top management. He acts as a friend in both directions, with his boss, and with his creative people. Understanding of the creative process is vital. It leads to the application of pressures, as well as to the use of patience. Remember, "creativity" is not continuously on tap, it is apt to occur in spurts. Think of possible barriers to creativity, and help to remove them, cultivate an understanding and tolerance for the creative temperament.

Especially in the scientific field, highly creative people often have the image of primadonnas, of strangeness. The public folklore pictures the creative individual in all kinds of ways not very attractive to management. This may require counter-action, correcting the false picture which your boss and management associates may hold of the creative people working with you. Their creativity, their contributions are vital to the success of the common endeavor. You must build bridges between some of your more temperamental creative individuals and the rest of the organization. It is a must, because no creative organization can exist without allowing for the individual values, the individual self-expressions, even the peculiarities of some of the creative contributors. A modern successful organization must allow for treatment of human beings as individuals. The supervisor of creative people must learn to handle each of them individually, and his management must allow him to do so.

The need for the highest competence and creative ability at all levels of the modern organization is self-evident. One of the most difficult creative problems is to be solved is the proper assignment of projects and responsibilities. It is the problem to which a good manager can make his greatest contribution. If you can select the individual properly, and make him feel a strong personal affinity towards a given project, if you can assign and motivate him to consider the project his own, he will be able to perform in the best possible and in the most creative fashion. Fascination, self-identification with the problem, other things being equal, is highly correlated with creative success.

Problems exist not only with the assignment, with the turning over of a project, but also with the termination, the taking away of a project. Taking away ideas from a creative specialist while he is still working on developing, or polishing the project, undermines his professional pride. It may cause resentment and hostility endangering future successes. On the other hand, the manager cannot wait too long after the idea has yielded to inspiration. Further action must follow, or else this can be again mis-interpreted as a lack of appreciation for the creative individual and his successful ideation. Thus, project assignment, project forward movement and termination of projects represent difficult exercises in creativity for the manager.

Another interesting problem arises from the desire of the creative individual to have as much freedom as possible. Freedom is a much-misused word. Most creative scientists, engineers and creative individuals in general insist on a high degree of freedom for creative work. On the other hand, an environment of urgency and certain pressures are known to stimulate creativity. Freedom first of all means encouragement to come up with new ideas and venturesome approaches. The creative individual wants to be truly treated in a professional way, not held back. He does not want to be pulled on a leash, nor harnessed. He must be left free to exercise his creativity towards the common goal.

Freedom means that while truly creative people always work best under pressure and with a sense of urgency, it is desirable that the pressure come as much as possible from within, that it be problem-generated, rather than generated by the supervisor. Once problems, projects and responsibility have been properly assigned, the supervisor can assist best by suggestions, by support, by smoothing the way, by providing inter-action with others, by removing time barriers. Active interest will accomplish a great deal more in dealing with the creative professional than requests, demands or orders.

199

The manager will provide not only encouragement, but inspiration. It is human nature that we are always ready to criticize, to correct or to complain when something is done wrong. The supervisor's natural inclination is to correct a mistake, to use it as an example to train for better performance. Far too seldom do we encourage, praise, or commend. The creative supervisor avoids criticism. While mistakes may have to be pointed out, there should not be any unnecessary emphasis. Praise is what really motivates, encouragement is what truly helps the creative individual.

Even after twenty-five years I have not forgotten the man in our company, who first was kind and considerate enough to write me a short note, when I was a young technical man. He stated simply that he enjoyed and profited from one of the few reports that I had written at the time. Encouragement, praise, has the beneficial effect of bolstering the confidence, the courage of your colleagues. This is particularly important when the going is rough, or if the performer is young and relatively inexperienced. Difficult problems yield their fruits with reluctance, any encouragement even only friendly interest, will be of benefit.

The supervisor, by personal evidence of optimistic courage, can do a great deal to prevent premature discouragement. He can keep the co-worker from giving up. One of the finest men I ever had the pleasure to work with, would come around smiling and cracking jokes, when he knew that things were going wrong. In fact, we used to tease him when he would smile, as to what was wrong today. His influence was tremendous.

Praise and one word of encouragement is worth ten criticisms. Very important: if you do have to criticize, do it tactfully, and especially do not criticize in front of others. "Criticize privately, praise publicly." The creative individual, even more than one whose creativity is not so pronounced, seeks recognition and is very sensitive to criticism.

Finally, when supervising creative people, one must be willing to put himself into the background. The creative supervisor must give credit to others, even though much of the credit may be his just due. The supervisor must be seen by his staff, by his co-workers, as a selfless, confident, alert individual, who puts their concerns above his own. Mutual confidence, mutual support and respect will pull any group together, will allow it to achieve creative results.

It is obvious that when working with creative people, communication is of utmost importance. All the lessons of communication will play a role in a creative working relationship.

Organization, a necessity, can be handled in such a way as to encourage creative group and creative individual efforts. It must not and should not stifle creativity. In the laboratory of organization, the supervisor, the manager, works like the chemist with a hundred human elements. If you possess the skills to combine them, you can produce food, drink, medicine, anything and everything of a material nature needed by mankind. Combine them in an undue way, and you produce an explosion. You can generate people problems which are beyond your ability to handle. The fault is not with the elements, but with the chemist; not with the people, but with the manager. The creative manager who succeeds in managing creative people is like the great chemist. He finds the right combinations, he carries out the proper reactions to get the desirable end result. He is a skilled creative practitioner in "human" chemistry.

EXERCISES

The next three meetings you attend, count the number of negative remarks, the cutoffs and premature judgments.

Before each meeting you call or preside over in the next three months, work out the purpose in advance on one sheet of paper. Check after the meeting whether it has been accomplished.

You ask somebody to do something. Write it down. Go over the write-up with him or her. Then hold yourself back, do not interfere any further for at least three days. Check your own reactions. Did you want to stay in the act?

Analyze, visualize, and group your relationship to the various organizations you participate in. Consider line, staff, project organization.

Draw an "upside-down" organization chart for yourself, your boss, one of your friends.

RECOMMENDED READINGS

Peter F. Drucker, "Management", Harper and Row, 1974.
John F. Fendrock, "Managing in Times of Radical Change", American Management Association, 1971.
Ralph M. Hower and Charles D. Orth, "Managers and Scientists", Harvard University, 1963.
Rensis Likert, "The Human Organization", McGraw-Hill, 1967.
James L. McKenney, "Simulation Gaming for Management Development", Harvard University, 1967.
Eugene Randsepp, "Managing Creative Scientists and Engineers", MacMillan, 1963.
Auren Uris, "Mastery of Management", Dow Jones – Irwin, 1968.

Peter Drucker's writings need no recommendation. Auren Uris' book is of special value, both as to its content and its method of presentation. His way of making the reader participate is especially noteworthy.

CHAPTER 13

DISCOVERY, INVENTION AND INNOVATION

Finding the truth.
Something new and useful.
Significant change.
Acceptance of a new order.
Forging links in the chain.

The passionate undertaking.
Risk and uncertainty.
The skills required.
Organizing for progress.
Time and patience.

The creative horizons of mankind are unlimited. This unique species, throughout its known history, has wrought wonders. From the caves of primitive man, to the conquest of the moon, humans have moved to ever-widening horizons. The wheels of progress are governed not by material limitations but by the boundaries of his potential, and the limitations of the individual. Discovery, invention, innovation . . . the sky is the limit. Only our feet of clay hold us back. Gloom and doom propaganda, the beat of frustrating news, endless stress on the negative, those are the chains that delay us, that slow and impede our forward movement. We can be mired in discouragement, succumb to hopeless attitudes, or we can free our creative talents, know that we will succeed. We will float above the barriers pleasurably free of all those self-made traps that are obstacles to discovery, invention, and innovation.

Discovery is *finding a truth*, locating something that is inherent in nature and society, a condition or reality that already exists. Science studies realities and it looks for truth and finds it in discovery. So does the law, in its search for justice.

Discovery has flourished greatly in the last few decades. Nine out of every ten scientists born into this world, are living today. However discovery in all fields has barely scratched the surface. We may have made great strides since the beginning of the century and especially in the last thirty years, but our knowledge, our understanding of truth is like a drop of water compared to the sea. Creative opportunities to discover new truths are everywhere in limitless numbers. In my field, Chemistry, every new piece of knowledge, every new truth learned, seems to pose numerous new questions, open up numerous new opportunities for discovery.

Our knowledge in most any field of human endeavor seems just an invitation for further creative search. Many basic questions escape our full understanding completely, such as time, human behavior, perception, transparency, nucleation, animal and plant life, to mention only a few. From the discovery of a new species of butterfly to radiation phenomena on the moon, there is no limit to future discovery.

Even though the process of discovery is searching for truth, for existing realities, for present hidden knowledge, it is a highly creative one. In fact, without the application of our fullest creative potential, discovery is left to chance and luck, important but limited tools for our extensive needs.

Invention, the application of our creative powers to *bring about something new and useful*, is generally considered, at least in the public's mind, the key to progress. Edison, Alexander Graham Bell, and other inventors are better know than most discoverers with the possible exception of Columbus and Einstein. The inventor holds a romantic spot in our world of images. He can easily be one of our heroes. Invention, inventorship, is a well-established goal of human endeavor. Invention has been enobled by social recognition. Our state has given it respectability by dealing with it in the constitution and by presenting each successful inventor with an elaborately decorated document called a patent.

Society is willing to encourage the inventor by granting him special rights in the exploitation of his invention. Society needs the new technology, the answers to its problems. Inventorship is creative performance, officially endorsed and documented. Still, the inventor, not only in this country today, but all over the world, complains bitterly about the barriers to success which society places in his way. Part of the complaint of the modern inventor is due to his inability: "not to invent", but to: "see something done with his invention". He invents a better mousetrap, but he cannot sell it. The invention ends with the issuance of a patent and nothing further happens. If the inventor doesn't have the necessary financial support, it may even be difficult for him to obtain a patent, since the filing process in most countries today is a lengthy and costly one.

Invention may be stymied, may be stopped, may be halted without the initiation of further changes, because the invention is really not worthwhile. The contribution to mankind, to society, is not sufficient to warrant any further activity. Clearly, many patents are in this category. I must admit, of my many patents, the majority could rightly be classified in this way. At the same time the invention was made, it was new, original, and potentially useful, a valid patent. It was new technology. However, it was not useful enough to warrant further action, to justify exploitation. Needless to say, few inventors will admit to themselves and to others that their latest invention is not really worthy of further effort.

Many inventions are out of phase with reality. They need a champion to bring their value to the surface. They call forth, they require the innovator. *Innovation* is *significant*, constructive *change for humanity*. It is the essence of progress. Without innovation, we not only stagnate, but quickly slide back to the stone age. Innovation, invention and discovery are linked to each other. Innovation is the arch built on the cornerstones of discovery and invention. Lagging discovery and invention will make successful innovation difficult. In the long run, innovation is unthinkable without a flourishing state of the sciences and humanities on the one hand, and creative inventorship and technology on the other.

Not only in the technical, but also in the commercial, the social and the cultural arena, discovery and invention are only the foundation of innovation, of progress. Discovery and invention may light the fuse to the rocket but it takes the rocket — innovation — to reach the sky.

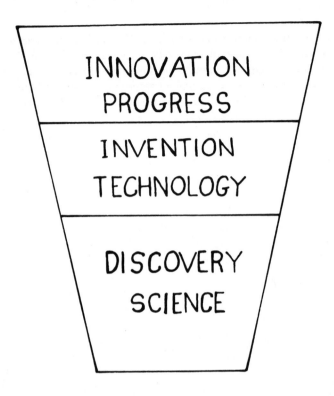

INNOVATION
PROGRESS

INVENTION
TECHNOLOGY

DISCOVERY
SCIENCE

The Supreme Court's desegregation decision, certainly a discovery of truth, put the U.S. on the road to major, significant social and cultural changes, but it took a long, arduous process of innovation for these changes to fully materialize. In fact, this innovation process is still in progress.

The invention of the transistor was a starting point for many of today's innovations, such as the electronic calculator and other solid state devices. However, without the separate and distinct efforts of numerous innovators, without their extensive innovative contributions, significant constructive change might not have occurred.

Innovation is the essence of progress. Discovery and invention cannot move us forward without innovation, significant constructive change-making. This holds for all areas of human activity: Government, education, the law, finance, business, and industry, even the arts.

Innovation is the payoff, and thus deserves our most creative attention and support. Innovation is the creative process by which we put the world together in a new way. Innovation is bringing significant constructive change to society. Innovation whether commercial, technical, social, cultural, or artistic is breaking new ground for progress and a challenging and different life.

We must be innovators to control our fate. History has shown again and again that we can neither go back or stand still, without suffering. It is the lot of mankind, to move forward, to innovate, to progress, or to suffer misery, death, and extinction. The artist may show us beauty, the scientist truth; and the inventor the possibility of new materials and new processes, but it takes the creative contribution of the innovator to translate beauty, truth and novelty into significant change.

With his importance to humanity, to the survival of civilization, one would believe that the creative innovator be given the highest praise, a place of honor in history. Not so, scientists, the inventor, even the great individual artist, may be idolized. The innovator, the entrepreneur, seldom captures the imagination, seldom obtains the recognition and the thanks of his fellow man. The innovator is a man who takes something new and useful and overcomes the barriers that society puts up against innovation. He carries his task to a successful conclusion, not to the applause of society, but against its opposition and resistance.

Today as in times past most of mankind will react to major changes with considerable reluctance. We usually find innovation, significant change a painful experience. Man is a creature of habit; new experiences break up cherished patterns and disturb his equilibrium. The creative innovator has the ungrateful job of breaking the mold and showing new ways, establishing a forward tilt to human activities. While ordinary man will resist innovation with all his might, the creative individual can and should participate. He should feel proud to assist innovative efforts, rather than opposing them.

Creative reception of innovation, acceptance can be hard, difficult for all of us. An accountant friend of mind, who spent most of his creative life proud of his ability to make books "talk" had extreme difficulties coping with the introduction of new computerized accounting systems. A professor devoted his life to studying how to put together the small pieces of pottery available from ancient times. Then came the aqualung, and all of a sudden, vast numbers of undamaged vases were brought up from the bottom of the Mediterranean. The aqualung innovation made his work obsolete.

In the excellent movie, "Why Man Creates", there is a scene where a scientist gives up on a project after seven years. Negative results, dead end; he turns out the light, and walks out of the laboratory. What next? In this world of accelerated changes, where innovations daily affect all of us, the creative individual has to develop a special open-mindedness, a flexibility. He must cultivate the talent to cope with, to live with, even to support and participate in innovation, regardless of his own suffering as a result of the change.

We cannot afford domination by the established order. As Eric Hoffer said, "We can never be really prepared for that which is wholly new." Creative man must develop the inordinate self-confidence to face drastic change without turbulence. Change we must face, change we must live with, change we must creatively cope with.

The changing times require from all of us who are being innovated upon, from all of us subjects, us victims, and those who benefit from innovation, a positive attitude towards significant change. The times when people could escape from innovation have passed, our planet is too small, too crowded, too populated. We are too interdependent, the reach of modern transportation, the possibilities of the future are too vast to allow isolation and retreat. Change, innovation, is too all-pervasive throughout this world of ours.

The creative individual living within the innovative society must creatively respond to change. He must expect it, even train himself to enjoy it. That is the answer to "future shock". Enjoy, expect, work for and participate in innovation, in the progress of "your" society. Use your creative potential towards new developments, expect and savor change. You can live more than one life, you can enjoy being part of one innovation after another.

Some of the men I have most admired lived more than one life. One of these was a successful industrial executive who in his early fifties changed to academia, and played a significant role in the establishment of a new university. Another started out in science, formed a successful company, and later returned to academia again to lend his creative talents to the inspiration of the young. A third, an extremely competent technologist, had to learn four different fields and reached excellence in each one of them. Innovators, truly modern, flexible, perceptive, creative individuals make the world go around.

Yesterday's freedom becomes tomorrow's constraint. Energy and abundance gives way to conservation. A coal economy turns into an oil economy, and back to a coal economy. Jazz, rock, country music, revival of the classics, we can truly enjoy the variety of change and innovation. Tramways are replaced by cars, and cars give way to new automated public transportation systems. We must be able to change specialization or to participate and lead in more than one specialization during a lifetime. We must not fight the change-makers but assist them, not condemn the innovators but appreciate them.

The innovator has an almost impossible task. He must furnish the energy, the driving force, the motivation for change. He moves the mountains of inertia, security, tradition, and disbelief in the possibility and value of change. For all this he is seldom praised or reconized, or fully rewarded, even if successful. Many, for example the men that built the railroads and some of our great industries, are depicted as exploiters, robber-barons, who enriched themselves at the expense of others.

Unfair! The innovator plays a very important role in society. We owe him recognition, praise, thanks for what he does to keep humanity's existence viable. However, the innovator is really not motivated by enrichment, success, nor our recognition and thanks. His activity, innovation, entrepreneurship, like gambling, like mountain climbing, is an obsession, an activity which is motivation and reward in itself. Like soaring, innovation is a thrilling, a fulfilling experience in itself.

Picture the innovator as a man riding an avalanche, as a lion tamer. He is gambler, mountain climber and expert fisherman all rolled into one. His motivation and satisfaction is in playing the game; he enjoys, he thrives on the risks, the uncertainties, the failures, and the successes of the innovative process.

That is why the role of innovator, of entrepreneur appeals to highly creative people. That is why the innovator succeeds in fulfilling the excessive demands of the innovation process only through utmost use of his creative potential. Innovation, entrepreneurship, requires the full man, the complete man, the creator to a greater extent than in any other human activity. This holds for any type of innovation, whether it be technical, commercial, cultural, social or artistic. Innovation require undeterred optimism, a stubborn will to succeed, an almost anti-intellectual unreasonable faith in the capability of accomplishment.

An innovator whose company later became a valuable part of a big chemical company started a new line by selling a tank car of biphenyl without even knowing what this chemical was, how it could be made, and that it had never been made in larger than beaker quantities.

Like a man, obsessed, even like a man possessed, the innovator carries the torch past all the barriers, real or imagined. The urge to innovate, to effect a constructive and lasting, a significant change motivates his willingness to look past and through obstacles, the willingness to try, and try again.

Innovation, the life-blood of progress, is not restricted to any one field of human endeavor. In today's society particular interest is focused on technological innovation, significant and constructive change that has its roots or its reduction to practice in technology. Technological innovation has been defined as "the process by which an idea or invention is translated into the economy."

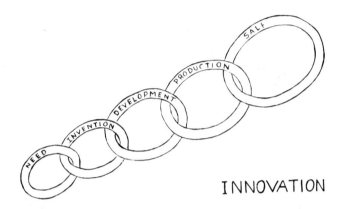

This process is composed of many steps, many fragile links in a chain that has to be forged in its entirety to be successful. Each of the links in the chain is vital to success. Only a complete, unbroken chain represents successful innovation.

The first link may be an invention, a technological opportunity, or maybe just a recognition of a human need. Major innovation may take place without a specific invention, or many inventions may be required along the way to make innovation possible. Thus the inventor can be the originator or he may be called upon in the middle of the chain to supply an important missing link.

The first link, the starting point, is often the recognition of a need, a market opportunity, a means of making a contribution to the consumer. The second link may be a way, a technology capable of filling the need. Ideally the start of innovation lies in the joining of these two links, the meeting between a need and the opportunity to fill it. Research in industry is aimed at forging these two links, making the creative effort of joining need and solution in an original way, bringing about effective surprise to generate innovation.

Forging this link demands cooperation, understanding, a constructive working relationship of the commercial man living amongst the "needs" and the technologist who can meet them with the "means". The commercial, the "real world" man sometimes has difficulties communicating with his technological counterpart and blames the scientist, the engineer for lack of recognition of the realities of the

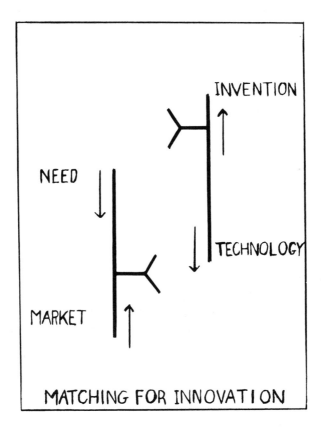

INVENTION

NEED

TECHNOLOGY

MARKET

MATCHING FOR INNOVATION

marketplace, lack of appreciation for the needs of the consumer. On the other hand, many technical professionals are prone to isolate themselves in their specialty, removed from the real needs of the public.

It is the innovator's job to serve as the catalyst, to coordinate, to forge the chain. He must study the needs, the opportunities, broaden them, manipulate them, move them until linking, a match, can be achieved. This is a true beginning of innovation.

There are many vital links in the innovation chain beyond the original concepts, that need to be developed. A feasibility study may be required. Development may be possible within the state-of-the-art, or uncertainties may exist, requiring new technology to assure feasibility of the innovation. Possibly additional creative contributions, inventions must be made. An early link in the innovation chain may well be funding of the necessary development expenses.

Links in the Innovation Chain
(An Example)

Recognition of Need	
Technological Opportunity	
The Entrepreneur	Concept
Initial Support and Funding	
Feasibility	
Design	
First Embodiment	Action
Prototype	
Test	
Trial	Evaluation
Social and Ecological Impact	
Continued Support and Funding	
Manufacture	
Marketing	Organization
Management	
Acceptance and Adoption	Implementation

A common link for most technological innovations is the prototype, the first useful demonstration of the innovation. Whether a product or a service, "doing it once" is apt to bring home that it can be done again. Vitally important is the concept of "doing" and "doing it simply" at this stage. Many an innovator has been blocked early by guesses and calculations, while an ingenious bit of action could have moved the innovation forward at slight expense.

Studies of innovations have shown that they take on a life of their own. Often success or at least initial promise is along different lines than anticipated even by the innovator.

In the successful introduction of the urethane industry to the United States through the transplanting of German know how, initital commercial success was not as anticipated in the urethane foams, but in wire coatings. Equally, the ultimate major success of the urethane foams in this country was based on polyether intermediates rather than on polyesters as employed in Europe.

Designs, prototypes are usually followed by test and tryout. This may be a test, a trial of manufacturing, of performance, or it may be a test of acceptance of salability, of use by the consumer in the marketplace.

There may be a need for new findings; there may be a link of organization. To the link of material assets, we may have to add the link of human assets, the necessary talents and skills. All these links may be interspersed at various points in the innovation chain.

With the tested working prototype comes the possibility of expansion. Totally new requirements arise in public relations, impact on society, on the environment, market introduction, and marketing as well as organizing for largescale manufacture. All these links finally lead to the successful adoption of the innovation, acceptance by those that benefit, and a profit to those who support it.

At this point, it is often desirable for the entrepreneur to seek new fields, new horizons, since his temperament, his inclination, his love is more in the promotion, the innovative process itself, than in the managing of the successful enterprise that he has created.

The innovator who gave us the long-playing record and the innovation of high--fidelity music in the living room was motivated by suffering through a symphony with the countless interruptions which the old style records entailed. He sold his idea against all the skepticism of the experts of the day, obtained financial support, built a team, and went to work. He overcame countless obstacles, developed new techniques, utilized inventions of others, including a new microphone just becoming available in Germany. He even catalyzed new inventions which became a vital part of the success of the hi-fi LP.

Successful technological innovation requires recognition that every link in the innovation chain is of vital importance. We need technological links in the invention, the manufacturing process, financial links, the development money, the original capital, and the money for growth. The key, however, to successful innovation lies totally in dealing with human beings. Acceptance in the marketplace, compatibility with the ecology, waste disposal, or cultural acceptability, all these are people problems.

The innovator's role is to assure that all the links are forged, that nothing is overlooked, that can hinder or prevent the innovation from being successful. Contrary to usual management tasks, which are manageable according to well recognized rules of cause and effect, or which recognize the normal risk taking so common to managerial decision-making, innovation takes place to a considerable degree in the sphere of "uncertainty".

The normal business organization and especially the big corporation, is not readily equipped for this job. It works on objectives, it wants measurement of results, it is designed to evaluate risk, to play the investment game, to bet in a careful manner. Uncertainty is a totally different affair. Here the odds are not known, the game does not lend itself to the usual way of playing it. You cannot manipulate your bet to improve your chances of winning. The only yardstick as to the probability of a new technical solution in the area of uncertainty, is the quality of your research organization. Adding more people will not make any difference. A hundred good engineers do not make up for the one genius who gets you from uncertainty unto the realm of risk.

Technological uncertainty involves the question of technical feasibility. "Can it be done", or more specifically, can it be done in the time and cost frame of the innovative process.

Thus, a successful LP required a new and improved microphone. The degree of uncertainty, whether a proper microphone could be developed, and the type of uncertainty, in fact that it was the microphone which was deficient, were unknown before and well into the innovative process.

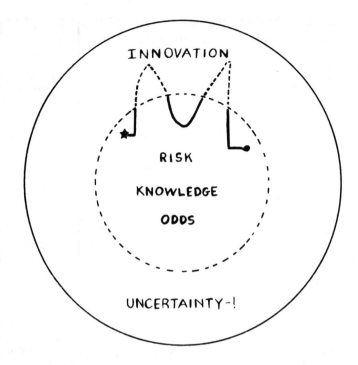

Technological risks and uncertainty today are seldom the task of individual inventors; groups of specialists, teams of well-trained technical contributors are required. They are creative, yes, but primarily equipped to be creatively effective in a limited field. Research and development, the translation of feasibility in the uncertainty region is expensive and requires organized effort.

Recent studies of the innovation process have brought us to the realization that technological uncertainty is not our only concern. In a broader view, we are always dealing with at least two kinds of uncertainty. Feasibility and acceptance . . . "can it be done" and "will it be accepted". Consideration of both these dimensions in technological innovation is a compulsory requirement today. What a waste of assets it would be if we developed an ingenious new product, only to discover that a simple study could have told us that it would be ecologically unacceptable or that the marketing problems are beyond our capabilities.

An excellent graphic device[1] and communication tool is the uncertainty chart used by Monsanto to bring out these considerations and put various projects into perspective.

---

[1] (Reference: M. C. Throdahl, MCM Meeting, New York, November 21, 1972. Also, Chemical News Interview with B. R. Williams, Chemical Week, February 28, 1973.)

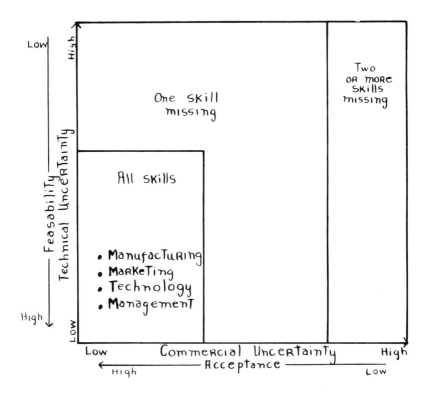

A successful project requires many skills in four key functions: "Manufacturing, marketing, technology, and management." In ongoing activities and their logical growth and extension, all four capabilities will be available. Thus, a new product with improved properties added to the line of an existing business group would fall in the lower left-hand box, with relatively limited technical and commercial uncertainties. Such projects can and do thrive in normal business surroundings.

Not so for projects with a high degree of technical or commercial uncertainty. These require special care, attention, special surroundings, which make creative innovation possible and compatible with the larger framework, with the objectives of the corporation. Many companies have special groups, special organization, to achieve this desirable result.

Creative understanding, creative leadership and participation in innovation requires emphasis of the all-important time factor. Contrary to media folklore, innovation requires a substantial investment in time. The 1973 National Science Foundation Study by Battelle: "Science, Technology and Innovation", showed that the time span from conception to realization was substantial, and not growing shorter as had been expected. For the 10 innovations examined, the average was about 19 years, the range from six to thirty-two years. A recent study of innovation in the British chemical industry[2] shows time periods of 9 years for a fine chemical, 14 years for a new drug, and 16 years for a new plastic.

In terms of creative participation this means understanding and patience. In terms of reconciling innovative efforts with current and shorter range objectives of an organization, it requires unselfish and farsighted management, since the individual terms of office of responsible executives in a given position seldom extends the full length of major innovative efforts. Most importantly, recognition of innovation as a long-term effort, brings realism to funding decisions. Continuity and stability are prime requirements of successful innovation. The innovation process is by nature lengthy, costly and time-consuming.

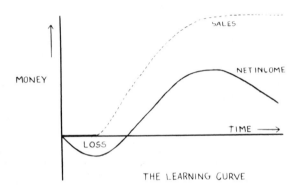

THE LEARNING CURVE

Not only extensive time periods but also considerable cumulative investment is required before the innovation can turn the corner and return its development costs and future profits to the organization. Major innovation will generate a very large negative cash flow before breaking even, and before profits can be realized.

Much has been learned in recent years through study of innovation but the record is as yet incomplete. One factor emerges clearly: The creative individual, whether as entrepreneur, as inventor, or as contributor, plays a key role. He occupies center stage in all successful innovations.

Our culture and society has been described as a "flow" society. It has been likened to a highway — one bottleneck, one accident, can bring to a halt or greatly slow the entire network. Thus, a few can affect our society, bring it to a halt, reverse progress, create havoc out of proportion to their numbers. Think only of modern day terrorism, plane hijacking or of our helplessness in the face of closed gasoline stations.

The flow society on the other hand, offers greater opportunity to each individual. Innovation is king. With the population explosion, media impact on human relations, increased activity in developing countries, and our expanding interna-

---

[2] (Reference: Alfred Spinks, Memorial Lecture, "The Changing Role of Chemistry and Product Innovation", Chemistry and Industry, September 15, 1973.)

tional trade, constructive change is more vital to mankind than ever before. The innovator has the world as his stage. Every creative individual, leader of, or subject to innovation can do his thing, make his contribution, participate in a creative, a positive way.

In the "flow" society the good and courteous driver, the flexible, humble, conscientious, interested, willing, creative individual keeps things moving and allows for constructive change. This contribution assures that we move up, not down.

Revolution, tearing down, may seem simple. Throwing a rock from a bridge onto moving traffic is not difficult. Attacking the hardworking, the busy, the creative, the innovator is the pasttime of the weak, of the incompetent. Our society, the world, needs positive action, new highways, better trains to avoid clogged traffic arteries. We need planes to fly over the stalled flow society. Innovations, solutions make the difference. Actions small or large speak louder than words.

Let me urge you to participate, to creatively get into the swing of it. Let me urge you that if you see a piece of paper or carelessly discarded beer bottle, pick it up — pick it up as a training act, if not as a participation in innovative endeavor. A highway sign I remember read: "The life you save may be your own". The Chinese have been respected for their patience in applying human endeavors to huge challenges, large dams, airports, highways, built by human hands using only primitive tools. It takes a large number of grains of sand to make a mountain, but every grain counts. The smallest link in the chain can be vital to its strength and performance.

In the "flow" society, our personal contribution is more vital than ever. The solutions for the future not only require technology but to a larger extent they require human behavioral changes. The radical drop in the death rate on the highway with the lower speed limits is a good example, that patience rather than killer impatience is a worthwhile innovation. Willingness to forego selfish needs for the common good are at the bottom of many innovations required for tomorrow. Dr. Glenn T. Seaborg, delivering the John Gardner lecture, said, "We are reaching a new stage in the development of man. One that involves new philosophy based on the different relationship between man and his planet, between man and his fellow man and aspiration and creative growth. We must find and practice this new humanity."

New solutions have to and will be found. One man's potential, each man's potential, is a driving force to constructive innovation. Your participation, your striving for excellence, will build the better future, the better world of tomorrow.

RECOMMENDED READING

Raymond M. Hainer, Sherman Kingsbury, and David B. Gleicher, "Uncertainty in Research, Management and New Product Development", Reinhold, 1967.
Christopher Layton, "Ten Innovations", George Allen and Unwin Ltd, 1972.
Robert Kirk Mueller, "The Innovation Ethic", American Management Association, 1971.

National Academy of Sciences, "The Process of Technological Innovation", 1969.

NBS Special Publication 388, "The Public Need and the Role of the Innovator", National Bureau of Standards, 1974.

NSF 6917, "Successful Industrial Innovations", National Science Foundation, 1969.

Donald A. Schon, "Technology and Change", Delacorte, 1967.

Wall Street Journal, "The Innovators", Dow Jones Books, 1968.

Donald Schon's Book "Technology and Change", is of great value to our understanding of the innovation process. Many of the other in depth studies make fascinating reading.

CHAPTER 14

A CREATIVE LIFESTYLE: THE PLACE IN THE SUN

Another look.
You are creative.
Your potential is great.
Practice originality.
Sharpen your senses.
Do it "your own way".

The early years.
Creative environment.
Living in a changing world.
Cultural nourishment.
A balanced view.
Innovation, wellspring of progress.

We have looked at ourselves — professionals, chemists, engineers, lawyers, students, bankers, and housewives. We have seen our limitations and our opportunities. Our potential is greater than our performance; artificial horizons limit our vision and only tradition and the habits of conformity hold us back.

This is a world of change, a time of transition, a dynamic surrounding. This world, full of the rapid currents of change, does not just flow around us, it pulls us, pushes us, requires our fullest capabilities to cope with it and to develop a truly creative and satisfying life style.

To live a satisfactory life, to accomplish our goals, to meet our targets, we must cultivate not only our own creative potential, but do our utmost to contribute to our society.

We have learned that there are many creativities. First, there is creativity as a human *talent*, our innate ability to create, the creative human potential. We distinguish this ability from our capability of thinking and from the skill of accumulating knowledge. Thought without creativity is like unleavened bread. Creativity is a separate talent. It can be applied to thought processes, or exercised independently. I do not have to think in creating a painting. Creativity flows from imagination and feelings independent of thought.

Next to innate creativity, the talent, we have creativity the *process*. Humanity survives by problem solving and only our extensive ability to solve complex problems makes modern civilization possible. Problem solving with the exception of machine problems, which are rare, is a creative process. Problem solving requires the application of creativity, the human talent.

Finally, we have the creative *product*, a work of art, a painting, an invention. The creative product is the result, the successful embodiment of creativity. It is the treasure at the end of the hunt.

Creativity is not easy to understand, especially when we want to apply this understanding to the talent, the process, and the product.

To help in the cultivation, strengthening, and training of creative potential, we have defined creativity in terms of:

Originality,
Action, and
Value.

Originality is the mystery of creativity. It makes us put elements together in a new and unexpected fashion. We achieve synergism. It is that magic way in which we can suddenly get the combination that is vastly superior to the component parts. We achieve "effective surprise". We astound ourselves, we accomplish the unexpected. We explore, we play around, we pick up and discard pieces, we see parts, and all of a sudden, "click" there is the image of a "new whole".

Visualization plays a significant role in originality. Our thinking world is oriented towards verbalization. We learn with words and sentences. Imagination, the world of pictures in our minds calls for visualization. Visualization is the powerful fountain of creativity, the shortcut to many an "effective surprise".

But originality alone, imagination, does not tell the full story of creativity. Something can be uniquely different, can be the product of effective surprise, and be only a fantasy, an unfulfilled dream. To be creative requires our action to implement the originality. Originality without action is nonproductive. Many a brilliant idea has been lost for want of action. Many a year has passed before a good idea was translated into progress. Due to the inertia barrier, we lose many a beautiful and original image, many a useful idea, that should have been translated into reality. To be creative, to solve problems, to achieve the creative product we have to act. So do not travel without pen and paper. Write down your ideas! Even the smallest move, the seemingly most insignificant act, can have large consequences. To be creative, take that first step.

Creativity also implies value. Planet earth and humanity demand from us contructive participation for the common good, in the common goals. This is not a time for hermits. Murder or suicide may be acted out with a high degree of originality, but this is not creativity. Creativity requires a positive contribution — building rather than destruction. This contribution may not always be recognized at the time of the creative act. However, action and value are necessary components of the creative product.

Value is measured on many scales. In our materialistic world we forget too readily the human values, the cultural values, and most importantly, the value of time. Considering our short visit to these shores, and the ever-accelerating needs of mankind, time is truly more valuable than money. It should be a significant yardstick of creativity.

Every human is creative. Creativity is a natural talent given to us at birth. Some are more heavily endowed than others, but cultivation of this talent, especially in the young, deserves an important role.

218

Modern research has shown that creativity is at its greatest height in the early years of our lives. Encouragement of imagination in the young, the pre-school children, all the way through school and into college is of vital importance to the future of society.

Korzybski talks about the types of mental health: sane, insane, and "unsane". Few of us are insane, but many of us are "unsane". We are not living up to our potential, we are not practicing a full and creative lifestyle. We squander our time, we let the routine beat of daily activities, the distraction and frustration of modern living, interfere with the exercise and practice of our creative selves. We allow rules, tradition, and other peoples' opinions to interfere with the creative performance of our assigned tasks. This antagonism between social pressures and creativity is unnatural. We are individual human beings; we must exercise our individuality and not succumb to the influences of conformity. The antagonism between education and creativity is hurtful, unnecessary, and to be opposed, if we are to make progress and surmount the many problems of the coming decades.

The creative talent with which we are born can and should be encouraged and cultivated from an early age. A child's imagination can serve as a fountain for his creative talents in future life. However, creativity need not stop, need not deteriorate, creativity can be stimulated, developed, practiced, at any age. Masterworks, technical scientific, legal, or artistic, are possible for an octogenarian. There is no retirement age for creative performance.

Perception, the skill of seeing, of fully using all our senses, has been much neglected. Perception training is one of the keys to creativity. This underlies the importance of teaching all of us to see, hear, taste, feel, smell, and fully perceive our surroundings. What have you missed? You have to sense life, experience and feel your surroundings to live life. You have to see and feel, to hear and taste, to be able to create. We must not let noise drown out the music, fog obscure the vision. Let us see what is around us, experience what is in us. If we can hear the birds, we can also hear the music in our minds. All perception is a creative act, it is a creation of our senses, an insight.

We interact with our world. We face problems daily, hourly, almost minute by minute. Very few of our problems are machine problems. Very few have only one solution. In the real world, in the world of human beings interacting among themselves and with their surroundings, few problems are simple, mathematical questions answered by an adding machine. There is always a human factor, there is much uncertainty.

Creativity is not chaos, but order. The creative process is an orderly method of applying our potential to the problems we face. Problem solving also supplies key motivation to the creative individual. But first, what is motivation? What is making us do? What supplies the drive for our behavior? Motivation is the release of energy; the creative individual acts in a motivated fashion. He is looking to a future condition that he is attempting to bring about. The motivated, creative individual is not primarily conditioned by the possibility of a reward, by the solution of the problem, but by the problem solving process itself. He is challenged, by the problem solving activity. He is striving for a desirable future condition, but he is striving for it in a creative, in an elegant way. This is personally satisfying. He is not solely interested in the solution of the problem, but also in the process and in that the solution be original.

Creativity, thus, is closely tied to motivation. It generates ideas of desirable future states. In problem definition, there is inherent the underlying idea, that a problem might be solved. There is seen an original, a challenging, a better future. Thus the problem provides the motivating stimulus for the creative human being to do his best to strive for excellence. Fully understood, properly applied, and properly practiced, the creative process is a necessity in our daily lives. It is the focal point of a successful life-style. This is especially true for professionals, since professionalism is, in essence, expertise applied to problem solving. The greatest expertise, the greatest store of knowledge, even the greatest capability of logical thought is helpless without the contribution of creativity.

Creative problem solving is:

Problem recognition
Preparation
Ideation
Incubation
Inspiration
Implementation

Subdividing the problem solving activity into steps is naturally somewhat of an oversimplification. Each phase poses its own new sub-problems to which the entire creative process must be applied. There will be a tendency of one phase to mingle with another. However, separate consideration of the phases of creative problem solving is of substantial value and assists us in the necessary discipline of performance. It is apt to increase our problem solving productivity.

Problem recognition or problem definition often is the basis of a solution. There is a danger not only in not recognizing that you have a problem, but also in defining problems in a way which interferes with a possible solution. It is vital not only to define a problem but also to define it without erecting barriers to a creative approach. Always ask the question, "Why?" before you are satisfied with the definition of a problem. The answer to the "Why?" may show you the real problem. The problem "as given" is seldom the problem "as understood". Make sure you understand the "real" problem.

Creativity is no substitute for hard work. It does not eliminate the need for craftmanship, for preparation. On the contrary preparation is a must for creative performance. Today the individual must perform at an ever-higher level of expertise, of professionalism. The growth of human knowledge places an ever-increasing burden on him. He must prepare, acquire the ammunition the background, the understanding from which creative ideas can spring. Preparation means in depth gathering of knowledge, of images, of pieces that might serve as the soil for the seeds of ideas.

There is a tendency for superficial preparation which is fostered by the media. News media are not effective in presenting balanced information in depth. The overkill of today's crisis topic leaves tomorrow's questions unanswered. This is particularly true for professional topics. This is not criticism of the media; it is a warning signal to use in-depth preparation. We have to prepare ourselves not only in areas of obvious relevancy, we must also explore related areas, look for clues in unobvious directions.

Equally, the professional has a greater responsibility not only of detailed preparation but also of honesty. Gather all the facts, not just those that fit your preconceived notions, or those that are fashionable or easy. Only with all the tools at hand can we produce solutions which will comply to the everrising expectations of modern society. Only the best prepared performance can avoid disappointing an already frustrated and skeptical public.

Ideas, ideas, ideas!

Ideation has always been a fascinating and intriguing subject. Much has been accomplished in recent years to understand the idea generating process. For ideas to flow freely we must check our critical faculties. We must leave prejudice, preconceived notions and premature evaluation at home.

Quantity is important; many ideas are likely to wield a crop of original ideas. The more the merrier. Let your imagination roam! Do not be satisfied with the obvious, the first idea that comes to mind. Keep hunting, exploring, seeking for unusual ideas! Have no fear of ridicule, do not judge your ideas. Try to improve them, not discard them.

Record, record, record!

We live in a world of noise and motion. We have lost the "art of the quiet moment". Give yourself a change of pace, a time free of tension, free of pressures, free of demands and restrictions. Ideas need incubating. Rest, relax, go for a walk, forget the problem, at least with your conscious mind, with your surface senses. Take a break! Time out for creative digestion! Incubation requires a mood, an environment, a pace that is favorable to the functioning of your subconscious. You still want to work on solving the problem, but you want it to simmer, you want it to be worked on below the surface. Incubation does not mean putting a problem aside for a more urgent different activity. Incubation is not compatible usually with activities that totally absorb us. You do not want to create competition for your subconscious. You want to create an atmosphere, an attitude in which all of your potential can go to work on the problem.

Inspiration is the most satisfying part of the creative process. Suddenly through the mist you see the solution. You know which idea to select and how to modify it to make implementation possible. Effective surprise sets in. It may not always be a "flash of genius" but it is "inspiration", "elucidation". You see the point. Just as laughter sets in when you see the point of a good joke, so satisfaction and pleasure is experienced when inspiration hits. This moment cannot be forced. Inspiration will be favored by a sound body and a sound mind. It may be connected for you with certain localities, a certain time of day, or you may experience inspiration totally at random. Creativity is like sex. You put it all together, but you do not necessarily control the climax.

With inspiration, much of the fun may be behind you. You may be tempted to go on to other things. However, the creative process is not complete without implementation. The most brilliant new discovery is useless, unless it is recorded and passed on. Otherwise it might be lost to mankind and be as if it never existed. A hazard for people having a high degree of imagination is the tendency to remain in the fantasy sphere. Action, return to reality and a coupling of the inspiration to the real world is vital. This is the finale of the creative process. Without it the symphony remains incomplete. Action is a vital requirement of the creative process. The solution of the problem must be implemented. Implementation is time dependent. Yesterday's inspiration, left too long without action, will be today's failure. Equally, a solution way ahead of its time cannot be successfully implemented in today's time span. Implementation must be timely.

We can practice the creative process and improve our ability to perform. The better our preparation, our ideas, and our inspiration, the more likely our success, a creative contribution. Practice makes perfect. Keep in mind that you are not following a cookbook recipe, you are exercising your individual "potential". You may be a morning man, or a midnight man. You may be a walking woman, or one who gets her ideas on a couch listening to music. You are a unique individual. Whatever the method, you are stimulating, strengthening, developing your unique creative potential. Creativity training must by nature be individualistic to be successful. Whether you write long lists of ideas or put them on small cards, whether you draw on the tablecloth or your shirt cuff, "your way" is important, "your way" is right. In any case, do it "some way", overcome the inertia barrier. Practice problem solving, engage in the creative process. Feel your way, and find the technique best suited to you. Soon inspiration will strike, often and frequently. Your solutions will be original and successful. That is the creative life style, it assures you a place in the sun.

You are not alone! Creativity and group effort are compatible; they are a lovely combination. Pooling and reinforcing each other's creative talents will yield magnificent results. In reality few of us successfully work with others. We have to learn the lessons of creative cooperation. In working together it is of utmost importance that all participants understand the problem. Combined and in depth preparation must be sound. Capabilities are multiplied, since each individual brings a different set of knowledge and background to the party. Premature judgment, harmful in your individual ideation process, spells resentment and breakdown of cooperation in the group. On the other hand the opportunities for enhancement and reinforcement of each other's ideas are unique.

Inspiration is an individual experience and more difficult to share. It takes particular skills of communication and cooperation to succeed in having the group accept a member's inspiration. This may be easier if it is the ultimate modification and reinforcement of ideas first generated by other members of the group. For implementation there is strength in numbers, and the opportunity of combining many skills for successful action.

Some very interesting methods have been developed to stimulate groups, to encourage them to go unobvious routes. These methods attempt to prevent the common pitfalls of group behavior such as fighting for leadership, or pouring cold water on each other's ideas. They also try to stimulate unusual ideas, encourage wildness, without permitting chaos to set in.

There are many lessons to be learned from the understanding of creativity, from the practice of the creative process, and from deliberate stimulation of our creative potential. First and foremost, there are those conclusions that concern ourselves, our motivation, our performance, our way of striving for a place in the sun. In essence, this is the call for a creative life style.

You are creative!

Regardless of age, sex, profession, you are a creative human individual. You can do things you never thought possible. You can draw, paint, do sculpture, write, act, be a photographer, be a film maker, and many more creative activities you may not now be practicing. Most importantly, you can apply any lesson learned in these activities foreign to you to the profession in which you are normally engaged. Even bird watching is likely to have a positive effect on your overall creativity. Do not fear ridicule. Try to be different. You, as a creative individual, are highly motivated. Overcome the barriers. Go into a new and different, a more worthwhile, a more creative future.

Your potential is a giant!

You may be a highly successful professional. You may be satisfied and rightly so, with what you have accomplished, your family, your position, your earning power. However, you can use a much larger portion of your potential. You are unique, and your potential is a giant. Many goals, you believe, you cannot attain are attainable. Many specific things that you think you cannot do can be done! Most importantly, exploit your special strength. You write well; have you used it only in your business? You have a knack of dealing with people; do you go out of your way to meet and talk to stangers? When you sit on that airplane, try to get to know that interesting and stimulating man or woman next to you. You can do many things that you do not now tackle. Overcome your shyness, prejudice and the ingrown social barriers. Get out of yourself, try the unusual. You have nothing to lose when you try to strike up a conversation with a stranger. You have nothing to lose in trying something unusual, something that you believe has low odds of success. If it can be done, you can do it.

Practice originality!

Try to be different. Stress your uniqueness. Put aside the obvious and look for the unusual. Explore freely without barriers and limitations. Let your imagination roam. Practice fantasy, play imagination games; no task is routine if you tackle it properly. Conformity is a curse that encourages mediocrity. Dare to be different in your actions, in your style, in your dress, in your life, your relationships with others. Ask yourself a new question every day, and do something a little different whenever you can. Look for those shortcuts which substitute ingenuity for time, money and effort.

Sharpen your senses!

Perception is in the mind, it is within you. Go and look at things within yourself. See, select, savor, enjoy, experience what is around you. There are visions, and sounds, and tastes, and smells, there are ugly and beautiful impressions out there. Select and digest what is of value. Look for the unusual. Store those impressions, those perceptions, which might help to strengthen your original, your creative lifestyle. Perceptions are your stock in trade, they are the components of your imagination. Perception is an exercise in creativity. Enjoy what you sense, and you will enjoy living. Sense and store the enjoyable, the constructive, the beautiful, and your creations will be worthwhile.

Recognize the problem.

Whatever your professional life's role, you are a problem solver. Recognize the problem; understand it clearly before you tackle its solution. The problem and the urge to solve it will motivate you.

Creativity requires input. Prepare yourself. Gather the pieces that can be useful to creative problem solving. Explore broadly to build your general stock in trade. Prepare in depth, and carefully, for a specific problem. Don't look narrowly; look where you have to, but also look in unexpected places for a contribution to your imagination. You can be both specialist and generalist.

Practice ideation!

Enjoy yourself. Generating ideas is fun. Look far afield to find unobvious ideas, speculate and dream. Do not hesitate to use idea-generating aids. Make ideation a game that will bring a smile to your face and to those of others. Develop a sense of humor. Think of ideas in threes. Take every idea and try to improve it. Will the opposite fit? Free-wheeling is a must. Apply the lesson of one specialty to the ideas for another. How would an ant do it? What if you were the machine? You can have ideas. You can have the original idea.

Time out for mental digestion.

Know when to change the pace. Make your subconscious work for you. Practice intelligent day-dreaming. Does your mind work best in the morning? Look inside yourself for the inspiration. Visualize the ideas for better incubation. Keep moving at rest. Inspiration is better than perspiration. You cannot command your subconscious, but you can create an atmosphere in which your total mind brings forth effective surprise. Inspiration is great enjoyment.

Do, do, do!

Overcome the inertia barrier. Move, do not stand still. There is no creativity without action, even the smallest step can have large consequences. Take that first step and the others will come easy. Practice the creative process . . . act. Create the product. Paint the painting. Carve the sculpture. Help that friend. Follow up that invention or inventive idea. Patent your invention. Commercialize, innovate, overcome the barriers that society puts in your way. You can be productive. You are a creative mover.

Whatever you do, do it your "own way"!

There is no firm formula for success. There is no "one prescription" for creativity. It is "your" personal potential, "your" creative style that you are developing. You are not the baby on planet 'X', you are *you*. Make your unique imprint, your unique contribution while you are on planet Earth. Find a way which is effective for you, practice it, improve it, enjoy it.

Most of our studies have been devoted to discussion of personal creativity, the discussion of how to improve our own creativity. It is equally important to move others, however, any contribution to society, any effort involving others begins with ourselves. The lessons of creativity apply to others you may be able to assist. There are creative remedies which need to be adopted by others, by our society.

Let's not waste the early years!

While somewhat exaggerated to make a point, it has been said that half of all the growth of human intelligence takes place between birth and age 4, another 30% between the ages of 4 and 8, and the rest is done by the age of 17. In creativity training, it has been well established that the early years play a very significant role. Experiences, influences on the young human are of particular importance to his creative performance in future years. A grid, a matrix is formed in the early years which has a major effect on future attitudes and capabilities. We are prisoners in a cage built by our early experiences. Kindergarten is more than play, it is a significant period of development for the imagination of the young. Kindergarten training of high quality is likely to have more impact on the creative potential of the individual than his last years in high school.

The early years, even experiences of the infant are crucial to future development of the person. The human organism is very readily influenced in early development. It has been found, for instance, that children who are exposed to constantly quarrelling parents show a stunting of growth. The growth hormone is produced at a much lower rate when young people are under stress. Remove these children to a conflict-free atmosphere, and they rapidly grow again.

Training of the imagination of young people influences their future creative performance and their ability to develop a successful, creative and happy life-style.

Creative Environment.

We are what we see and hear. Wherever we are, young or old, our environment, in the home, at school, at work, in our cities, plays a major role in terms of supplying our creativity with the necessary raw materials and encouragement. The full extent of the influences played by the human environment, especially in the early formative years, is still unknown. Animal studies have confirmed that sensory and environmental deprivation have a profound effect on development. The quality of the environment is of major importance to human performance, creativity and happiness.

The beauty of the world around us lies in the eyes of the beholder. There is beauty in a tree leaf, a blade of grass, and the tall lines of the skyscraper. How do we get to see beauty? Experiments have shown that children exposed extensively to fine art not only show a greater appreciation of beauty, but also reflect a capability of creating more beautiful forms in their drawings and activities. Nelson Rockefeller, whose mother was instrumental in establishing the great Museum of Modern Art in New York and who all his life has been surrounded with sculptures and paintings of a high degree of originality could not be a reactionary. Environment plays a major role in our attitudes, it greatly influences human creativity.

We must then see to it that we create an environment of challenge, beauty, and inspiration. That extra dollar to erect a building that is beautiful, to build a fountain, to have room for a park is as important as the dollar spent for functional purposes. Demand, support, insist on more beautiful surroundings for yourself and your children. Beautify, then, your city, your street, your home, your office. Stimulate yourself daily with gay colors, with works of art, with attractive furniture. Even if you do not consciously see your surroundings, you are exposed to them at all times. Cut down noises, eliminate unpleasant odors. Dress well. Suggest that others contribute to the quality, the atmosphere of your life.

Art education for better perception.

When we have problems, we look to technology to bail us out. We are dollar and machine oriented. However, as we have seen, most of our problems are people problems. Science is handcuffed and limited where people problems are concerned. Centuries of studies have shown scant results where human behavior needs to be modified.

Quoting from the fascinating book by Duane Preble, "Man Creates Art Creates Man":

"A technologically explosive society needs the integrating rewards of art experience. The arts and sciences can work for man in different ways. Science looks for and finds factual answers to questions related to our physical world. The arts help to answer our emotional and spiritual needs and can help to shape our physical environment as well."

The arts not only help our perception, but meaningful participation sharpens all creative skills. It can yield true satisfaction and enjoyment.

Living in a changing world.

We are only one of millions, but we too can exert a positive influence on our society. Change, dynamics is a characteristic of our time. This, then, puts special requirements on creativity and creative approaches. What was true yesterday is out of date today. This requires a great degree of imagination, a willingness to look at the world in a unique and original fashion. Living with change puts a premium on learning "how" to, rather than "what" to do. The "what" of yesterday is not likely to be applicable to tomorrow. The world of change puts a great demand on style, as well as performance. We need the ability to cope with many a new situation. Knowledge is not enough, since last year's knowledge may well be inapplicable to today. Change requires of all of us a creative acceptance and a willingness to live with new situations. Change offers great challenges and great opportunities.

Education is a life-long process.

With the dynamics of our fast-changing world, continuing education assumes great importance. Yesterday's learning is not adequate for today's and tomorrow's needs. Individualized learning is a must! The conditions and materials of learning must be tailored to the needs of the learner as an individual and his time. We are studying, we are learning, not for yesterday, not for today, but for tomorrow. We once thought of education as the expertise, the skills required for a profession. We went to school to get it. Once we passed, we had it for life. This is not enough in today's time.

Only those specialists can creatively cope with the real world, who have acquired the skills of problem solving, who can apply their knowledge and gather new knowledge as it is needed for a creative solution. Thus, education in the old sense is out of date as fast as it has been acquired. The education process, the learning process never ends. The high school graduate, the college graduate, are only at the beginning of further learning. To find solutions in the ever-changing society we must apply the methods of creative problem solving using every new material, gathering every new information to bring about the original, the "effective surprise" future.

Cultural Nourishment.

Learning, studying our specialties is not enough. To be creatively alive, we must have cultural nourishment, we must be exposed to other specialties, to hobbies, to the arts. In our country as a whole, our society, we must encourage this type of activity in order to have the opportunities for ourselves, our children, our friends, and our co-workers. This means support for symphonies, for museums, for good books, for all those many sources of creative food for our imagination and that of our fellow travelers.

It is said that reading is the national pastime in Russia. The Russian professional reads many more good books than his counterpart in other countries. In America we have many pastimes. Careful thought must be given to support and encourage those activities and products which serve as the cultural nourishment for our citizens. As an individual, you can make yourself felt by supporting creative activity in your community, in your state, and in the nation.

Encourage the understanding of the power of language.

Language distinguishes us from the animals. Yes, we all have studied English in school. Still we do not have a fine mastery of the language. We must encourage the understanding and the teaching of the language skills. Communications is vital to social peace, and to the success of our institutions. We must be aware of the power of the spoken, the written word. We must be aware of the need for imagery, the ability to describe, to paint with words the pictures which can communicate ideas. We must foster the full understanding of the great opportunities which our language offers to us. Idea communication, the transmission of the inner image from one person to another is not easy, but much is known, and much can be done to improve the understanding and use of language in our society.

It is particularly important that we encourage the tearing down of the barriers which foster separate languages for separate professions. We must abolish languages which are not readily understood by their audiences. The super-specialized language of medicine makes it difficult to communicate with the patient. Often words hide our ignorance. The super-special language of science, totally unnecessary in most cases, has separated science from the rest of the citizenry. Language is a tool, a beautiful tool, that can bring us together. We must encourage its study, and its understanding.

Not just English, but a full understanding of the art of language must become part of education in all our schools. Nobody should progress through college who cannot master the language, who cannot read, write and speak in such a fashion that he can truly communicate.

A balanced view.

For most of us, TV is our window on the world. TV has assumed a special role in our lives. Assuming that you agree that creativity is vital to your well-being, your performance, then you should be particularly worried about the impact of commerical television on you, your family, and your friends. TV, by nature, has to sell time, it has to attract the largest possible number of viewers. Therefore it is geared to the common denominator. Very little is programmed to emphasize originality, TV is not geared to be different. Most importantly, TV, tastes aside, does not surround you with beauty, or challenges. It is more likely to present violence, the sensational, thus stunning your senses, inhibiting your creativity. A creative life style requires a balanced, careful selective approach to TV. Yes, there is a need to view the news, to keep informed. Yes, there is a call for some recreational uses of TV, some viewing of sports. However, viewing TV is a passive activity; it seldom stimulates. Creativity requires a perception of the real thing; at best, TV is a limited, often superficial substitute.

Your creative potential requires not only balance in looking through the TV window at the world; it requires balance in many fields of activities. Think about balance of:

> Technology with Art
> City Life with Country Trips
> Television with Books, Plays and the Real Thing
> Routines with Games
> Work with Hobbies
> Schooling with Experience

228

Classroom with Internship
Words with Images
Sights with Sounds

I am sure many other such balances will readily occur to you. But let me urge you to exercise your creative potential with a sense of humor. Balance the sublime with the ridiculous, and the serious tasks with a good joke.

Creativity Training and How to Teach Creatively.

Creativity can be nourished, it can be stimulated. A human talent, it can be fostered, it can be developed. Teaching creativity means to learn about the various ways by which other people have succeeded in stimulating their creativity. Creativity teaching cries out for unusual approaches, for originality, for novel ways, for short-cuts to make people break through the barriers of tradition, and repetitious performance. That means training not according to some magic formula, but individual training of candidates with all their strengths and weaknesses. Try to help them fulfill their potential along the lines of their own patterns, their own best way to succeed. Creativity training must shun all formal cast-in-concrete prescriptions.

Creativity training means, that it is not enough to transmit to the next generation the vast store of knowledge which has been acquired through the years. We must teach young people how to learn, where to learn, and what to learn "in the future," rather than just at present. Creativity training means to teach "inquiry," to teach "creative approaches," to teach the "creative process" as a way of life.

Innovation — Well Spring of Progress.

To shape the future, we must create beyond the selfish needs, wants and desires of the day. We must not only discover new truths, but we must encourage and support and stimulate innovation. Populations continue to grow at an ever-alarming rate. We need to feed ever-more people, and we need to preserve the environment in which they live. Add to that the revolution of rising expectation. In our increasingly affluent, leisure-oriented societies, people want a better life, a higher quality, less restrictions. This will require ever new ways of achieving the impossible. We must continue to innovate in the areas of food, housing, health, environment. Most importantly, we need to innovate in the area of human behavior, we need to innovate in the solution of major people problems. We need to innovate in the field of communication cooperation, understanding among human beings, whether they be our neighbors down the street or across the ocean.

The creative human "can do" it!

"Creativity"	is intensely human
	is action, value, originality
	is attitude and environment
"Creativity"	is not intelligence
	is not knowledge
	is not reserved to the few

"Creativity"	can be taught
	can be stimulated
	can be reawakened
"Creativity"	needs perceptive skills
	needs a sense of humor
	needs imagination
"Creativity"	fosters human understanding
	fosters human communication
	fosters human cooperation
"Creativity"	results in discovery
	results in invention
	results in innovation

EXERCISES

Reread chapters one, two, and three.

Review your education, your learning processes, those of your children. Write out a 2 year plan for creativity training.

Education is a lifelong process. What changes require your action to catch up. Do it.

Participate in a cultural way, do something you have not done in a long time. Opera? Theatre? Lectures? Visit to a court trial? Museum? Concert; Take your pick.

D